AUDIT AND THE ART OF THINKING DIFFERENTLY

By thinking differently about audit, this transformational book establishes that the conceptual core of audit itself is the art of thinking differently: the making of those new connections that inspire the creativity and confidence to challenge established thinking and provide actionable insight. Audit is reconceptualised as a vital, creative, engine of progress – in society, the economy, the environment and in the appropriate use of technology. Progress requires confidence in the future. Audit addresses whether an audited entity is deserving of confidence and capable of developing – with deserved confidence flowing from creativity, sustainability, resilience and fair treatment. Audit becomes a form of social conscience, responding to, evaluating and influencing the ideas and ideals that a society or an entity within a society holds dear.

Through such framing, audit no longer observes from the sidelines but drives progress in business and society more generally. Whilst audit's traditional notions of conformity, control and compliance can be readily captured by a machine, the insight, imagination and inspiration that comes from thinking differently is fundamentally human. In this respect, the future of audit and of humanity converges. This book is not just for auditors and accountants concerned about the future of their profession but is an invitation to all with an interest in the future well-being of business and society to reformulate how they view audit.

David Hatherly is Emeritus Professor of Accounting at the University of Edinburgh Business School, Edinburgh, UK.

Christopher Humphrey is Professor of Accounting in the Accounting and Finance division of the Alliance Manchester Business School, The University of Manchester, Manchester, UK.

AUDIT AND THE ART OF THINKING DIFFERENTLY

Making the Connections That Inspire a Better Future

David Hatherly
Christopher Humphrey

Routledge
Taylor & Francis Group
LONDON AND NEW YORK

Designed cover image: Getty Images/Sukanya Sonlila

First published 2027
by Routledge
4 Park Square, Milton Park, Abingdon, Oxon OX14 4RN

and by Routledge
605 Third Avenue, New York, NY 10158

Routledge is an imprint of the Taylor & Francis Group, an informa business

British Library Cataloguing-in-Publication Data
A catalogue record for this book is available from the British Library

ISBN: 978-1-032-72127-9 (hbk)
ISBN: 978-1-032-72124-8 (pbk)
ISBN: 978-1-032-72129-3 (ebk)

DOI: 10.4324/9781032721293

Typeset in Galliard
by Newgen Publishing UK

CONTENTS

FIGURES

TABLES

ACKNOWLEDGEMENTS

We would like to acknowledge our families, friends, students, editorial and library support, and colleagues in both academia and beyond who encouraged and inspired us to think differently about audit, and then to think again. In particular, we are grateful to Heather and Kendra for their patience and understanding. We have benefited from our engagement with those with experience from the worlds of business, investment and finance who have thought about and formally reported upon the future of audit, notably John McFarlane and Sir Donald Brydon. We have drawn upon the ideas of other disciplines such as physics and philosophy, and the intriguing insights of contemporary writers on those subjects such as Carlo Rovelli and Iain McGilchrist. Our thanks to Andrew Hatherly for drawing our attention to the latter.

We also recognise that a good number of those who engaged with our thoughts and ideas did so in spite of, and perhaps because of, their puzzlement as to why audit was such a fascinating topic – and seemingly capable of consuming endless hours on telephone calls and computer keyboards, or locating and delving into library archives, buying up old editions of auditing textbooks and searching for meaningful references to the significance of audit across different disciplines.

The outcome of all of the above has been the realisation that audit is the art of thinking differently and the unearthing of new connections and perspectives that deepen understanding of both business and society and help to enrich people's lives. Our final acknowledgment is to the ability of audit, if properly conceived and applied, to inspire a better future.

1

AUDIT AS TRANSFORMATION

In January 1942, in the middle of a world war, *The Accountant*, which claims to be the oldest and most prestigious accountancy publication in the world, published a series of four anonymous articles on the future of auditing. The first argued that the financial audit is inadequate, even for satisfying the needs of shareholders. The second emphasised the growing interest of society in good management and the third reviewed the methods of preventing 'anti-social' behaviour in industry. The fourth discussed the part society might require the accounting and auditing profession to play and asked what the attitude of the profession should be. The fourth article on 24th January (Anon., 1942, p. 45) stated that "the trouble with the profession at the present time is that its leaders seem bent on doing nothing more than maintaining the status quo ante". The article envisaged the role of the auditor as providing supervision of organisational health, falling into three broad divisions relating to finance, ethics and management effectiveness. It argued that the task of financial supervision, pure and simple, is relatively the least important. The audit client of the future was seen to be society in general.

This discussion is as relevant today as it was 80-plus years ago. In our book, we envision audit as the engine of progress – financial, ethical, societal and personal. But all of these are deeply interconnected and any study of audit exposes the complexity and dynamics of society, the connections, transactions and human values that form society and the challenge of understanding and representing these realities in terms of 'progress'. So auditing is not just supervision and monitoring in a passive sense but a function that drives and shapes progress; progress that requires action based upon new thinking (creativity); new thinking that is delivered by audit. Audit is in a state of tension between control and creativity, a tension that should itself be challenging and

DOI: 10.4324/9781032721293-1

creative, but we argue fails to be so because of the dominance of control and conformity.[1] Whereas control comes from regulation, standards and the ability to provide evidence through repetition, creativity is a break with the past and the regulation and standards that have been developed there. Creativity in this sense can almost be seen as inviting a feeling of being 'out of control'. There may well be areas of society, which are out of control, but we should not just see auditing as being rooted in notions of control. If society desires progress, it must also nurture and inspire creative action; and, in turn, we have to contemplate audit and its capacity to impact society in more ambitious and creative terms.

Accordingly, whilst audit has traditionally been associated with the audit of financial statements and in particular with the financial statements of commercial enterprises, we do not start here. We start with the challenge of society understanding itself and its situation better, including key reciprocal relations between organisations and individuals. This challenge is the social essence or purpose of audit. Audit is the function within society that is charged with the task of helping society not only to understand itself better but also to become better.

To meet this challenge, the audit needs to understand itself better. In turn, organisations need to understand themselves better, their performance and their connections to stakeholders, including society as a whole. At this latter point, key considerations become the organisation's values, how they are constructed and represented and the organisation's success in progressing them – not just commercially or economically but also in terms of an organisation's societal contribution. We do not belittle the importance of commercial success or a successful economy but, in the final reckoning, financial value is a means to an end and not the end in itself. As David Flint (1988) emphasised, "audit is a social phenomenon" (p. 4), whilst Michael Power (1997), through his idea of the 'Audit Society', invites the notion that society be viewed as an audit phenomenon. With both perspectives, the connection between audit and society is clearly important but how it is drawn evidently has significant consequences in terms of the way the social functionality or value of audit is represented. For us, the fundamental social justification for audit and what gives it its dynamism is that audit must contribute to social development and enhancement. This is the core test and expectation for something that is represented as a public interested function.

These are important times for the audit. In the UK, for instance, restoring trust and confidence in audit has been the subject of a fairly recent government white paper (BEIS, 2022).[2] But like most so-called audit 'reforms' – and there have been many over recent decades – the central focus remained one of restoration; of going back to where we were (or were supposed to be) rather than re-thinking audit to identify and release new potential.[3] Our book steps into what we regard as a very evident but, overly long-standing, vacuum. It re-thinks audit. This is a process inspired by our belief that audit has been in serious need of a deeper and broader conceptual analysis and cannot seek to rely or place faith in regulatory quick fixes. Moreover, it is driven by a stance that such re-thinking and re-conceptualising should not be a one-off event but is, as it were, the very essence of audit. Following this line, we suggest that audit is not so much about locating a set of uniform concepts or ideas that can be applied over and over but is a continuing search for different ideas and conceptual thinking that allows audit to improve understanding of society (or understanding of a particular entity within society); and, through such understanding, audit can enable that society (or a specific entity) to 'progress' and, through such achievements, for audit itself also to progress.

The book, therefore, initiates a journey with no end in terms of the delineation of one, definitive form of audit and related audit practices. Instead, it establishes a philosophical foundation from which we expect the practice of audit and its societal significance to flourish. The central conceptual baseline is that 'audit is thinking differently' (Humphrey, 2020), making audit a dynamic, ever developing, progressive function in terms of its practical application. The result is a fundamental challenge to existing representations of audit and a demonstration of how a different appreciation of audit's core conceptual base promotes innumerable development possibilities for audit practice whilst, at the same time, illuminating the dysfunctional nature of conventional debates over an auditing expectations gap. Once it is recognised that audit is, by definition, not a static function, it becomes evident that the discussions we need to be having in public policy and professional circles are not about what auditing is or is not, but what auditing can become and what auditing can enable to happen or prevent from happening.

Serving the public interest

The importance of working in the interests of the public is evident in the formal constitutions and public statements of bodies such as the Institute of Chartered Accountants of Scotland (ICAS), the Institute of Chartered Accountants in England and Wales and the Association of International Certified Professional Accountants.[4] However, we do not believe that at present the received education or experience of auditors provides a sufficient philosophical and conceptual grounding to meet broad-based aspirational commitments to serve (and challenge) society, and thereby protect the public interest; nor to provide the intelligence required to clarify and influence a complex and changing world. In particular, we believe that the connection or relationship between audit as expertise and audit as public interest is deserving of more explicit attention. Indeed, we believe this inattention has left the (auditing) profession and its practising professionals in a highly vulnerable position. An important motivation for our book is the belief that it is possible through conceptual analysis and re-thinking to allow audit to develop in ways that it has not done before and ways that allow it to serve the public interest better.

A typical view of the social contract between the auditing profession and society is given by Satava et al. (2006, p. 281), who concluded that: "the role of the audit function is 'covenantal' to the degree that the audit profession represents itself as a guardian of the public interest (Caldwell and Clapham, 2003, p. 249). As a quid pro quo for being certified by society as professional and competent, auditors owe society a citizen's duty (Manville and Ober, 2003) to follow principles as well as rules faithfully".

Satava et al. are talking here more broadly of ethical (rather than just accounting) principles, which they categorise, citing Hosmer (1994), as "the basic principles that have been proposed to ensure a 'good society'. A good society is one in which people willingly cooperate for the benefit of all" (p. 274).

Satava et al. insist that the duties owed by auditors must be based on unchanging ethical principles that reflect a commitment to honour "duties to society that encompass the public interest and the welfare of all stakeholders" (p. 274). Adapting Hosmer's (1994) work on the ethical and moral principles to be considered by management, Satava et al. then present ten ethical 'perspectives'[5] to be considered in a pragmatic fashion by auditors on behalf of society. They leave the precise connection between ethical 'principles' and 'perspectives' unspecified but the implication is that the presented 'perspectives' provide frames through which auditors can pragmatically determine how best to apply and follow the ethical principles and fulfil their societal duties. They agree with Paine (2003) that ethics and morality are 'a highly practical invention', "because society expects business and its leaders to fit within contexts that endow human activity with meaning, prescribe standards of behavior, and establish expectations for how we should treat one another" (p. 281). Satava et al. (2006) suggested that the effect of bringing together their ten ethical perspectives was to demonstrate how the ethical foundation had to and could move beyond a predominant, narrowly specified, rules-based approach.

We would argue that thinking in this way offers a capacity not just to reconceptualise auditing ethics but to reconceptualise audit itself. Contemplating audit in terms of what it can contribute towards ensuring a good society (and having a range of (ethical) perspectives through which to structure analysis of the various dimensions of audit's social contract) is not something that is, or should be, static. We can also contemplate how to develop a better society and what auditing can contribute in terms of stimulating and helping to deliver such improvement. For instance, the public can have an interest in society (and the entities within it) making progress rather than just being preserved or maintained, and developing a better understanding of themselves and the connections between them so that they can progress.

If society's framing of acceptable ethical behaviour is a complex blend of different ethical perspectives, then it is possible to see the essential spirit of audit as being both an interrogative and informative function that assesses and advises, through particular determined modes, dimensions and practices, on societal well-being. Audit oversees, investigates, remembers, reminds and invigorates, helping society to establish, maintain and develop acceptable forms of social functionality (ethical behaviour) – but in ways that can also support progress and advancement.

If audit's social contract goes beyond preserving the past, then it also extends beyond appreciating and maintaining principles. It involves understanding the connections between 'principles', 'perspectives' and 'progress'; of finding and contemplating new perspectives, developing new principles, seeking and becoming better. Encompassed here is an essential dynamic spirit – a society committed to advancement and an audit function, ever flexible, reflective and responsive, so as to facilitate such advancement and to caution against detrimental patterns of behaviour. As such, when we talk about the need to reconceptualise audit, it is important to recognise that this is not just a one-off, one-time only remedy. It is about recognising that the deepest, conceptual or philosophical roots of audit are embedded in the very essence of dynamism. Audit conceptually cannot be treated as a static practice or activity; audit has to be stimulating, invigorating, regenerative, advancing, ready and willing to think differently. The very idea of a 'good society' or the very notion of 'progress' and the creative tension between permanence and progression, between continuity and discontinuity, are all open to different interpretations and representations[6] – but that is why we need an audit that is conceptually rooted in and committed to thinking differently. This has to be the very core sense of what is required when we talk of audit 'working in the public interest'. It not only requires audit to embrace subjectivity and to work in ways that inform and reassure society but also encourages it to question and to challenge society, as to its state of progress and whether this is occurring in the best possible fashion.

Audit and society

Hence, of particular importance is understanding better the capacity for society to shape audit and for audit to shape society. At present, audit and its long-standing presumed purpose are framed in something of a vacuum – a public interested function whose shape has almost been predetermined without any explicit derivation as to how and why such a form best serves the public interest. The persistent nature of the audit expectations gap makes such a position all the more puzzling because it is evident that there is a persistent, significant difference between what is justified and defended as audit and what stakeholders (including the public in whose name the audit profession has been constructed) want, or deserve, from audit. The profession's response is a form of justification capable of being classified as a 'take it or leave it' theorisation: you may feel dissatisfied with audit, sense that it is not meeting public expectations and want something different... but, typically, your desires are deemed (by the profession) as not being well informed.

Another way of classifying such a state of affairs – of an audit function that does not appear to have been visibly shaped by, nor secure in its capability to satisfy, the public interest – is to suggest that the interactive connection between audit and society, between audit values and societal values, appears to be broken and needs to be sorted. The auditor is a part of society and cannot function without regard for or, at least, reference to the common values which hold society together. Indeed, it is possible to argue that for auditors to be trusted by society, they need to judge those being audited using the values of society – making audit a form of social cognition. However, at the same time, the public interested auditor can also be represented as an important, guiding, influence on those values and upon their own dynamic. In turn, such framing suggests that the audit expectations gap has to be seen in at least two dimensions. It cannot be represented in a one-sided fashion, and we should no longer accept or live with any such representations. Society legitimately can and should expect more from auditing, whilst the audit profession can and should have the ambition to offer more than society has expected!

In his book *The Master and His Emissary: The Divided Brain and the Making of the Western World*, Iain McGilchrist (2012) argues that the difference between the brain's left and right hemispheres could help to explain the history of Western civilisation. Western culture, he claimed, oscillated between the left and right hemispheres' engagement with the world – the former tending to emphasise order, control, rationality, agency and bureaucracy and the latter tending to prioritise experience, change, empathy, freedom and openness.[7] Consequently, given the above-noted interdependence of audit and society, an audit that engaged left hemisphere characteristics would push society towards those characteristics, whilst at the same time, a society that prioritised left hemisphere characteristics would expect audit to do the same. Power's (1997) well-known Audit Society thesis, where audit is increasingly embedded in society as a matter of ritual verification and monitoring, can be taken as an example of such a left hemisphere dominated behavioural pattern.

According to McGilchrist, history represents periods of left hemisphere dominance followed by collapse and periods of right hemisphere dominance (and subsequent collapse). An interesting potential implication for audit reform and development is that if society is seen as increasingly 'left-brained', then audit should be increasingly 'right-brained' (and vice versa), acting as a 'balancing factor' (countervailing force) to protect society from either left or right hemisphere dominance. If the audit is thinking differently, then the audit has to be prepared to contemplate thinking differently about society. It should seek not just to follow society but to influence society to think differently, too. 'Influencing' in this respect has to be regarded as an essential characteristic of the role of the auditor within society.

There is, however, another possibility. It is that the divided brain leads to an increasingly divided society – divided into those who engage with the world primarily through their left hemisphere and those who engage primarily using their right hemisphere. In so far as this is the situation, the audit cannot think differently from (all of) society since society is divided. Instead, the audit must act as the connection between society's left and right hemisphere oriented thinking. According to McGilchrist (2021, p. 841), such a coincidence of opposites can be profoundly creative.

This opens up the conceptual possibility of audit and auditors making connections in ways that create or inspire a 'better' society. What we learn from this discussion of the connection between audit and society is the importance of balance as a kind of duality. On the one hand, the auditor, as a member of society, shares, or at least has to recognise, society's values. On the other hand, the auditor has a responsibility to think differently from the rest of society in order to influence its values, bringing divergent ways of thinking together and helping, in the process, to create a better society. The auditor's social acceptance depends upon thinking the same as society but the pursuit of societal progress demands that auditors must also think differently – meaning that the auditor has to manage both acceptance and progression, and both convergence and divergence.

Moving from the classic view of conceptualisation

Perhaps the most influential conceptualisation of audit to date has been *The Philosophy of Auditing* (Mautz and Sharaf, 1961). David Hatherly recalls:

> In 1973 when I took my first academic post at Glasgow University, Professor David Flint, my new boss, called me into his office, handed me a copy of *The Philosophy of Auditing*, Mautz and Sharaf's 1961 classic for the American Accounting Association and stated that before I did anything else I should

> read this book. Professor Flint explained that I had to understand audit as philosophy. No-one in the major audit firm where I had worked before had talked in these terms, let alone classified audit as a philosophy of thought! I subsequently had the privilege of spending time with Bob Mautz when he visited Scotland at the invitation of David Flint. We discussed the nature of audit evidence, a major contribution of his book.[8]

To Mautz and Sharaf, the primary auditing concepts are evidence, due care, fair presentation, independence and ethical conduct. They also have a set of postulates or premises for their theory and these are explicitly rooted in the traditional financial audit. So, though undoubtedly providing a historic classic, Mautz and Sharaf still function in a restricted way by fitting or matching the philosophy and concepts of audit to a pre-existing delineation of what audit is or isn't.[9] As they openly acknowledged, the "postulates that we offer here were devised after careful study of the nature and activities of audit. They were then carefully explored to determine their implications, completeness and consistency" (p. 41). This is an analytical journey that ultimately narrows things down conceptually – a 'justifying' travel path that, from our perspective, essentially becomes one of thwarted ambition. Our conceptual development path is more expansive. It is less centred on substantiation and on seeking to fit conceptual standpoints to existing audit practice. Instead, its direct intention is to use conceptual analysis in a more creative way that can inspire practice development.

Concepts are abstract ideas that we all use in, and develop from, everyday life (and auditing concepts can similarly emerge from, or out of, the everyday lives of auditors). However, it is one thing to apply concepts and another to understand their connections with each other. The development and refinement of connections are critical to the book's primary aims of reconceptualising audit. Whilst a set of concepts form a platform that both helps people to think through and create human activity, they are themselves a human construct and not set in stone. Thus, concepts are a product of our thinking, and at the same time, our thinking is a product of the concepts we use. We must be prepared to re-evaluate our concepts; to understand them better in the light of experience and, where the opportunity arises, reformulate them in order to release innovative thinking or improve their power to explain. From a pragmatic perspective, concepts, like principles, are not theoretical but practical and temporal in the sense of helping us to understand until a better opportunity for understanding comes along. So, whilst concepts serve to establish a framework for cognition, reconceptualisation is key to creativity.

As such, there is a tension to be managed between stability based upon enduring concepts and the creativity of novel concepts that might deliver progress. This tension was explored by Bergson who elaborated a philosophy that rejected static values of permanence and uniformity in favour of values of motion, change, evolution and novelty in experienced reality. For Bergson, change constitutes reality.[10]

Whilst Bergson developed a philosophy (called 'process' philosophy) based upon the rejection of permanence and uniformity, we prefer a more pragmatic (observable) approach of seeing human activity as both seeking uniformity (a process of convergence) and seeking novelty (a process of divergence).[11] You cannot think differently if there is no such thing as thinking the same. You cannot think outside the box if there is no box. In this sense, it is the successful management of opposite processes (convergence and divergence) that is key to progress. This is management as a skill or judgement rather than a science or procedure, although we can and do learn from how science and nature manage such opposites.

For pragmatists, "experience – perception, thought and enquiry – is a whole in which we are not merely passive recipients of sense-impressions but actively inferring and conceptualising a world and justifying our beliefs about it by reference to how they hang together – a 'coherence' view of justification." (Grayling, 2020, p. 331). So, according to the pragmatists, truth is in some sense a dynamic search for agreement between our ideas (what is in our mind) and reality. Grayling stresses the Kantian flavour to this in terms of how our minds are deemed to work. For human knowledge, both senses and understanding are necessary. In his use of the term 'understanding', Kant was referring to the organising function of the brain, which, through concepts and rational argument, imposes order on incoming sensory data received by eyes, ears, touch or indeed through second-hand reporting.[12] The application of this organising function to the incoming sense data creates 'experience', being 'the world as it seems to us'. Kant essentially distinguishes the world as it is (the world in itself) and the world as it seems to us (Grayling, 2020, p. 262). We see the world through the lens of our own representation or interpretation of it. When we re-represent it to others, as an auditor does, there is an additional organising function involved on the part of the auditor's brain and by the brain of the recipient of the audit report. The auditor attempts to anticipate how the recipient's brain works – in cognitive terms, a form of mindreading. As such, audit can be regarded as the representation and re-representation of the world to others.

The spirit of auditing

If audit is to draw together both sides of society's brain, both the left and right hemispheres, then it has to be spiritual as well as analytical. As illustrations of the underlying, essential spirit of auditing, we turn to phrases such as 'seek the truth' and 'dare to know'.

The first of these, 'to seek the truth' ('*quaere verum*'), is the motto of ICAS. This promotes a journey of conceptual development that is openly ambitious, though one in which, given ICAS' role as a guardian of practice, practical and conceptual development could move in ways where the former dominates the latter. In other words, it can become a journey in search of a pragmatist's version of truth. However, the ICAS motto does not define 'truth' and does not have to be bound by pragmatism. The truth seeker can take the search for truth beyond current thought and experience to reconceptualise, potentially giving a more coherent understanding and creating a 'better' world based upon 'better' truths (Baggini, 2017, pp. 105–106). The idea of 'better truths' implies that truth is both relative and dynamic.

The second phrase – 'dare to know' ('*supere aude*') – originates with Kant and is quoted by Julian Baggini in his book, *A Short History of Truth* (Baggini, 2017, pp. 30–31). Drawing on this, we like the idea of the auditor being 'daring', since it implies that audit is a challenge and goes beyond the comfort zone of established practice and thinking. Baggini highlights the connection of truth with attitude, especially attitude towards authority, given the power of authority to create a so-called 'post-truth' world of alternative 'facts'. Alternative facts can also emerge from an absence of authority combined with an abundance of connection, such as that which exists in today's 'social media'. Thus, truth can be created as well as found and this creation or emergence can either be to the detriment or to the benefit of society. There are also clear parallels to audit in the way that Baggini represents the pursuit of truth as a blend of individual opinion and an awareness or recognition of broader sentiment and context – commenting that seeking truth is a matter of thinking for oneself and not allowing anyone to make up your mind for you, whilst being open to different perspectives and recognising the benefits of collective enquiry.

Truth, it seems, is itself a concept held in place through its relationship (connection) with other concepts or ideas such as time and space, belief, fairness, holism and representation. What is true for a while in one place may not be true for another time and/or another place or context – truth is both static and dynamic. A representation can be true in a limited sense without being fair, because the context is missing – suggesting that a fair representation of truth needs to be holistic. Truth's connection to other concepts, such as fairness and (re)presentation, again has clear parallels as to how formal audit reports are typically presented – and how, philosophically, a reader attributes meaning to words, phrases and sentences used by auditors, particularly in terms of how meaning is attributed to words such as 'true' and 'fair'. Such attributions can vary depending upon the reader's belief system as to how one truth relates to another and what is encapsulated and considered when assessing the appropriateness of actions, behaviour and description.

Baggini (2017, pp. 106–107) concludes his contemplation of truth in the following terms:

> We tend to think of truths as like shiny pebbles: hard, unchangeable, clearly defined, collected in the mind as though it were a kind of rock garden. Truth is actually more like a real garden, an organic, holistic system where everything relates to everything else. While some features are as good as permanent, others grow, change or die. And like a garden, truth needs nurturing or else it becomes overgrown with the weeds of myth, distortions, misunderstandings and lies.

This quotation highlights the tension between a tendency for us to think of truth as unchanging and permanent, when such a view needs to coexist with the realisation that truth is part of a holistic and dynamic system and the recognition, above all, that truth needs to be developed and nurtured or it will die. Applied to the notion of audit, it becomes readily possible to see the role of the auditor as one of developing and nurturing truth; both searching for, and building respect for truth.

For McGilchrist (2021, p. 389), truth is never 'single, timeless and correct' but 'multiple, contingent and fallible'. He says, "It is uncertain not because it is *empty* – but because it is *full* – rich, complex, manifold". The contingent nature of truth suggests that truth might take the form of an 'if… then' statement. Accordingly, McGilchrist[13] represents and frames the issues that surround truth and the search for truth in the following terms:

> If reality is such that our knowledge is intrinsically not accidentally, incomplete; if it is intrinsically, not accidentally, uncertain; if it is intrinsically inexpressible in everyday language, requiring exceptional, non-denotive, highly metaphoric, 'poetic' use of language to get beyond the limits of language; if we must deal not with facts but with connexions; if entities are never wholly separable from other entities; if the process of a knower coming to know is interactive or reverberative, each changing the other – not distanced, inert and owing nothing to the presence, and possibly the nature, of the one who comes to know; and if any attempt to model it reduces what is continuous and moving, to what is static and discrete – if all of this is true, it is clear which hemisphere will be better suited to discerning it. Once more, the right hemisphere's take seems more veridical.
>
> (McGilchrist, 2021, pp. 1017–1018)

'If all of this is true' and a core element of audit is to seek the truth then, following McGilchrist, audit must engage with the incomplete, with the uncertain, with the inexpressible, and with the connections and interactions between entities – including the way their representation brings our world into existence and the extent to which such representation is reductionist (i.e., whether a world that is continuous and moving can be adequately represented and explained in terms that are static and discrete). If there is too much reductionism, so much of the richness, complexity and diversity of the world will be missed from any such representations and, in so far as the world is susceptible to human activity based upon a lack of representation and understanding, the richness of the world is potentially driven out and becomes less significant.

An auditor's understanding of truth and the search for this understanding – the audit process – are evidently challenging but also quite fascinating and, in our view, much in need of fresh conceptual consideration and analysis if audit is to have an intellectual basis from which innovation and societal enhancement can readily flow.

Structuring our analysis

The next four chapters (Chapters 2–5) of the book build our (re) conceptualisation of audit through a detailed exploration of the form and nature of audit engagement. We develop and analyse audit from the conceptual standpoint that treats audit as the search for a better society encompassing a better truth. Figure 1.1 provides a diagrammatic representation of this conceptualisation, delineating the core dimensions of audit's social functionality or purposefulness.

The ambition includes a better reality, a fairer society and a truer representation – collectively facilitated by, and symbolising, the existence of a more purposeful audit. 'Better', 'fairer', 'truer' and 'purposeful' are all value-laden words and consequently 'values' are central to Figure 1.1. Any such values are not static but have an interactive connection with each of the four contributing elements of what could be classified as the 'societal audit network'. The ellipse at the heart of Figure 1.1 is a repository for, or an embodiment of, the particular society's values and, in that sense, acts as 'central bank' for the network.

The ellipse's vertical connections take up the idea that truth is the relationship between representation and reality, a relationship overseen through audit, but one brokered by societal values that, to varying degrees, nurture and respect truth. The ellipse's horizontal connections are between audit and society, connections discussed earlier in terms of the need for audit to be a balancing factor to protect society from either left or right hemisphere dominance and to use any divisions in society as a source of creativity rather than conflict.

Values reverberate between audit and society to give a shared sense of social values. Audit provides a continuing challenge and influence but ultimately society determines what is to be seen as fair and reasonable. Following the central bank analogy, 'values' may be taken to be the currency of the societal audit network; a common currency that enables the exchanges (flows and counter-flows) that form the connections between audit and society. Figure 1.1 deliberately does not detail different stakeholders nor contexts but both differing stakeholders and contexts can be mapped or superimposed to provide a more individualised and contextualised audit network.

A holistic overview of the societal audit network takes us around the perimeter of Figure 1.1 in both clockwise and anti-clockwise directions. Such clockwise and anti-clockwise movements should not be treated as alternative or sequential but as being conducted simultaneously.

Going clockwise from the bottom of Figure 1.1, reality generates evidence which audit evaluates to provide an understanding of reality. This understanding forms the basis of a representation communicated by auditors to society to help society's understanding of reality. This understanding informs society's purposeful action – action that, in turn, helps to shape or reshape reality.

Going anti-clockwise, society's experience of reality (experience shaped by reality's inherent uncertainty and unpredictability) can lead to disruption in the sense that society's intended purposes are not fulfilled. This experience

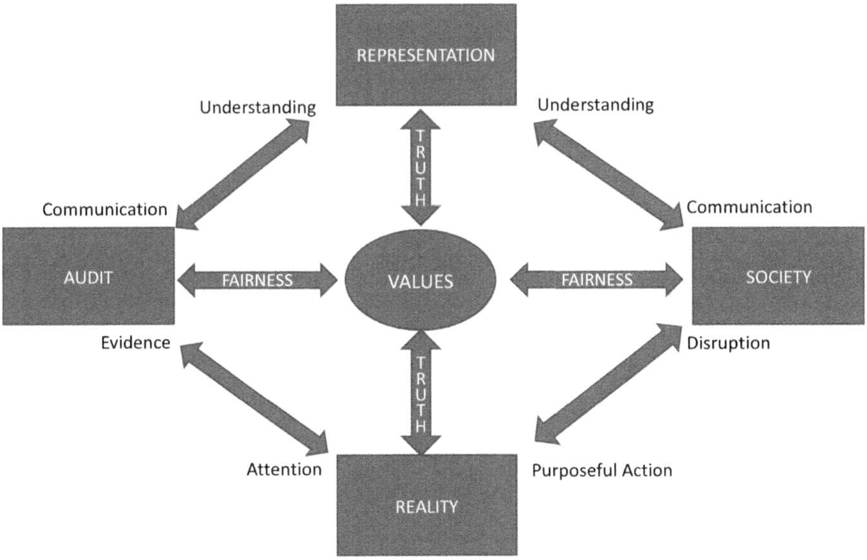

FIGURE 1.1 **The societal audit network.**

drives society to re-assess its understanding and to revise ('re-present') the existing representation of reality. This re-presentation is communicated in varying fashions and forms to the designated auditor who, in turn, re-assesses audit's understanding and the aspects of reality to which attention should be given by the audit. Changes in the focus of audit's attention can have the effect of changing the nature of reality, with implications for the next round of both clockwise and anti-clockwise movements.

Figure 1.1 is also a vehicle for introducing and explaining the basic structure and approach taken in Chapters 2–5 – where we reflect in more depth on how the elements of Figure 1.1 and their connections (associated flows and counter-flows) contribute to the societal audit network, with the purpose of the network as a whole being a better (understanding of) society.

To provide a better understanding of the nature of connections in the societal audit network, Chapter 2 draws on ideas from physics and its attempts to represent reality. The chapter identifies connections through time and through space and considers whether such connections are continuous or discrete, dynamic or static. Of particular relevance are ideas from quantum physics whereby, 'in reality', connection might be both continuous and discrete, or both divergent and convergent at the same time. If so, in the physical world, connection can coexist with disconnection to create the 'unity of opposites' similar to that seen in a progressive society. Another important idea is that of the 'conjugate pair' where bringing one of the pair into sharper focus leads to less clarity for the other, highlighting the need to attend to the pair holistically. Holistic (bigger picture) understanding is a crucial skill of the auditor. If the world is inherently uncertain and our knowledge of it inevitably incomplete, then the more we know, the more we realise what we don't know – making the role of audit one of guiding, cautioning, stimulating and, even, leading society through a journey of learning and knowledge development.

Chapter 3 looks at the two connections shown in Figure 1.1 that serve to shape reality. The first is the relationship between reality and society. Society takes action with the intention or purpose of impacting reality for the better, but with inevitably incomplete knowledge of an inherently uncertain world, purposeful action at some stage leads to unintended consequences and disruption. Consequently, reality can have an unwanted or unexpected impact on society. The second connection is between reality and audit (evidence). The auditor's perception of reality (following Kant) is of two kinds: that for which there is audit experience (evidence) and that which lies beyond experience and for which, therefore, no evidence is felt or seen to exist, except perhaps in the imagination.

Reality for which there is evidence is also of two kinds: that to which attention is given by the auditor and that to which attention is not given. This boundary is determined by audit judgements of materiality. This is the traditional concept of materiality, being a determination as to when evidence matters. Reality for which there is no evidence divides into that within the human imagination (of the auditor) and that which lies beyond human imagination, with the boundary between the two following the limits of the auditor's imagination. The audit question here is when does imagination matter – or what could be described as the materiality of imagination. In this way, it becomes possible to see that, as well as the nature of reality yielding evidence that influences the audit, the auditor's attention and imagination (reflecting an ability to think differently and the resulting capacity to change boundaries) are influential (material) in shaping the nature and perception of reality.

Chapter 4 investigates the two interconnections shaping the representation of reality. The first is between representation and the understanding of reality that audit gains through the identification and evaluation of evidence. Representation has a reciprocal relationship with understanding since representation relies on understanding but, at the same time, understanding also comes from the act of representation. The second relationship is between representation and society's understanding and perception of reality. Representation is a coming together or synthesis emerging from a discourse between audit and society, between their respective experiences and value judgements – essentially, a discourse as to what is true, what is fair, what is valuable, and how it should be valued; relating to questions of what is progress and what are the opportunities for its achievement? Representation, in this respect, is an exercise in social cognition. Where a common view emerges, there is a single joint representation but if not, perhaps because of the auditor's 'different thinking', then a separate representation by the auditor is necessary. This chapter seeks to develop a better understanding of 'representation' through its connections with other parts of the societal audit network and underlines the importance of representation being balanced in order to avoid left or right hemisphere dominance in society – and the role that audit plays in securing and retaining such balance.

Chapter 5, taking the premise that the world is 'in reality' intrinsically uncertain and that our knowledge of the world is intrinsically incomplete, focuses on how purposeful human activity inevitably leads to disruption (both positive and negative) and consequently a re-purposing of activity. The connections or pathways between purpose and disruption shape human activity, including the everyday life of the individual and the relationship between audit and such life. These pathways and relations are demonstrated through the medium of two thought experiments. In these experiments, the audit subject, performer of the audit and beneficiary overlap or merge – demonstrating that having these three classifications separate is not crucial to a conceptualisation of audit. For example, an audit permits and enables the separation of principal and agent but is not dependent upon the existence of such a separation. In subsequent chapters, the relations between audit and the individual are shown to be relevant to relations between audit and both organisations and society. Thinking differently becomes the driver (dynamic) of audit at the level of the individual, the organisation and society, and is key to understanding the connection between these levels.

Advancing audit, business and society

A primary vehicle used to assist us in developing our conceptualisation of audit, its core attributes and cognitive facilities, is to contemplate a range of 'audit as...' depictions, scenarios or perspectives (with the titles of the first nine chapters of the book beginning with the words 'audit as...'). Collectively, Chapters 2–5 establish a number of core conceptual standpoints as to the functionality of audit and its professional and intellectual obligations and commitments. Chapters 6 and 7 focus on reframing or reimagining what an audit is or what an audit could become. Specifically, they explore how an audit contemplates and connects (1) the environmental, societal, economic and technological realities faced by the entity that is subject to audit; (2) the activities of the entity; and (3) the confidence the entity deserves from its stakeholders (including society).

The consideration of connection and the role of audit in Chapters 6 and 7 is undertaken from the perspective and context of a limited company – where understanding of connection is crucial both to the financial value of the business and the interaction of business, society and audit in generating that value. We believe that companies, including those not statutorily required to have an audit, can benefit significantly from a reconceptualised audit that stimulates different thinking about their business, both in terms of the impact on the business and its overall social connectivity and purposefulness.[14] The resulting vision is one that extends the concept of audit beyond notions of 'fair correspondence' to incorporate consideration of 'fair progression' and it is this duality or combination of perspectives which establishes a firmer conceptual basis for claims that audit serves the public interest.

Chapters 8 and 9 further illuminate the significance of our re-conceptualisation of audit by considering its implications for notions of corporate governance and corporate financial statements. We consider what our reconfigured audit implies for management (including its stakeholder relationships and patterns/processes of investment) and what it implies for the nature and presentation of corporate financial statements.

Taken as a whole, the book's philosophical analysis extends our thinking beyond the boundary of a contemporary business or society. A business or a society is just a selected boundary that a given set of people or groups of people have determined as being important, which, by implication, means that anything beyond this boundary is deemed not to be important or to be of less importance. Such a position or perspective has profound implications in terms of considering whether and how audit works in the interests of a society or a specific group of stakeholders – and whether what audit is currently doing is framed in unduly narrow terms.

Subjecting a particular society or an entity within society to an audit helps to reinforce the boundary forming that society or entity. However, we argue that a 'public interested' audit function must also be an instrument for crossing that boundary and giving effect to the mutual connections with the outside that help to define existence. In this sense, audit not only reflects but also creates and crosses boundaries. The truly public interested auditor has to consider the connected and possibly competing interests of different publics, different entities and different societies...a social animal not restricted to one society but who considers trans-societal interests.

We close the book, in Chapter 10, by emphasising that the conceptual heart of audit **is** 'thinking differently' and highlight the profound implications that this has for the future of audit. Thinking differently requires engaging both hemispheres of the brain – new rationality and logics associated with the left hemisphere, combining with new intuitions, senses and feelings associated with the right hemisphere. When we think differently, we both feel differently and employ new logics. If we translate audit into 'thinking differently' then, in terms of Figure 1.1, audit is the catalyst that leads to 'betterment' – more truthful representation, a better reality and a fairer society – both inspired by, and helping to inspire, a better audit.

Conceptually, it is acknowledged that Figure 1.1 is itself a representation and a macro-one at that. As with any representation, it will always be open to improvement and development. This is not just in terms of the greater specificity to emerge from consideration of different social contexts and different stakeholder groupings and relationships, but also in terms of developing both our own, and a broader societal, understanding and appreciation of the overall nature of core connections and the connected. What is most attractive to us in terms of the book's contribution is that it can set the future of audit on a more exciting and inspiring path.

A different 'audit' society?

We will say more on this in the later stages of the book but it is worth reflecting on the potential consequence of connecting our desire to think differently about audit with the analysis provided by Iain McGilchrist of the societal significance and influence of left and right hemisphere thinking. The implication is that any representation of society or an entity within society should not be dominated by judgement and feeling (right hemisphere) or by logics and metrics, including financial metrics (left hemisphere) but by a medium that connects – crosses the boundary between – the two. Power (1997) made no reference to the metaphor of the left and right hemispheres of the brain in framing his notion of an Audit Society but he essentially describes a society in which the left hemisphere of the brain has come, and continues, to dominate both society and the audit. Implicitly, any innovation and improvement (whether in audit or society) that requires the involvement of the right hemisphere of the brain is being squeezed out, in the interest of 'making things auditable' – and, consequently, reducing audit to what Power classifies as 'a ritual of verification'.[15]

Power (1997) concluded that breaking out of an absence of official scepticism and critical diagnosis and enabling audit to "become part of a broader organizational learning process rather than an empty ritual of verification for merely disciplinary purposes" (p. 145) requires a confident society which is "capable of knowing when to trust, when to trust trust and when to demand an audited account" (p. 146). We agree with this but any such society also has to be confident that it really does understand audit, not only in terms of what audit is but what it could become with better conceptual fundamentals. At its core, audit is epistemological; that is to say, audit is about the nature of knowledge and how we come 'to know' and 'to know our feelings and what matters'. Thus, a contribution of audit to society is one of enabling society to know itself better and to trust audit as a means to such knowledge. Audit creates knowledge by bringing together opposites – for instance, the comparative transparency of logic and reason with the comparative obscurity or opaqueness of emotion and instinct. Hence, audit (judgement) is neither fully transparent nor fully obscure.

To become a society confident in and about audit, we need to bring the conceptualisation of audit and, consequently, society into a fresh, brighter, and more optimistic light. Our book lays down the conceptual foundation for a very different way of looking at audit and the potential existence of a very different form of Audit Society – or rather a society in which audit is directly associated with innovation and 'betterment' through the promotion of balance and understanding of interaction between the two hemispheres and their different takes on the world. Audit becomes making things better, not making things auditable. Audit has to break free of the conceptual restrictions and traditions that prevent it from doing and being more, a point recognised by Power (2011) when noting that the fundamental nature of audit is "more or less taken as a given, albeit as something in need of reform" (p. 324). Whilst Power's impressive work on the Audit Society has been a major influence on academics,[16] there is far less evidence of it motivating an effective societal push back against the growth of the Audit Society depicted by Power. Our book is written in the hope of motivating such a countervailing movement. We seek to enable this by taking readers on a journey in search of a society in which there is deserved confidence[17] in progress and the future because of audit; why not have a society that is better served by audit, even a society that is better because of audit? We see an audit that promotes thinking differently as challenging the why with the why not; an audit that thinks differently and deeply about progress – what it is and how to recognise and achieve it.

Notes

1 For an illustration of the tension between control and creativity, albeit in the fashion industry rather than auditing, see Jeacle and Carter (2012). Clearly there are differences but perhaps also some similarities between audit and fashion.
2 In January 2026, the government announced that it was scrapping its intended Audit Reform Bill "to avoid significant new costs for large firms" (www.gov.uk/government/news/business-secretary-backs-british-scaleups-with-growth-package-and-red-tape-review).
3 According to Theodore Limperg (whose auditing papers in 1932 and 1933 were translated from Dutch into English in 1985 – Limperg, 1985), trust and confidence of the public in the audit function is the essence of auditing, powerfully noting that without such trust audit was useless. Society's reform of audit has tended to focus upon, and be motivated by, one-off restorations and maintenance of society's trust in audit. To his credit, Limperg did not see audit as static but as dynamic, responding to change in society and change in audit techniques. Limperg saw the auditor as an agent of the public interest.
4 For example, see: www.icas.com/about/governance/icas-charter; www.icaew.com/about-icaew/who-we-are/icaew-overview; and www.aicpa-cima.com/about/landing/about.
5 The ten ethical perspectives (and their sources) are self-interest (following Protagoras), utilitarian benefits (Bentham and Mill), personal virtues (Plato and Aristotle), religious injunctions (St. Augustine), government requirements (Hobbes and Locke), universal rules (Kant), individual rights (Rousseau and Jefferson), economic efficiency (Adam Smith), distributive justice (Rawls) and contributing liberty (Nozick).
6 Later in the book, for example, we will talk of 'progress' explicitly in terms of creativity, sustainable delivery, resilience and the engagement of citizens and stakeholders. But, of course, this is only one possible set of considerations as to what constitutes 'progress'.
7 For a succinct and enthusiastic review of the book, see Willis (2010). The provided characteristisations of left and right hemisphere thinking are taken from this review. What matters for the argument of our book is not so much the specificity of where the different personal characteristics reside in the brain, but rather that the brain in general functions (thinks) by recognising and synthesising (bringing together) opposite characteristics.

8 David Flint set out his own thoughts on audit in his 1988 book *Philosophy and Principles of Auditing* (Flint, 1988). Sikka's (1989) review of the book questioned Flint's failure to address adequately 'issues of power, authority, domination and ideology'. Flint argued that audit should serve society as a whole whereas Sikka expressed concern that, in practice, this was not the case.
9 Philosophical analyses of the conceptual underpinnings of audit have also tended to stress the importance of recognising and negotiating the limits of audit (for a discussion, see Arthur, 2001). Our primary concern is with developing the potential and possibilities of audit.
10 See Gunn (2004), chapter 2, *The Reality of Change*.
11 Jacoby (1912) discusses whether Bergson might be considered a pragmatist and suggests that he was not. He states (p.98) "....to Bergson's mind philosophy begins where pragmatism ceases ...".
12 Kant's ideas are more fully discussed, amongst many others, by Kenny (2012, pp. 612–623), Grayling (2020, pp. 256–268) and Russell (1946, pp. 731–739).
13 In McGilchrist's *The Matter with Things* (McGilchrist, 2021), Volume 1 is titled *The Ways to Truth* and should help the audit profession shape its future. It covers the question of what is truth (Chapter 10, pp. 379–403) whilst other chapters discuss possible paths to truth.
14 Our new conceptualisation of audit (including its incorporation of the concept of deserved confidence) is also highly relevant to public sector entities – with increased value of the entity to the public clearly capable of flowing from developing understanding of the connections between (1) the activity of the entity; (2) its societal, economic and environmental pressures; (3) technological opportunity; and (4) the audit. Public sector audits, in addition to financial audit, can include performance audit and programme evaluation. Lindeberg (2007, p. 348) saw these three as more of a continuum rather than justifying separate categorical distinctions. We consider that all three should embrace notions of thinking differently as outlined in our book. In respect of programme evaluation, thinking differently is significantly constrained if the auditor is not allowed to comment on or question policy.
15 In his earlier work on *The Audit Explosion*, Power (1994) did identify two styles of audit (style A and style B) and, although he did not make the connection, they might roughly be taken to correspond to the left (style A) and right (style B) hemispheres of the brain. Power (p. 7) observed that the audit explosion had involved an overwhelming priority for style A. Style A has become increasingly dominant and created the Audit Society. In subsequent work, Power (2009) argued that style A dominance in risk management is a consequence of style A dominance in audit. Rather than audit, he represented 'Business Continuity Management' as an opportunity for creativity and progression based upon a recognition of the importance of interconnectedness.
16 See, for example, Bottausci and Robson (2023) and Gendron (2024).
17 The Brydon Report (Brydon, 2019) introduced the term 'deserved confidence'. It is neither confidence in (a strictly) emotional sense nor is it a statistical confidence, but rather a confidence that draws together both hemispheres of the brain.

References

Anonymous, 1942, 'The future of auditing – IV', *The Accountant*, 24th January, pp. 44–47.

Arthur, A., 2001, 'Evidence and argument: Another look at audit fundamentals', *Critical Perspectives in Accounting*, 12, pp. 247–267, https://doi.org/10.1006/cpac.2000.0414.

Baggini, J., 2017, *A Short History of Truth: Consolidated for a Post-Truth World*, (Quercus Publishing, London).

BEIS, 2022, *Restoring Trust in Audit and Corporate Governance: Government Response to Consultation on Strengthening the UK's Audit, Corporate Reporting and Governance Systems*, (Department for Business, Energy and Industrial Strategy (BEIS), London), www.gov.uk/government/consultations/restoring-trust-in-audit-and-corporate-governance-proposals-on-reforms.

Bottausci, C. and K. Robson, 2023, '"He hears": An essay celebrating the 25 year anniversary of the audit society', *Critical Perspectives in Accounting*, 97, December, www.sciencedirect.com/science/article/abs/pii/S1045235423000291?via%3Dihub.

Brydon, D., 2019, *Assess, Assure and Inform: Improving Audit Quality and Effectiveness, Report of the Independent Review into the Quality and Effectiveness of Audit*, https://assets.publishing.service.gov.uk/media/5df8edfced915d0938597e1f/brydon-review-final-report.pdf

Caldwell, C. and S.E. Clapham, 2003, 'Organizational trustworthiness: An international perspective', *Journal of Business Ethics*, 47:4, pp. 349–364, www.jstor.org/stable/25075151.

Flint, D., 1988, *Philosophy and Principles of Auditing: An Introduction*, (Macmillan Education, New York, NY).

Gendron, Y., 2024, 'The audit society: Opening up a meaningful epistemological agenda', *Qualitative Research in Accounting & Management*, 21:1, pp. 7–20, https://doi.org/10.1108/QRAM-09-2021-0173.

Grayling, A.C., 2020, *The History of Philosophy: Three Millenia of Thought from the West and Beyond*, (Penguin, Random House, London).

Gunn, J.A., 2004, *Bergson and his Philosophy*, Gutenberg e-books, www.gutenberg.org/files/5717.

Hosmer, L.T., 1994, 'Strategic planning as if ethics mattered', *Strategic Management Journal*, 15:S2, pp. 17–34, https://doi.org/10.1002/smj.4250151003.

Humphrey, C., 2020, *Thinking Differently is 'Audit'*, (Audit Futures, ICAEW, London), https://icaew.access.preservica.com/portal/asset/sdb%3AIO%7C3c14db66-e5bb-4aa0-b043-90c3a0b3f472.

Jacoby, G., 1912, 'Henri Bergson, pragmatism and Schopenhauer', *The Monist*, 22:4 (October), pp.593–611, www.jstor.org/stable/27900398.

Jeacle, I. and C. Carter, 2012, 'Fashioning the popular masses: Accounting as mediator between creativity and control', *Accounting, Auditing & Accountability Journal*, 25:4, pp. 719–751, https://doi.org/10.1108/09513571211225114.

Kenny, A., 2012, *A New History of Western Philosophy*, (Oxford University Press, Oxford).

Limperg, T., 1985, *Social Responsibility of the Auditor: A Basic Theory on the Auditor's Function by Professor Theodore Limperg (1879-1961) of the University of Amsterdam with some recent comments*, (Limperg Instituut, Amsterdam), https://limperginstituut.nl/archivefiles/2004/Publicatie_The_social_responsibility_of_the_auditor.pdf.

Lindeberg, T., 2007, 'The ambiguous identity of auditing', *Financial Accounting & Management*, 23:3, pp. 337–350, https://doi.org/10.1111/j.1468-0408.2007.00432.x.

Manville, B. and J. Ober, 2003, *A Company of Citizens: What the World's First Democracy Teaches Leaders about Creating Great Organizations*, (Harvard Business School Press, Cambridge, MA).

Mautz, R. and H.A. Sharaf, 1961, *The Philosophy of Auditing*, (American Accounting Association, Sarasota, Florida).

McGilchrist, I., 2012, *The Master and his Emissary: The Divided Brain and the Making of the Western World*, (Yale University Press, New Haven).

McGilchrist, I., 2021, *The Matter with Things: Our Brains, Our Delusions, and the Unmaking of the World*, (Perspectiva Press, London).

Paine, L.S., 2003, *Value Shift: Why Companies Must Shift Social and Financial Imperatives to Achieve Superior Performance*, (Harvard Business School Press, Cambridge, MA).

Power, M., 1994, *The Audit Explosion*, (Demos, London), https://demos.co.uk/wp-content/uploads/files/theauditexplosion.pdf.

Power, M., 1997, *The Audit Society: Rituals of Verification*, (Oxford University Press, Oxford).

Power, M., 2009, 'The risk management of nothing', *Accounting, Organizations and Society*, 34:6-7, pp. 849–855, https://doi.org/10.1016/j.aos.2009.06.001.

Power, M., 2011, 'Assurance worlds: Consumers, experts and independence', *Accounting, Organizations and Society*, 36:4-5, pp. 324–326, www.sciencedirect.com/science/article/abs/pii/S0361368211000614.

Russell, B., 1946, *A History of Western Philosophy*, (Allen & Unwin, London).

Satava, D., Caldwell, C. and L. Richards, 2006, 'Ethics and the auditing culture: Rethinking the foundation of accounting and auditing', *Journal of Business Ethics*, 64:3, pp. 271–284, https://link.springer.com/article/10.1007/s10551-005-0556-y.

Sikka, P., 1989, 'Philosophy and principles of auditing: An introduction: D. Flint, Macmillan (Basingstoke, 1988)', *The British Accounting Review*, 21:2, pp. 200–202, https://doi.org/10.1016/0890-8389(89)90203-5.

Willis, J., 2010, 'A tale of two hemispheres', *British Journal of General Practice*, 60:572, pp. 226–227, https://doi.org/10.3399/bjgp10x483779.

2

AUDIT AS CONNECTION

Whilst subsequent chapters work through the specifics of the clockwise and anti-clockwise flows and connections of the societal audit network (as represented by Figure 1.1, Chapter 1), this chapter deals with the primary, overarching, issue of the nature of connections and their significance to audit and the interconnected world in which audit operates. In order to provide a better understanding of the nature of connections, this chapter draws on ideas from the philosophy of physics (notably the connected nature of time and space as recognised by Einstein) and from perspectives in quantum physics on the nature of reality (which emphasise the fundamental importance of connections).

For non-physicists such as ourselves, an introduction to quantum theory is well explained by Stephen Hawking (1988) in *A Brief History of Time* and by Carlo Rovelli (2021) in his book *Helgoland*. In the inside cover of *Helgoland*, Rovelli states: "One idea more than any other, has transformed our understanding of the fabric of reality: Quantum physics". He writes:

> The discovery of quantum theory, I believe, is the discovery that the properties of any entity are nothing other than the way in which that entity influences others. It exists only through its interactions. Quantum theory is the theory of how things influence each other. And this is the best description of nature we have.
>
> (p. 69)

Rovelli's favouring of this relational interpretation of quantum theory sits well with our relational conception of audit, which frames audit (as per Figure 1.1) in terms of (1) its relations (interactions) with society and (2) its

DOI: 10.4324/9781032721293-2

role as the connection between reality and representation.[1] This is premised on understanding that the existence of any 'thing', whether it be a physical particle, an object, an idea, a feeling or an entity comprising more than one of these, can be expressed in terms of its relations with (connections to) other things; things that are both similar to and different from itself. The relational interpretation can connect the physical world and the mental (human) world, bringing them closer together. For example, relations between the human and physical worlds are the subject of academic work labelled Science and Technology Studies (STS), in which objects may be assigned a purpose, being the purpose of the human who uses them. Thus, objects become a stakeholder in human endeavour and part of an extended cognition that connects a rational understanding of the physical world with the world of human requirements, desire and feeling.[2]

Every 'thing' or entity is a story of relationships or connections that, when made by humans, may be either rational or emotional, or a combination of both. Judgement, including audit judgement, can be regarded as the connection between the rational (logic and analysis) and the sensory (emotions, feelings and intuitions, perhaps based upon experience). As we will discuss later, it can be treated as a coming together of the left and right hemispheres of the brain and a connection that is itself managed by the right hemisphere. If every 'thing' exists courtesy of its relations or connections with other 'things', whilst at the same time connections exist courtesy of the existence of the things they connect, this must also apply to the idea of 'connection' itself.

Understanding the nature of connection depends on exploring the relationship that the idea of 'connection' has with other big ideas such as classification, networks, space, time, order, complexity and, of course, audit. In particular, networks require classification (things to connect) and classification requires judgement to determine the boundaries of 'things' or 'entities' based upon the two opposites of similarity to, and difference from, things other than themselves. Classification creates boundaries and crossing those boundaries through movement, flow and conversion generates evidence of the state of connection. Thus, 'connection' has a relationship with boundary crossing in the form of 'flow' – flows that can link together and superimpose one on another, in different ways to form different types of network (including the societal audit network of Figure 1.1, a network that connects reality and representation).

This chapter represents audit as a key to a system of connection that crosses boundaries, enabling flow, including both physical and sensory flows. It is through its relationship with the big ideas of 'reality' and 'representation' that audit connects to ideas from the philosophy of physics – ideas which we will see include not only representation of the behaviour of very small particles but also representation of the whole universe of time and space, where Einstein's theory of relativity applies. It is through its relationship with society that audit connects to the sensory ideas and values shaping society. Ultimately, an audit is a coming together of the sensory and the physical, of truth and fairness with reality and representation; a coming together that has the potential to be creative and generate progress through new insight.

This chapter comprises three key analytical segments. The first contemplates audit as a study of classification and connection and of the nature of connectivity, with creativity being closely connected to the development of our understanding of connectivity. Since audit is concerned with representation, the second segment of the chapter develops the idea of networks as a means of representing classification and connection. However, connections are made across space and over time and so the third segment of the chapter considers the context of time and space, and how space-time impacts our understanding. Collectively, the three segments illuminate how 'understanding' depends deeply on the making of connections and how such connections come from both the left and the right hemispheres of the brain working together. In this respect, conceptually, audit can be regarded as the study of connection and the nature of connectivity. At the same time, the chapter highlights the complexity and depth of the connectivity that audit represents, a complexity and depth that has to be explored through thinking differently across a range of different perspectives.

Segment 1 – Classification and connection

The mental construction of classifications underpins the human idea of existence as a network of connections. When two 'things' are identical, they cannot be separately categorised or classified. Similarly, were two things to be completely different, they cannot be separately classified because there is no medium through which to express a difference. In the first case, there is no disconnection between the two things, whilst in the second, there is no connection. Therefore, the separate existence of a 'thing' in the form of a distinct classification or categorisation depends on there being both an element of difference from, and an element of similarity with, other things. Existence, in the form of a separate classification, may be lost over time. For example, a hot body and a cold body have in common the experience of temperature and come together (connect) to create two warm bodies. When they are the same temperature, the two bodies can no longer be classified separately on the basis of temperature and the distinguishing adjectives 'hot' and 'cold' are dropped. The two bodies are each converted into, and conserved as, 'warm' bodies. In being converted into 'warm bodies', the 'hot' and 'cold' bodies cease to exist or, at least, cease to fulfil their previous categorisations. This is a disconnection or discontinuity. Of course, the two bodies continue to exist physically and now share the more general classification or description of 'a warm body'. Temperature apart, the hot, cold and warm bodies all share the same physical attributes and this provides the element of continuity and connection. The use of language in respect of classification is intimately linked with a notion of existence – through the coexistence of connection and disconnection, of continuity and discontinuity and of conversion and conservation.

To give some illumination to these ideas, suppose X is a 'tree' and Y refers to 'the retention of leaves', with Y1 being a deciduous tree and Y2 an evergreen tree. Suppose we can form a hybrid tree, Y3, by the active physical operation of grafting a deciduous tree with an evergreen. The hybrid retains what is common to Y1 and Y2 (they are all trees) but the clear differences between Y1 and Y2 are not retained, as the hybrid emerges with its own pattern of leaf retention. The action of hybridisation causes the differences between evergreens and deciduous trees to come together. Suppose we plant trees together (contiguity) so W is a wood, W1 is a wood of similar trees and W2 is a wood of mixed trees. In this case, the effect of placing trees together is to create a new classification – a wood.

According to philosopher, David Hume, the mind is capable of making connections due to resemblance, because of contiguity in time or space, or because of (observable) cause and effect (see Grayling, 2020, p. 245). In terms of Hume, deciduous, evergreen and hybrids all resemble trees, all woods are formed of trees contiguous in time and space, and hybrids are the product of cause and effect. Cause and effect implies action and appears as a flow or movement from the cause to the effect. In the physical world, cause and effect are often irreversible but in the human world, anticipation of the effect may 'cause' a different choice of action.[3] Each of Hume's associations or connections (resemblance, contiguity and 'cause ---> effect') is represented in the tree/wood illustration, as is the process of 'connect <---> disconnect'. Trees are connected through what they have in common (resemblances such as a trunk, branches and leaves) and disconnected by their differences (deciduous, evergreen, hybrid). Similarly, woods are connected through what they have in common (contiguous trees) and disconnected by the mix of trees they contain, as well as geographical location. Collections of trees might also be disconnected (classified) by size. A copse, a wood and a forest are connected by each having contiguous trees but disconnected by the number of trees they contain. A copse is small, a wood is medium and a forest is large. The boundaries are not explicitly expressed in a specific number (of trees) and, in this case, the boundaries are fuzzy and the chosen description or category is a matter of judgement – so, although categorisation sits comfortably with the left hemisphere of the brain, its execution also involves the right hemisphere, which must also be involved in the judgement as to the appropriate number of categories.

To sum up, existence as a distinct category or classification requires both connection and disconnection – being a coincidence and coexistence of opposites. So, there is no separate existence without disconnection, whilst without connection and interaction, separate existence is meaningless in the sense that there is no point of reference.[4] Each classification represents a 'thing' or 'idea', which consists of both properties X that connect with, and properties Y that disconnect (or distinguish) from another classification. The (relative) information we learn about one thing from another depends upon the materiality of what they have in common relative to the materiality of their differences – and materiality is a right hemisphere judgement that depends upon context. It is context that determines the ability of one thing to represent or provide evidence for another. What the 'trees' illustration shows us is that the world, as seen through our minds, develops spatially in response to the rhythm of 'connect <---> disconnect'. New mental spaces (classifications) are formed by, and to facilitate, mental operations of disconnection and connection.

Classification in society and in accounting

Consideration of accounting classification is given in 'The Finitist Accountant' (Hatherly, Leung and MacKenzie, 2008), which takes finitism to cover the analysis of how people classify or represent activities and states of all kinds.[5] Classification is part of the human effort to create order and a form of discrimination necessary to facilitate logical argument (understanding) but which can also promote good or bad feelings. The management of classification, therefore, is part of the management of the balance between the left and right hemispheres. In this connection, it is arguable that, whilst a 'classless' or 'classification-less' society is unlikely to develop or progress (because of an absence of recognition, analysis and understanding of difference), the introduction of classes with boundaries that are difficult to cross can cause bad feelings and potentially an unstable society. Interaction (connection) requires the crossing of boundaries but also the maintenance or creation of boundaries to cross. Consider the business and the community: whilst business is the survival of the fittest, community is the support of the weakest and the term 'society' covers both – a coexistence of opposites. Management of both business and the community requires judgement in connecting these opposites but also in maintaining them as opposites. Whilst some may wish to change businesses into communities or communities into businesses, it is also worth remembering that the fittest businesses and strongest communities are likely to be those that interact the best with each other.

The important point here is that the 'resolution' of opposites does not always come from exchange, substitution or standardisation in order to minimise differences. Sometimes opposites (and differences) need to be maintained and to find a way of co-operating and coexisting, just as the left and right hemispheres of the brain (need to) co-operate and coexist. The detailed mechanics of this coexistence can be mysterious (as they are far from being understood), but coexistence implies balance (in that neither hemisphere of the brain is dominant). Coexistence within a society might be explained in terms of equality and diversity being two opposites but opposites that arguably coexist in the most 'progressive' of societies. Here, coexistence should not imply stasis and an absence of disruption but should be seen as a creative 'co-incidence of opposites'. In the sense that more equality does not lead to greater diversity and vice versa, then the one does not directly lead into, flow or convert into the other. Instead, both diversity and equality flow, interact and are drawn together and engage with each other through a third concept, being the 'progressive' society. Thus, equality and diversity are not substitutes and cannot be exchanged without impacting upon progression. The progressive society is one that skilfully manages equality and diversity as a pairing.

Classification permits the logic of accounting, being the subtraction of activities classified as expenses from activities classified as revenue to form the hybrid notion of accounting profit or surplus. Revenues (income), expenses and profit/surplus are contiguous in space (in the sense that they belong to the same company) and contiguous in time (belonging to the same time period). Profit emerges from the calculative space that is the left hemisphere but then needs to be picked up by the right hemisphere for evaluation in context in order to understand (including to get a feel for) the connection between the business and its financial performance. Later chapters in the book will suggest that a crucial contribution of audit might be to ensure that not only are the classifications and calculations completed appropriately but, more radically, that the right hemisphere oriented 'evaluation in context' is suitably conducted, by incorporating it as part of an audit. Audit is often described as a 'process' and process might be associated with the left hemisphere, but the audit process is not strictly mechanistic, linear and sequential and can and should engage the left and right hemispheres, incorporating both analysis and feeling.

The importance of context is emphasised by McGilchrist in discussing the work of the phenomenologist, Edmund Husserl, phenomenology being the study of lived experience. The idea is that our view of the world is shaped by our experience of it and by the experience of others. Husserl came to the conclusion that reality was constituted by empathy for others and shared experience, a shared experience made possible by our embodied existence alongside other embodied individuals (McGilchrist, 2012, p. 144).

McGilchrist states

> In this emphasis on the body, the importance of empathy, and intersubjectivity (which forms part of what I mean by 'betweenness') Husserl is asserting the essential role that the right hemisphere plays in constituting the world in which we live. He too emphasises the importance of context: things only are what they are because they find themselves in the surroundings in which they find themselves, and are connected to whatever it is that they are connected to.

Empathy and shared experience should coexist with classification – classification that highlights both the connectedness and the differences between people, their feelings and experiences.

Audit as a coincidence of opposites

Audit is about managing the interaction of opposites; it is the management of connection and disconnection, of similarity and difference. In this regard, an audit can be conceived of in terms of the workings of the human brain. While differences are associated with the left and right hemispheres of the brain, the two hemispheres are connected by the corpus callosum in a coincidence or union of opposites that can be profoundly generative. When the left hemisphere and right hemisphere of the brain have a common situation to be dealt with, they come together to produce a response to that situation. Thus, in any one human brain at any one time, both hemispheres will be actively involved (McGilchrist, 2012, p. 10). However, managing the contributions of the left and right hemispheres to produce the response to a situation is done by the right hemisphere. The corpus callosum also serves to keep the two hemispheres apart so that they do not confuse each other but retain their separate (opposite/different) functions (McGilchrist, 2012, pp. 17-19). It seems the two hemispheres are simultaneously connected and disconnected. Similarly, an audit can be regarded as a 'brain' function and one that parallels the corpus callosum by simultaneously connecting and keeping apart.

Discussion of the coincidence or union of opposites has a long history in philosophy, going back to early Greek philosophers. Empedocles suggested that the elements (earth, air, fire and water) were joined through the attractive force of 'love' and split apart through the repulsive force of 'strife', to make up everything in the world (reported in Baggott, 2012, p. 1) – in essence, suggesting that the emotional opposition of love and strife account for (connect with) the classification of the physical elements. McGilchrist (2012, pp. 268–270) reports that for the pre-Socratic Greek philosopher, Anaximander, opposing principles are of crucial importance. "They balance one another, and it is this giving and taking, this ebb and flow of opposites, that gives rise to all things ...". In relation to Heraclitus, McGilchrist reports (p. 269)

> If we are able to attend to experience, rather than to our pre-conceived ideas about experience, we encounter, according to Heraclitus, the reality of the union of opposites. Appreciating this coming together, wherein all opposing principles are reconciled, was the essence of sophia (wisdom, the root of philosophy) for Heraclitus. Opposites define one another and bring one another into existence.

In the conclusion to chapter 21 of his 2021 book (a chapter entitled 'The One and the Many'), McGilchrist (2021, p. 879) points out that we need both similarities and differences, the general and the unique, not in sequence but simultaneously. If they are not simultaneous, then we are liable to experience them in sequence and this can both lead to and result in instability.

The resolution of opposites or differences in the form of contradictions is central to Hegel's dialectic method. Hegel believed that every notion or thesis contains within itself a contradiction (antithesis) which is resolved through synthesis. But he argued that every synthesis also contains its own contradiction, resolved through a new synthesis, so that there is endless development. The organising function of the mind is progressing all the time. In discussing Hegel, William James (1909, pp. 39–40) states that

> Empirical instances of the way in which higher unities reconcile contradictions are innumerable ....Somehow life does, out of its total resources, find ways of satisfying opposites at once ....Peace we secure by armament, liberty by laws and constitutions.......Our mistrust of mistrust engenders our commercial system of credit, our tolerance of anarchistic and revolutionary utterances is the only way of lessening the danger.....the way to certainty lies through radical doubt.....by obeying nature we command her etc. ..... It sounds paradoxical, but whenever you once place yourself at the point of view; of any higher synthesis, you see exactly how it does in a fashion take up opposites into itself.

Hence James recognises the importance of perspective, being the ability to place oneself at a different viewpoint in order to resolve opposites.[6]

McGilchrist (2012, p. 259) refers to a Hegelian theme as follows: "union cannot exist without separation and distinction, but separation and distinction are of no use unless they form the prelude to a later, greater union or synthesis". This ties together the resolution and maintenance of opposites and the achievement of progress over time.[7]

The language of audit adopts the language of duality

If the philosophy of audit is similar to the philosophy associated with the coincidence of opposites, then the language of audit should be expected to have a 'duality' capable of both expressing the creation of boundaries (disconnecting) and the crossing of boundaries (connecting). In fact, we do see this and the following paragraphs give examples of terms much used in auditing – materiality, sense, understanding and value – where this duality exists, although auditing policymakers and practitioners may not openly recognise it and its relevance to the union of opposites. In so far as this is the case, the duality is 'opaque' and understanding, including an understanding of understanding itself, may be limited. In the conclusion of this chapter, we suggest that the term 'audit' itself contains a duality that is not widely recognised, and one which our book seeks to expose.[8]

In referring to duality in the following paragraphs, we examine how certain words can both divide (create boundaries) and bridge (cross boundaries). They highlight how language has developed to capture the simultaneity of difference and similarity. The duality of the word 'materiality' is reflected in its capacity both to separate and bring together the worlds of physics and audit. In physical terms, materiality or matter means possessing substance (i.e., being tangible), whereas, in auditing terms, it means possessing a value, financial or otherwise that matters, that is important to a societal, commercial or investment decision. In one sense, the two views of materiality separate the physical from value but, in another sense, the term materiality brings the physical and value worlds together – in both worlds, the term 'material' brings something into existence, into play.

'Sense' plays a dual role in both separating and bringing together emotion (sense as feelings) and logic (sense as 'making sense'). Sense as feeling is how we observe and absorb the world around us and our connection with it. It can be intuitive but it can also be influenced by what makes sense. Through a coming together of sense as logic and sense as feeling, we validate both the feelings and the argument but such validation is, of course, still a feeling. Thus, sense as 'feeling' and sense as 'making sense' are both different and yet similar – coming together, in an audit context, to provide (the mental interpretation of) audit evidence. The duality of sense extends a duality to understanding. There is understanding in making sense and understanding in an appreciation of, or sensitivity towards, something embodied in the feeling of empathy – a key element in the construction of mental connection between humans.

The duality of value also plays an important role in both separating and bringing together the two hemispheres: value expressed in purely financial terms (counting value – left hemisphere) and value expressed in emotional terms (what we value – right hemisphere). Both relate to what we regard as important. If we are willing to pay for something, it is a statement that we regard it as important. If we behave according to our moral values or beliefs, then it is a statement that we regard those moral values as important to us. Just as both value and values are important to us as individuals, they are important for companies and for society. We shall see that the duality of materiality, the duality of both sense and value, plays an important part in the audit's role of bringing together the different worlds of the physical, the emotional and the financial. Duality is applied to anything that simultaneously both divides and brings together, that connects and disconnects; that creates boundaries and crosses boundaries, following the activity between the two hemispheres of the brain.

The power of language is that it not only creates boundaries by attaching labels to different things (recognising their differences) but it also enables boundaries to be crossed (recognising similarities) and this extends to crossing the boundary between one human brain and another (communication) to help joint cognition. Language is a boundary-crossing instrument as well as a store of cultural value (right hemisphere) and a store of knowledge through classification (left hemisphere).

Connecting across time and changing the viewpoint

Returning to the earlier illustration of the wood, whatever the wood's (spatial) classification using size of wood or mix of trees, in time, the older trees will die and will be replaced by new seedlings. Introducing time alongside space, essentially, produces intergenerational connections. The regeneration of the wood can result in the mix of trees and/or size of wood changing as some trees regenerate better than others (survival of the fittest). It introduces a natural dynamic that might result in the classification of the wood changing.

An example of a non-natural dynamic would be to cut down the wood in order to construct a housing estate. To make the connection across time in this case, we can define 'A' as the land common to both periods of time. Whilst the total of land is conserved, the transference, or flow, of land from woodland to housing represents a loss (of land) for woods set against the benchmark of conserving woodland and a gain for houses set against the benchmark of conserving land for houses. The mix of land use changes with trees preceding, or existing before, houses. We can regard time as just another property of A so that A1 is a (mental) space for A at time period 1 and A2 is for A at time period 2. The space A1 is occupied by trees and the space A2 by houses, and the new generation of humans has more houses but fewer trees.

Market prices, effectively a rate of exchange[9] (in this case between trees and houses), might suggest the houses are more valuable than the trees, giving an accounting profit – but this profit is not sustainable if society is unwilling to continue to allow the (further) destruction of trees. At some point, society faces a difficult choice since it values both houses for its citizens and a natural environment for its citizens to enjoy, plus, of course, the climate change implications. Ideally, an alternative brownfield site could be found on which to build more houses but, if not, society has to decide which of its responsibilities matters most. Materiality is a matter of choice; a matter not just of importance but of relative importance which might change over time and is, therefore, fundamentally dynamic. In other words, the political exchange rate between trees and houses will change over time as more houses are built, more trees cut down and the availability of alternative land (on which to build houses) changes.[10]

It is interesting that before the construction of the housing estate, the pattern of connections and disconnections is presented with the tree as the origin or starting point. Trees are also present in all of the subsequent connections. Once the housing estate exists, the origin (focus) shifts to land, which is common (universal) to both the wood and the housing estate. Thus, the action of building the housing estate changes the origin of the universal from trees to land. A change in origin corresponds to a change in context or viewpoint and consideration of context is a right hemisphere activity. This shift in the origin reflects a shift in priorities (materiality) from trees to houses – but this change in priorities is liable to shift back again as more and more houses are built.

With each shift, policy (on house building and forest preservation) presents itself more as a wave than a straight line of progression. Progress is seldom linear. Included in any assessment of a house-builder's future is an assessment of the future shifting pattern of social and political priorities (the future political exchange rate). When the origin or focal point of policy attention shifts, we see things in different terms and vice versa – i.e., the perspective changes.

Thus, a loss from the perspective of conserving woodland becomes a gain from the perspective of developing land for housing. Housebuilding can cause a material loss of woodland, whilst the retention of woodland can have a material impact on housebuilding. This can be called conjugate materiality, conjugate in the sense that woods (W) and houses (H) have to be considered together as a (conjugate) pair by asking the question: 'Is combination WH2 a material improvement upon WH1?'.[11]

The idea of a conjugate pair is taken from physics, where bringing one of a pair of variables into sharper focus leads to less clarity for the other, highlighting the need to attend to the pair collectively or holistically. Holistic (big picture) understanding has to be a crucial, principled, commitment and commensurate skill of an auditor. Though the different classifications given to date correspond to physical/natural properties (such as whether trees lose their leaves in winter) and also size perceptions (such as a specific number of trees – or, less precisely, 'a lot of trees'), classifications can also relate or correspond to intrinsic qualities such as 'beautiful' trees – a classification that connects the sensual and the physical.

The connection of the physical/natural with the numerical and the sensual allows for further refinement of the original classification (e.g., a wood of mixed trees might be beautiful but a forest of evergreens might not) and potentially an improved thought process – with greater accommodation of both the quantitative analysis of the left hemisphere and the sensuality of the right hemisphere. Indeed, thought processing using both hemispheres can connect the physical, the natural, the emotional, the financial, the empirical, the logical, the intuitive and the imaginative. It can do so with the intention of representing the world 'as it is' or as representing a world of possibility, imagination or idealism. That said, it also has to be noted that, individually, we are only able to see the world as it 'appears to us' – what we see as the world is what we understand it to be rather than 'what it is' in any absolute sense. No representation of the world as it appears to us is ever going to be complete, as it is only based on what we see and have experienced. However, this does not make redundant the desire to understand the world better and to represent any such personal understanding in the most comprehensive manner.

Segment 2: The representation of classification and connection through networks

Audit as a boundary-crossing instrument

It is relatively easy to create boundaries and, therefore, new classifications or categories, but developing the means of connecting, crossing or integrating across, these boundaries is much more difficult. The IIRC (International Integrated Reporting Council) was formed in 2010 to develop and promote integrated reporting but after several mergers, it was disbanded in 2022 (See O'Dwyer, Humphrey and Rowbottom, 2024, for an analysis of the demise of the IIRC). The IIRC suggested five dimensions (categories) for the business environment in addition to the financial, making six business dimensions in all – which they referred to as 'capitals' (being manufactured, natural, human, intellectual, social and relationship capital). The IIRC model is now to be found as part of the IFRS' Integrated Reporting Framework (IFRS, 2021). The model does the relatively easy bit in creating boundaries (the six capitals) (p.19) but it is harder to deal with boundary crossing; that is, how the six capitals come together and whether one combination of capitals is preferable to another.

The IIRC's (now IFRS') Integrated Report and its accompanying Integrated Reporting Framework hoped to encourage integrated thinking (p.5) and an understanding of how the six capitals come together with the organisation and its business environment to create value, but on this, there has only been limited success. The IFRS' integrated report requires (p. 14) a statement from those charged with governance (not the auditor) about whether the integrated report is in accordance with the Integrated Reporting Framework, thus headlining conformity rather than creativity or improvement. Whilst there is some common ground with what we are advocating in our book, we approach the need for connection, combination and integration from the perspective of audit and an audit that gives leadership based upon thinking differently and its associated creativity. Integrated thinking that follows an established framework is not necessarily creative in terms of new classifications or connections. We shall argue in Chapter 8 that governance, like audit, should be thought of in terms of improvement and not just conformity.

A major contribution of our book is representing audit as a study of connection (connectivity) and its connection with creativity; a study developed in the context of, and pioneered by, audit. We see the audit as both a boundary making and a mediating instrument[12] that can identify (new) categories or classifications and make connections between them in different ways – offering scope for audit to be deeply creative by contemplating, bringing together and drawing attention to different analytical dimensions and ways of thinking.

To illustrate in simple terms, let the audit introduce, in a commercial setting, three classifications or dimensions – being the financial value of the business (F), the environment for the business (E) and the business activity (B) itself. At this stage in our analysis, the 'FEB' network and its audit serve as an introduction to the idea of audit as a network of connections. The initial FEB network detailed below will be taken further and deepened in Chapter 7 when what society values in the shape of resilience, sustainability, creativity and fair treatment of stakeholders is added to provide an additional layer of considerations when undertaking an audit.

Suppose that within F there are further different dimensions of the financial value of the business (e.g., F1 = book value, F2 = market value added); that within B there are different business activities (B1, B2, B3 etc.) and within E there are different aspects of the business environment, including the natural environment, technology and the economy (E1, E2, E3 etc.). The function of a financial audit (the financial dimension of audit) might be to search for and investigate the connections (in both directions) between all F, B and E that explain F1 and F2. An environmental audit (the environmental dimension of audit) would see the focus being upon the impact on the environment, E, or one particular aspect of it, say E1, and to explain E1 in terms of its connections with E2, E3 etc., all B and all F. Similarly, a business audit (the business dimension) could be focused on explaining the set of business activities in terms of their connections with both the financial value of the business and its present and future environment. The future pertinence of audit, as a whole or combined function, might rest on understanding how best to identify, contemplate and assess this collective set of FEB connections.

This FEB assessment can be supported by measures of 'F improvement' (being how well the financial performance has been maintained and improved), 'E improvement' (being how well the environmental performance has been maintained and improved), plus the 'conversion rate' (exchange rate) between F and E. The appropriateness of the exchange rate depends upon the financial and environmental contexts. Any change in business activity B, including the adoption of innovative practices, is intended to improve performance across such measures but the overall, final judgement on performance is something that comes from the right hemisphere and is explicitly concerned with conjugate materiality; that is, judging the particular effectiveness or desirability of the achieved FEB combination. Such judgement is much more than providing assurance separately on environmental and other non-financial information. B improvement, being the maintenance and improvement of the business, is, in effect, maintaining and improving the desirability of the achieved FEB combination. Is FEB at time 2 an improvement upon (and how big an improvement upon) FEB at time 1? Ultimately, this is the audit judgement on the performance of the business – a judgement (and interaction) designed to stimulate still further improvement.

Crossing boundaries: A study of possible connection

In this and the following sections, we demonstrate that highlighting connections such as the FEB set of connections leads to networks that increase in complexity and depth, and that as the complexity and depth increase, the role of judgement in understanding and interpreting the network also increases. The conclusion is that increasing the analysis (left hemisphere activity) of connections leads to complexity that makes the interpretation of the analysis (a right hemisphere activity) more important and more difficult. The implication is that understanding connection more deeply requires expertise from both the left and right hemispheres of the brain.

In this section, we shall consider the possible mappings of the FEB network, an essentially left hemisphere activity, whilst also recognising the need for right hemisphere interpretation and judgment. To combine a financial and environmental audit into a business audit (an FEB audit network), we need to explore the possible connections between F, E and B and consider how they apply in the circumstances of the particular FEB audit, whilst at the same time recognising that the increasing complexity of the connections requires right hemisphere engagement. We start with simple connections and then build to an integrated network and illustrate its latent or 'hidden depth'. We argue that increasing the analysis of connection (left hemisphere) has to be matched by an increasing role for the right hemisphere to address and deal with the resulting complexity/opacity.

Assume that the conversion from one thing to another, such as B to F, is treated as a flow that can be represented as 'B------->F'. B leads to F as a sequential flow starting with B. Alternatively, the flow might be in reverse and shown as 'B<--------F'. If B is impacting (flowing into) F at the same time as F is impacting B, then the flow is in two directions at once, shown as 'B<-------->F'. Such a flow may be described as 'reverberative', a term taken from McGilchrist.

If business activities B connect with F and E, and flows between B and F, and B and E, are not reverberative, a range of different simple networks can be constructed. Depending on the directional flow, it is possible to categorise these as a network of divergence (Figure 2.1) or convergence (Figure 2.3).

In Figure 2.1, B impacts F and E, which are said to be connected with each other through their common origin in the business' activities. Relations between F and E exist courtesy of their relations with third party B. In Figure 2.3, it is the simultaneous impact of F and E upon B that shapes and creates the business and its activities. Additionally, it is possible to conceive of a linear sequential channel where one thing leads to another (e.g., Figure 2.2 where F leads to B, which in turn leads to E). This is also capable of being reversed as an EBF pathway (although this is not shown in Figure 2.2). In none of these cases (Figures 2.1–2.3), is there a direct relationship or connection between F and E, a condition that is relaxed in the next section.

In Figure 2.1, B is a 'field' that impacts both F and E (that is, the whole network), exhibiting divergence. In Figure 2.2, B is an 'intermediary' (channel)

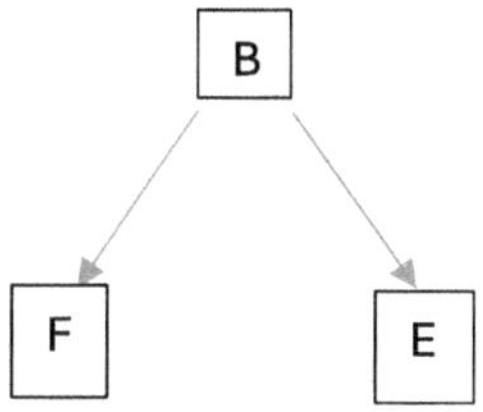

FIGURE 2.1 **B as a field.**

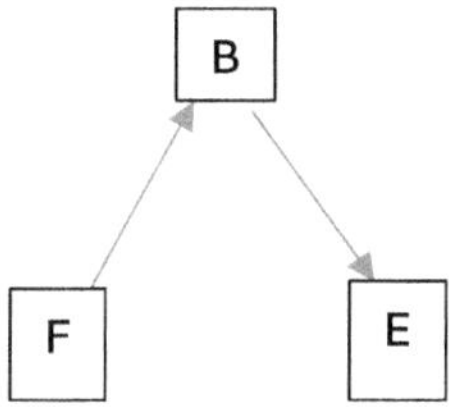

FIGURE 2.2 **B as an intermediary.**

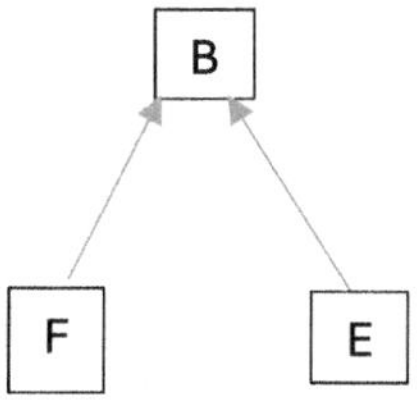

FIGURE 2.3 **B as an entity.**

between F and E, with FBE forming a linear pathway. In Figure 2.3, B is a 'particle' or 'entity' that exists due to the coming together or convergence of F and E, both of which might be considered 'stakeholders' in B.

The three 'networks' in Figures 2.1–2.3 show that a business' activities (B) are capable of being a field or an intermediary or an entity. A field is pervasive in the sense of flowing to and impacting all other entities in the network. An intermediary takes the flows it receives from an entity and subsequently passes them on to other entities in the network. An entity is created by the coincidence of flows received from other entities in the network. The significance of a business being two or more of the three – a field, an intermediary and an entity – is that it substantially increases the complexity of the network. For example, if the business were able to operate simultaneously as a field and as an entity, then there would be simultaneous divergence (Figure 2.1) and convergence (Figure 2.3), and connections (flows) between B and F and between B and E would both be two-way. Simultaneous divergence and convergence is a coincidence of opposites capable of creating disruption that is either positive (an opportunity) or negative (a threat).

Introducing a direct EF connection

In this section, a direct connection between E and F is introduced. For instance, a poor environmental performance could result in fines, and applying such an EF connection to Figures 2.1–2.3 gives Figures 2.4 (introducing a roundabout way to get from B to F), Figure 2.5 (circularity) and Figure 2.6 (introducing a roundabout way to get from E to B).

In Figure 2.4, roundaboutness is a superimposition of B as a field, coincidence (F as an entity), and linear flow (E as an intermediary on the linear pathway BEF). An example would be where business (activity) B generates financial performance F but simultaneously has an (adverse) environmental impact E, and this adverse environmental impact, perhaps sometime later, comes to have an adverse effect on financial performance. Timing and uncertainty issues serve to make this impact less immediately visible or

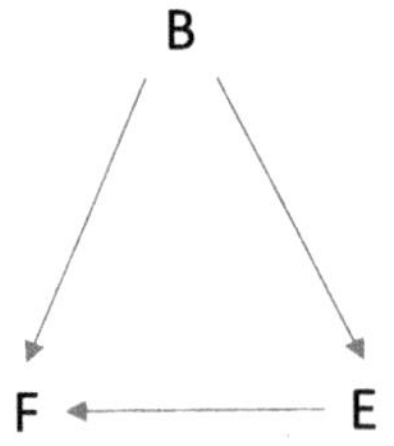

FIGURE 2.4 **Introducing a roundabout route from B to F.**

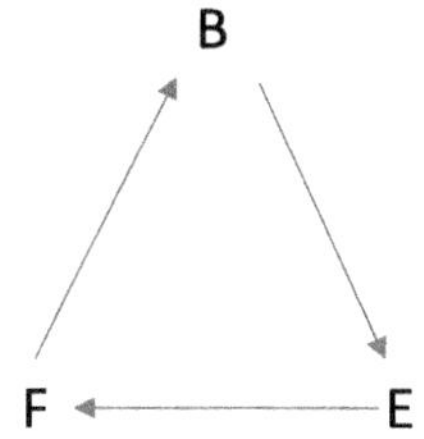

FIGURE 2.5 **Introducing circularity.**

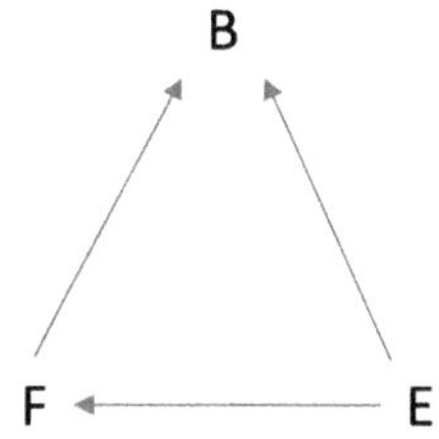

FIGURE 2.6 **Introducing a roundabout route from E to B.**

anticipated, hence the notion of 'roundaboutness' and its association with hidden risk and disruption.[13]

Introducing the EF connection to Figure 2.2 gives the circularity of Figure 2.5. With circularity, B, E and F are acting as intermediaries (with each being at the centre of an individual linear pathway). Whereas Figure 2.2 gave a roundabout way of getting from F to E, there are now additional (roundabout) routes from E to B and B to F. A positive example of this would be where the business designs its products to improve its impact on the business' environment E, thus gaining a wider product acceptability and an improved financial performance, enabling further investment in product development. Circularity can be associated with the business' pursuit, over time, of sustainability. This is clockwise circularity or flow but anti-clockwise circularity can also be present.[14] For example, if the business were to invest not in improving the environmental impact of its products but to invest directly in (improving) the environment, then this may have a positive impact on the reception of the business by its customers and consequently improve its finances, allowing further investment in the environment. The direction of flow here would be financial>environmental>business>financial, being an anti-clockwise circularity that introduces a direct FE connection.

Introducing a reverberative network

Many businesses (organisations and societies) will operate simultaneously as a field, an intermediary or channel, and an entity. Operating simultaneously as a field and as an entity can be represented by superimposing Figures 2.1 and 2.3 (divergence and convergence), resulting in reverberative connections between B and F, and between B and E. Introducing to this superimposition a direct and reverberative connection between F and E now gives the fully reverberative network of Figure 2.7. In Figure 2.7, not only B, but also F and E act simultaneously as a field, an intermediary and an entity. Thus, in this network, B, F and E are fully interchangeable and as a consequence the same network can be used to explore and understand all three through their connections with each other. It follows that the audit of one element such as B cannot be achieved without an audit of F and of E and the only meaningful audit is that of the FEB network as a whole. This analysis implies that a standalone financial audit (F) is inevitably only partial and, therefore, potentially misleading.

What is particularly important to appreciate is that a fully reverberative network such as Figure 2.7 connects with (and is built up from) forms of divergence, convergence, linear sequences (pathways), roundaboutness and circularity; each of which is a network in its own right, potentially superimposing with the others. Understanding these individual networks and how they come together, often through superimposition, to form the fully reverberative network, provides a fuller appreciation of how a business (and its activities) connects with its financial and environmental performance.

Understanding Figure 2.7 (and what underpins a fully reverberative network or what it collectively represents) can be compared to appreciating a great painting that is built from many layers and can be interpreted and appreciated at numerous levels. In respect of art work, McGilchrist (2012, p. 409) states, "We come to see not the work of art, but the world *according to the art work*, as Merleau-Ponty says, necessitating that it is neither opaque nor wholly transparent, but 'semi-transparent'". In this respect, Figure 2.7 has, arguably, provided a view of the business that is semi-transparent since, apart from the evident scale of reverberation, none of the other network layers (divergence etc.) are fully transparent in Figure 2.7. As the representation of the world becomes more complex and sophisticated (a triumph of the left

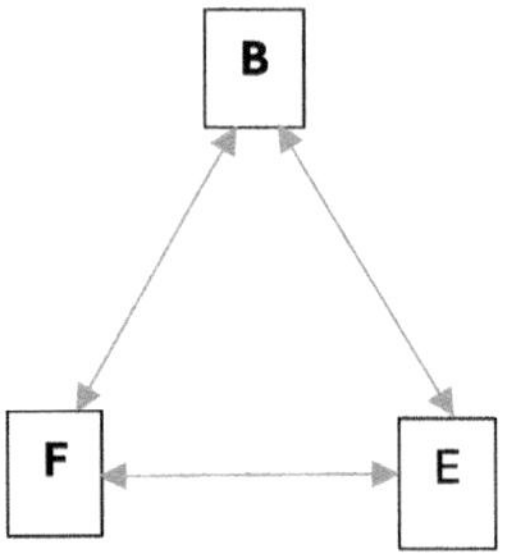

FIGURE 2.7 **A reverberative network.**

hemisphere), it also becomes more dependent on the right hemisphere to see through the representation to the world beyond; that is, beyond the surface to the many layers and levels underneath.

To see and feel the world beyond, through or according to the network, it is necessary for the right hemisphere to see and feel the network's many interconnected layers and levels of interpretation and how they come together. The left hemisphere analyses and the right interprets. The analysis assists and improves the interpretation but it is the right hemisphere that is the master and has the final say.

Our ambition in the above sections discussing the FEB flow diagrams is to indicate the connections and layers of connection that an integrated,[15] holistic audit (one that integrates F, E and B) needs to consider. This not only suggests that greater clarity requires greater attention to complexity but that seeking such clarity, in itself, can generate further complexity as it reveals things that may previously have not been known, but now may need to be explored further. Such a pattern of exposing and making sense of what was previously hidden suggests that a core quality of audit is its innate hidden depth – and the emphasis this places on the importance of auditor insight and judgement. For instance, in terms of knowing and reconciling what questions to ask, what different thoughts to entertain and determining what analysis is sufficient. Audit is about knowing and appreciating when the pursuit of clarity serves to inform or to confuse, to discourage or to inspire and to know when confidence or doubt is justified and treated or managed appropriately.

Segment 3: The context of time and space

A flow such as B to F has the property of order (direction) being the order B then F. It occupies the space between B and F, and it takes time to complete the journey from B to F. It may be a continuous flow or it might take place intermittently at either set or uncertain times. The remaining sections of the chapter explore in more detail the significance of order, time and space to our understanding of connection, starting with a discussion of time and space together, followed by the significance of order, leading to the final section on the order of time and space.

Time and space are key to Einstein's general theory of relativity, as explained, for example, by Stephen Hawking in *A Brief History of Time*:

> Before 1915, space and time were thought of as a fixed arena in which events took place, but which was not affected by what happened in it...... Bodies moved, forces attracted and repelled, but time and space simply continued, unaffected......The situation, however, is quite different in the general theory of relativity. Space and time are now dynamic quantities: when a body moves, or a force acts, it affects the curvature of time and space – and in turn the structure of space-time affects the way in which

> bodies move and forces act. Space and time not only affect but are affected by everything that happens in the universe. In the decades that followed this new understanding of space and time was to revolutionise our view of the universe. The old idea of an essentially unchanging universe that could have existed, and could continue to exist forever was replaced by the notion of a dynamic, expanding universe....
>
> (Hawking, 1988, p. 33)

In effect, Einstein recognised the reverberative nature of connections involving time and space on the one hand, and physical bodies that occupy time and space, on the other. Space-time is the gravitational field that 'connects' bodies and is one of the 'force' fields of physics that draws them together.[16] It is the force fields of physics that keep things connected and enables/powers connection and innovation in the physical world. We argue that we should identify the force fields that enable connection and innovation in society and business.

The ideas in our book could be regarded as a step towards the building of 'a general theory of audit' in which we replace the physical bodies and forces that constitute the physical universe with the moving bodies and forces that form society, whilst physical space and time is replaced by audit space and time – a canvas upon which the moving bodies and forces of society can be recorded (evidenced), represented, interpreted and responded to through action.

As in the physical world, this canvas is not neutral – how society is evidenced and represented impacts the very forces and moving bodies that form society. Audit and society, as shown in Figure 1.1 in Chapter 1, are interdependent and interconnected. In particular, a dynamically developing society could be said to require a conceptualisation of audit that, itself, is fundamentally, dynamic – in recognising that the construction and representation of what audit can (and needs to) be is not fixed; audit conceptually has to be capable of responding/adapting to, and influencing, different social and business contexts.

Order, time pressures and truth

Audit is often represented as a series of discrete steps and when those steps form a linear sequence, it could be referred to as an 'audit pathway'; a pathway in which order can be very important, especially when the choice of later audit steps depends upon the outcome of earlier steps. Typically, an audit pathway is represented in terms of 'space <---> time' reflecting their substitutability or transferability. For instance, when there is a shortage of time, we can divide (reduce) an audit pathway into a large number of short-term moves (disconnections) and execute them in parallel, execution being followed by subsequent reconnection. Space, in an audit context, can be taken to be access to audit staff resources, to client staff and to evidence, in contrast to audit time, which is the time for which that access exists. When there is a shortage of space, for example, in the form of a shortage of staff resources, the space available (the available staff) is used to conduct audit events in series over a long time period. Thus, when time is scarce relative to space, the space-time exchange rate favours time (time is valuable) and when space is scarce relative to time, it favours space. If the exchange rate is capable of changing, then the plot of audit time against audit space can become bowed or warped, a familiar characteristic of Einstein's space-time.

The introduction of some form of 'order' constrains the ability to substitute (exchange) time with space and vice versa, whilst the plot of time against space becomes discontinuous. For example, when the order in which audit steps are carried out is important, it may not be possible to relieve pressure on time by conducting the steps in parallel since they should be conducted as a linear sequence. Similarly, if there is pressure on space, for example, by adding additional audit objectives and requirements, then the audit might need to take more time but a timely audit report is generally a requirement of its users and so the necessary time may be unavailable.

The simultaneous pressures on financial auditors' time and space coming from regulators, management and investors have been articulated in detail by Martyn Jones, a former president of the ICAEW (Institute of Chartered Accountants in England and Wales) (Jones, 2021). He classified the potential irreconcilability of such pressures as the 'elephant in the audit room', with colleagues in the audit profession often complaining that regulators increase audit requirements whilst investors refuse to sanction delays in the audit report. Consequently, more audit work has to be done in parallel. The network in Figure 2.8 represents audit steps in a financial audit being carried out in parallel. To get from B to F and F to B in the required timescale involves audit steps S1 and S2 being carried out in parallel and subsequently reconnected. If the reconnection is to happen quickly, then S1 and S2 should be in a frequent dialogue during their conduct; in effect, a 'reverberative' connection as shown in Figure 2.8.

Figure 2.8 follows the pattern of Figure 1.1 (Chapter 1) in being two parallel intermediaries (in this case, S1 and S2) between the reality of the business activity (B) and its financial representation (F). The line with arrows in each direction drawn directly between B and F is the reverberative 'line of truth'

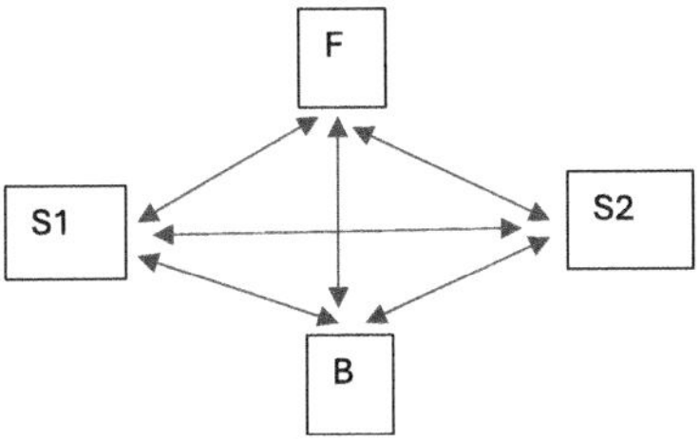

FIGURE 2.8 **Audit work in parallel.**

connecting business reality (B) and its financial representation (F). Carrying out too many actions in parallel can hinder the connected learning potential of audit. For example, if (instead of just S1 and S2) there were multiple steps carried out in parallel, most of which needed to be in regular dialogue, then the volume of required communications within a very limited time period might become unmanageable. If so, it would affect the strength and insightfulness of the connection between reality and representation provided by the audit.[17]

The importance of order

Any act of ordering is an act of classification in the sense that it requires both commonalities/similarities and differences. In the case of a hot body next to a cold body, the commonality is the temperature scale and the difference that generates the ordering is between the relative position of the two bodies on the scale. If heat is transferred so that the temperatures converge, then full convergence is achieved when the bodies have the same temperature. At the point of convergence, there is no difference in respect of temperature and no ordering on this criterion is possible. This is the equilibrium point often referred to as the point of maximum disorder. It is a disorder in the sense that no ordering is possible with respect to temperature.

Of course, the two bodies have characteristics other than temperature and these might still permit classification and ordering. The idea of entropy is that a closed world, such as the two bodies, moves from order towards disorder. Once equilibrium is achieved, the two bodies can no longer be ordered and the previous ability to order the world (on the temperature scale) is lost. This loss of order can be seen as the 'price' of the heat transference or exchange.

Hence, as with classification, order is lost both when everything is the same and when everything is different. Things that are completely different cannot be placed in any meaningful order – a meaningful order being one that fulfils a purpose or gives understanding. Equally, when all things become identical, any classification and ability to order collapses. The importance of order is its connection with a sense of direction and movement; in the case of what is called entropy, this direction is from everything being in order to the 'disorder' of either everything being the same or everything being completely different. Whilst entropy, the trend towards disorder, dominates the physical universe, much human activity and organisation is designed to promote order.[18] Thus, both disordering and ordering involve movement across space and time[19] and order, time and space are deeply interconnected in society, business and audit just as they are in physics. Of course, these interconnections are not and (as this chapter implies) cannot be, completely understood – and the role of audit, at least in respect of the societal world, is of necessity one of seeking to understand the interconnections better.

The order of audit work is important if the audit of P then the audit of X, gives a different result, evaluation or impression than that given by the order of doing X then P.[20] Suppose P is connected to (interacts with) X so that P can provide evidence of X and vice versa. The impact of such order effects is to create uncertainty unless the audit steps (P and X) are carried out in both directions and the outcomes evaluated together (co-evaluated).[21] To the extent that these conditions are recognised and allowed for, then there is no order – or order effects are neutralised. Co-evaluation means the two pieces of work are considered together as one to assess the overall implications for both P and X. The co-evaluation employs a conjugate materiality (co-materiality).

To illustrate auditing that is undertaken in both directions, we can take the case of an environmental audit and a financial audit. If we start by evaluating the environmental impact of the business and then move to the financial, we can discover any instances of the environmental impact being underrepresented or missing from the representation of the company's finances and financial value. If we start with the financial audit, we can discover fines, legal claims, expenses to repair environmental damage (a disruption that has happened) or expenses to develop environment-saving technology or expenses to prevent environmental damage (to prevent disruption). We can then evaluate whether the environmental impact of this financial expenditure is appropriately represented in the environmental statements. This is an important example where the auditor, as far as possible, co-evaluates – assessing both the results from E to F alongside the results of F to E in the form of a 'co-audit' that seeks to understand and represent the connection and flow between the financial and the environmental. This understanding takes into account that the business' activity as a channel or intermediary brings F and E into contact – meaning that there is an important role for understanding the environmental values that the business, organisation or society believes in and how those values influence (connect with) its activities.

The order of time and space

In addition to understanding current contact between the business (organisation or society), its finances and its environment, the audit must enhance understanding of how such connections play out and change over time between the past, present and future. Audit is, therefore, concerned with the temporality as well as the spatiality of connection. The past, present and future are not independent of each other but are phases of the time element within a space-time continuum. Consequently, you cannot, for example, understand or evaluate a business without relating its present to its past and to its (anticipated) future.

The flow of business is like the flow of a melody that cannot be appreciated one note at a time. It follows that an audit seeking to appreciate spatial connections between a business, its environment and its value should make these connections between the past, present and the future as a single exercise in 'flow'. Consequently, the audit advances from being concerned with spatial connections at a point in time to addressing the flow of such connections across time. Connection is seen to exist in a space-time continuum but this is not represented in current financial or audit reporting. For instance, today's company financial statements contain information about the past, the present and an increasing amount of information dependent on the future but the haphazard way in which the future is addressed means they fall short on explaining the movement or flow of connections over time.

In the case of a business and its activities, it is an understanding of this flow that gives rise to the business' financial valuation. For a successful business, the whole is greater than the sum of the parts, just as a melody is greater than a collection of individual notes, and the representation of the business should reflect and explain this inequality. The commercial company can be broken down into its component parts (disconnection), evaluating each component separately. At the same time, the whole company can be judged as a holistic entity.[22] In terms of its financial position, it is a meaningful connection between the sum of the parts (e.g., as represented by book equity) and the whole (taken for this purpose to be market equity) with which current accounting and audit practice fails to engage. Of course, current audit practice also fails to engage with those externalities not adequately taken into account by the equity market. What is needed is an audit function that, through its insight and influence on investors, increases consideration of externalities in equity market pricing.

There are two ways of thinking about the order of time (see, for instance, Grayling, 2020, p. 326). The first is the ordering 'past-present-future'. An event changes its category with respect to this ordering. It can start being in the future, appear in the present and thereafter be in the past. The categorisation of an event is, therefore, one of change. Employing this categorisation can provide a representation of the flow of value from the future through to the present and then the past. A second ordering is to place an event either before or after another event. This categorisation is fixed, provided the order of the events does not change. This categorisation can be employed in the execution of a 'pathway'. Duration is the period of time between any two events on the pathway – a period of time with no change (no events take place) might be taken to constitute the present.

In the financial world, a simple discounting model can convert a future income stream into a financial value at a point in time, a capital value which the mind finds easier to work with and can form the basis of trading capital. The model essentially converts the future to the present using an exchange rate between the future and the present (the interest rate used as a discount rate). It provides a measurement or observation of capital value and demonstrates how financial value and value flow (the income stream) are connected with respect to time. For the model to deliver, the choice of discount rate has to be an input with which the user of the model is comfortable. To the extent that the discount rate is a judgement (based in part upon a feeling or sensation), then the output from the model is also a judgement. If the (central bank) interest rate is persistently low (in recent times in the UK it has even been negative in real terms), the implication is that the present is valued highly relative to the future and accordingly societal, organisational, business and economic progress is not in demand and unlikely to be delivered. A confident society sees a future that is much improved over the present. It sees a creative opportunity capable of rewarding those who forego current consumption for investment in such an opportunity. A low (real) interest rate signals a society that lacks confidence in the future or is unwilling to make the current sacrifice for a better future.

We explore further the significance of the interest rate for audit in Chapter 7 but referencing it here is done with the intention of illustrating the sheer scale and depth of considerations and connections capable of being required in the undertaking of an audit – and helping to appreciate the reverberative nature of audit's investigative processes.

Overall, the intention of this chapter has been to recognise both the depth of audit analysis and to realise that analytical depth may resolve existing questions but can also raise fresh ones (highlighting issues that were previously unknown or hidden – but now brought more into view and requiring further analysis). This raises the question of a stopping point in audit and how to determine what is an appropriate residual level of uncertainty, confidence and insight. As subsequent chapters will demonstrate, such judgements and associated expressed opinions on the part of the auditor are what ultimately determines and are determined by the framing and exercising of auditor judgement – and what it means to be a public interested 'professional'.

Summary and conclusion

This chapter has taken the philosophy of physics associated (a) with the relational interpretation of quantum physics and (b) with Einstein's ideas on space, time and relativity, and considered their relevance to a philosophy of audit. Whilst audit thought is familiar with the ideas of space, time and order, such thought has been less influenced by the ideas of quantum physics. Consequently, the chapter has focused somewhat more on the potential influence of the latter.

According to the relational interpretation of quantum theory, everything exists courtesy of its relations with other things; relations that can be expressed in terms of opposites, being similarities (connections) and differences (disconnections). Existence requires the coexistence of similarities and differences that give rise to classification and order.

A big issue for audit is to understand and establish the existence of (for instance, in the case of the financial audit) assets and liabilities, revenues and expenses along with their classification and ordering. Existence connects to other audit issues such as ownership/access, timing and valuation (measurement). Does the access exist? Does the value exist? Did the events take place when recorded? All of these are the very basic audit questions students learn in a typical introductory auditing course. This chapter pushes well beyond such questions to consider how duality, in the form of both creating boundaries and crossing boundaries simultaneously, plays a key role in the construction of multiple interactions or networks. Simple network constructions include divergence, convergence and intermediaries and these can be brought together (superimposed) to create more complex and sophisticated networks. Understanding such networks requires a coming together of analysis and judgement and is central to our understanding of audit – of what it is and what it could become.

As an illustration, this chapter has considered an audit that integrates business activity with its financial condition or status and with its environment. It has demonstrated the connections and layers of connection of such an audit and highlighted its (hidden) depth. Audit can be seen as a process of both introducing and exposing, acknowledging and unearthing, this depth. Such an audit requires consideration of a 'conjugate' materiality that is premised on the assumption that there can be significant differences across combinations of financial and environmental performance and business activity and that, consequently, the materiality of financial performance, environmental performance and business performance cannot be considered separately. This adds both complexity and depth – but it is important to appreciate that this is a complexity and depth that has to be explored through thinking differently from different perspectives.

A foundation of quantum theory is that P then X does not give the same result as X then P. These are order effects and similar such effects can apply in audit when the impact of conducting audits or audit work in one particular order is different from the impact or impression gained by conducting work in a different order. This can create a need for work to be conducted together in both orders (both directions) and co-evaluated *in order to* minimise order effects.

A key insight from quantum physics is that the world is inherently uncertain and that our knowledge of it is inevitably incomplete. Indeed, the more we know, the more we realise we don't know. If it is logically impossible to know how much you don't know, then this insight must be from the right hemisphere. That is to say, an assessment of how much you don't know is based upon experience and feelings rather than logic. The more connections you come across in the audit, the more you might feel there are further connections that you have not yet come across. This is important because, if so, then more knowledge can provide both more confidence and more uncertainty simultaneously. Understanding becomes associated both with trust and with its opposite, doubt. Holistic understanding as a crucial skill of the auditor becomes seen as a unity of opposites, opposites that can be characterised in many ways, including confidence and doubt. "The way to certainty is through radical doubt" (James, 1909, p. 39) may have been intended as a way to express this unity of opposites. Rovelli (2021, p. 130) makes a similar point:

> I believe that one of the greatest mistakes made by human beings is to want certainties when trying to understand something. The search for knowledge is not nourished by certainty: it is nourished by a radical absence of certainty. Thanks to the acute awareness of our ignorance, we are open to doubt and can continue to learn and learn better.

The chapter makes the important point that there are 'opaque' dualities in so far as the duality of terms such as materiality, sense, understanding and value is not fully appreciated in current audit thought. Indeed, we need to understand more broadly audit as a theory of connection and creation that embraces both duality and opposites. The idea that audit simultaneously creates and connects both confidence and doubt shows the (hidden) duality of audit as a coincidence of opposites. This duality might be hidden not only in the sense of not being recognised but also when more confidence serves to create more doubt. The capacity for audit to inspire and generate progress lies in this reverberation of confidence and doubt and the respective degree to which audit investigation reveals, stimulates, and/or resolves such competing standpoints and perspectives on the audited entity.

Notes

1 There are other interpretations of quantum theory to that favoured by Rovelli, such as Quantum Bayesianism (Qbism). For discussion of Qbism, see Rovelli (2021, pp. 58–61).

2 From this perspective, human activity is treated as an exploitation of the physical world. Such exploitation is represented as the basis of human 'progress' until the point of 'over-exploitation' is reached. Identification of this point relies upon human judgement.

3 In the physical world, the second law of thermodynamics is often cited as an example of irreversibility. Heat flows from a hot body to a cold body but not the other way round.
4 '....to attribute properties to something that does not interact is superfluous and may be misleading. It is talking about something that has no meaning: for there are no properties outside of interactions' (Rovelli, 2021, p. 70).
5 Donald MacKenzie introduced 'finitism' to David Hatherly when they were jointly supervising Dave Leung's doctoral thesis, a study inspired by Hutchins' *Cognition in the Wild* (Hutchins, 1995) and the idea that cognition extends from the individual mind to a network or group and to collective tasks (see also Leung, 2011).
6 In geometrical terms, this suggests the importance of circularity since a sphere is circular from any vantage point (it is symmetrical, a physical property associated with stability and resolution), linking circularity with the resolution of opposites.
7 The way algorithms are often used by 'big data' business is focused on similarities (associations). If you watch film X and film X has a strong similarity (an established connection) to film Y, you will find yourself being recommended (associated with) film Y. The algorithm encourages incrementalism (a left hemisphere engagement). It does not encourage the more challenging experience of watching a very different film, which would exercise the right hemisphere in bringing the two very different experiences together. Too much focus on similarity may not be good for creativity and progress. This follows the philosopher Deleuze who felt that difference was more fundamental than similarity. To Deleuze 'all identities are effects of difference' (Grayling, 2020, p. 501).
8 In physics, De Broglie is the one credited with exposing the electron's duality as both a wave and a particle. Kumar (2009, pp. 143–154) calls De Broglie the 'Prince of Duality'.
9 Where any action results in different outputs from a set of inputs (or a different mix of outputs to the mix of inputs) then to compare before and after (that is to measure transference in terms of creation, gains and losses) requires rates of exchange (rates of conversion) between the various inputs and between the inputs and outputs. The different capitals cannot remain disconnected. To assign an exchange rate is to assign a similarity or equivalence to two things that are otherwise dominated by difference.
10 Whilst commerce (in this case, house builders) generally benefits from more people to whom to sell, the environment benefits from fewer people – producing a tension between opposites, the resolution of which requires creative thinking.
11 Economists such as Ricardo and Malthus recognised that land was not scalable and, therefore, what society chooses to do and allow to be done with its land is a crucial decision.
12 Miller and O'Leary (2007) explored the functionality of capital budgeting as a mediating instrument between science and the economy. In a similar fashion, it is possible to view auditing (as connection), in the case of a business, as a mediating instrument between the business environment (that includes the natural world, science, society and its economy), the business (activity) and its finances. We go on to argue in the book that the mediating potential of audit has been fundamentally restricted by its historically presumed or accepted attachment to a business' financial statements.

13 It can be noticed that roundaboutness comes from the combination of divergence (from B) and convergence (on F). Thus, the network provides a combination or connection between opposites – opposition that might give rise to either creativity or disruption or both. Hence, roundaboutness could be associated with creativity and/or disruption.

14 Replacing an EF with an FE connection and applying it to a reverse pathway of Figure 2.2 results in the anti-clockwise circularity BFE. Introducing an FE connection to Figure 2.3 results in FEB being a roundabout route from F to B.

15 We use the term 'integrated' here as a representation of the fully reverberative nature of the connections that form the audit network. As such, our notion of an 'integrated' audit is conceptually much broader than is currently associated, in a US context, with an audit that combines or 'integrates' an assessment of the presentational fairness of a company's financial statement and the effectiveness of the company's internal controls over financial reporting (e.g., see https://pcaobus.org/oversight/standards/auditing-standards/details/AS2201).

16 For example, see David Tong, April 2018, 'Quantum Fields: The Real Building Blocks of the Universe', www.youtube.com/watch?v=zNVQfWC_evg. The four fundamental force fields of physics are gravity, electromagnetism, the strong and weak nuclear forces. They are responsible for shaping the universe we inhabit.

17 Later, in Chapter 7, Figure 2.8 is adapted (Figure 7.1) to form the auditor's mental model.

18 Although the proliferation of laws, regulations and standards associated with today's society could be construed as moving towards the 'disorder' of everything being the same – i.e., when everything conforms to the same standard, no ordering is possible.

19 The concept of order (reorder, disorder) is very similar to the concepts of organisation (reorganisation, disorganisation) and presentation (representation, misrepresentation). The opposite of a 'representation that provides understanding' is 'misrepresentation' – being a presentation that generates misunderstanding.

20 If measuring P alters X or during the measurement of P, X changes, then measuring X first and then P gives different results than measuring P first and then X. The bigger this difference the more important the order effect (based on Rovelli, 2021, p. 94).

21 As a practical illustration, an auditor concerned with the completeness of stock could identify possible misstatement by starting the audit from the stock records (P) checking that recorded lines of stock are being held as stock at the company's warehouse (X). This check, however, would not identify a line of stock held in the warehouse that had never been recorded or entered in the company's stock records. This misstatement would only be identified if the auditor starts with lines of stock held in the warehouse and checks (in the reverse direction) that they are also listed in the stock records.

22 Grayling (2020, p. 394) reports the philosopher Quine's version of holism as "our statements about the external world face the tribunal of sense experience not individually but only as a corporate body.... Scientific statements are not separately vulnerable to adverse observations, because it is only jointly as a theory that they imply their observable consequences". This also holds for accounting statements intended to give observations on company performance, a company being a corporate body.

References

Baggott, J., 2012, *Higgs: The Invention and Discovery of the 'God Particle'*, (Oxford University Press, Oxford).

Grayling, A.C., 2020, *The History of Philosophy: Three Millenia of Thought from the West and Beyond*, (Penguin, Random House, London).

Hatherly, D., Leung, D. and D. MacKenzie, 2008, 'The finitist accountant', in *Living in a Material World: Economic Sociology meets Science and Technology Studies*, Pinch, T. and R. Swedberg (eds.), pp. 131–160, (MIT Press, Cambridge, MA) Ch. 4.

Hawking, S.W., 1988, *A Brief History of Time: From the Big Bang to Black Holes*, (Bantam Press, London).

Hutchins, E., 1995, *Cognition in the Wild*, (MIT Press, Cambridge, MA).

IFRS Foundation, 2021, International <IR> Framework, www.ifrs.org/issued-standards/integrated-reporting/framework/.

James, W., 1909, *A Pluralistic Universe, Hibbert Lectures at Manchester College on the Present Situation in Philosophy*, (Reprinted by Dodo Press, 2007), www.gutenberg.org/cache/epub/11984/pg11984-images.html.

Jones, M.E., 2021, 'It's time to deal with the 'elephant in the audit room'', *ICAEW Insights*, www.icaew.com/insights/viewpoints-on-the-news/2021/sep-2021/its-time-to-deal-with-the-elephant-in-the-audit-room.

Kumar, M., 2009, *Quantum: Einstein, Bohr and the Great Debate about the Nature of Reality*, (Icon Books, London).

Leung, D., 2011, *Inside Accounting: The Sociology of Financial Reporting and Auditing*, (Routledge, London).

McGilchrist, I., 2012, *The Master and his Emissary: The Divided Brain and the Making of the Western World*, (Yale University Press, New Haven).

McGilchrist, I., 2021, *The Matter with Things: Our Brains, Our Delusions, and the Unmaking of the World*, (Perspectiva Press, London).

Miller, P. and T. O'Leary, 2007, 'Mediating instruments and making markets: Capital budgeting, science and the economy, *Accounting, Organizations and Society*, 32:7-8, pp. 701–734, https://doi.org/10.1016/j.aos.2007.02.003.

O'Dwyer, B., Humphrey, C. and N. Rowbottom, 2024, 'From institutional integration to institutional demise: The disintegration of the International Integrated Reporting Council (IIRC)', *Critical Perspectives on Accounting*, 99, March, https://doi.org/10.1016/j.cpa.2023.102699.

Rovelli, C., 2021, *Helgoland*, (Allen Lane, London).

3

AUDIT AS THE SEARCH FOR REALITY

Physics and audit are very different subjects and seldom studied together and yet they have one big thing in common: they can both be presented as a search for reality, reality comprising everything that 'exists' in the world and beyond. Accordingly, in principle, audit and physics might learn from each other and share a common philosophy of existence. This was the thinking behind Chapter 2 and its consideration of the philosophy of physics and how this led us towards the development and interpretation of audit as a network of connections and, ultimately, a philosophy of existence.

Reality is everywhere and everything. It is pervasive. It provides the environment and context for the societal audit network, an environment that is natural, social (political), technological and economic. These are the pervasive force fields of reality, which interact with the audit, with society and with each other. Furthermore, what we learnt from Chapter 2 is that with greater understanding of these interactions comes additional doubt and so reality always exists beyond our understanding and experience. We engage with reality through the lens of our senses, our observations and our intellect. Accordingly, our contact with and understanding of reality is never complete.

In framing the relationship between audit and society, Figure 1.1 (in Chapter 1) highlighted two points of engagement (two connections) between reality and the rest of the audit societal network. The first was the relationship between reality and society and the second was the relationship between reality and the audit. The greater the audit's engagement with the force fields of reality, the stronger the audit's connection with reality. We shall concentrate on reality as a pervasive field or collection of fields but reality also 'exists' as an entity or classification (that is, the metaphysical question of what reality is – its formal existence) and as a channel/pathway connecting society and the audit.

DOI: 10.4324/9781032721293-3

As regards the audit, we shall concentrate on audit's operation as a channel, connecting reality and society, as shown in Figure 1.1, directly through shared values and indirectly through representation.[1] Nevertheless, audit also 'exists' both as an entity (raising the question of what audit is?) and as a pervasive field that influences both society and reality. It is the latter – audit as a pervasive field – that leads us to see a much bigger opportunity for audit in shaping the world around us.

Turning to society, from an audit perspective, it is society or an organisation within society or possibly a particular action taken by society, that is the 'entity' subjected to audit. We can regard society as an entity formed by the combined forces of reality itself and the understanding of reality delivered by the audit. We can also consider society as a pervasive field influencing both the audit and reality, and as a channel between audit and reality. Arguably, from an audit perspective, reality is primarily a field, audit is primarily a channel and the auditee (in the case of Figure 1.1, society) is primarily an entity, whilst the 'audit–society–reality' network may be considered to incorporate all three, comprising interactions between the particular fields, channels and entities that form the network.

The chapter proceeds as follows: the first section looks at 'performativity'. In Figure 1.1, clockwise flows between reality, audit, representation, society and forward to reality again, give a channel or pathway in which the audit (directly and through representation) influences society to take action, thereby influencing reality. Continuing in a clockwise direction, this new reality is then represented by the audit, once again influencing society etc. Thus, the societal audit network is a circular network and the first section of this chapter explores the potential consequences of this circularity in terms of audit's performativity. Performativity is the ability to generate action and we want this action to result in progress, not regress.

In the second section of the chapter, we look at how the nature of reality (and the fundamental assumption that reality always exists beyond our understanding and experience) places a limit on the operation of audit as a channel within the audit societal network. This limit is associated with materiality – materiality being a judgement that introduces a boundary or limit beyond which the auditor does not search. To an extent, this limit is a function of limited imagination, and we then show how imagination and thinking differently can reshape boundaries, including the audit assessment of what matters (materiality). The audit, therefore, can be regarded as a coincidence of establishing boundaries through materiality judgements and removing boundaries through thinking differently.

The third section of the chapter addresses thinking differently through the lens of research and development. It argues that research and development conducted by the subject of the audit resembles thinking differently by the auditor. The two domains of 'thinking differently' each provide progress through a greater understanding of the connection with the realities of the societal audit network's environment. This suggests that research and development should be a crucial influence on the shape and direction of the audit and, by implication, the audit should be a crucial influence on the shape and direction of research and development.

We then look at the societal audit network of Figure 1.1 as an anti-clockwise pathway that coexists with the network's clockwise pathway. A dominant feature of the anti-clockwise flow is disruption. Purposeful action shapes reality, but because of our limited understanding of reality, it ultimately invites disruption. Disruption reshapes society and, in so far as society is a channel between reality and the audit, disrupts the audit as well – generating unexpected evidence and requiring the auditor to think differently in response, and in particular, where to give attention. The penultimate section of the chapter addresses the human dimension of the societal-audit pathway since, being conducted by humans and requiring human judgement, audit is susceptible to human bias and conditioning. Nevertheless, judgement is an inevitable and crucial part of the audit and one in which the right hemisphere of the brain is heavily involved.

Building on the ideas presented in the chapter (namely, ideas from the philosophy of physics and, in particular the idea of existence as a network of connections), we conclude that through its existence as a search for reality, audit can in significant ways, similar to physics, be seen as a philosophy of existence.

Since this chapter is a discussion built upon Figure 1.1, this is a good point to remind ourselves that Figure 1.1 is itself a construction or representation. It is not reality but a representation of reality (i.e., how we see reality at a point in time and a vehicle through which to contemplate the fundamental conceptual basis or underpinnings of audit). Clearly, it also can be regarded as something open to further development through re-imagination and new thinking, but it firmly establishes that audit, as a discipline, is the search for (improved) understandings of reality and is something that has a close relationship with cognition, in terms of how we come to 'know' and understand.

Performativity

As shown in Figure 1.1, the connection between reality and audit involves attention (i.e., what does the auditor attend to?) and evidence (i.e., what evidence should be gathered?), whilst the connection between reality and society involves purposeful action and disruption. If we assume that society instructs action and wants the best possible credit from the auditor for what it does, then whatever (evidence) the audit pays attention to in assessing society, society pays attention to and amends its action accordingly. This influence of audit upon societal action, action that changes reality, can be deemed to be performative, and this chapter starts with a discussion of performativity.

Performativity originated with the work of language philosopher John Austin (1962), who referred to the capacity of speech and communication to act or to consummate an action. Austin differentiated this capacity from descriptive, 'constative' language, which can be 'evaluated as true or false'.

For example, in Austin's terms, a representation of business (such as an audit report) can be evaluated as 'true or false' or as 'performative'. Audit exists to inform its audience (whether it be society or an organisation and its stakeholders) and to show how that information might be used as the basis for action. To maximise its value, an audit needs to bring about a certain effect in its audience through the transmission (communication) of both understanding and information; a transmission that translates into action, rather than the transmission of mere statements of fact and whether they be true or false.

In this regard, there is much scope for improving the value of the current audit report by improving its performativity. Although the current statutory company auditor's report has become more detailed and explanatory, it remains, at heart, constative, in the UK, using the term 'true and fair'. Binary audit opinions (such as 'OK' or 'not OK') tend to be descriptive when given as 'OK' (especially if 'OK' is the expected, anticipated, state) but performative (as well as descriptive) when given as 'not OK', especially when this 'not OK' opinion is unanticipated – where it then becomes a cry for action, although such incidents are rare.[2]

Performativity can operate in anticipatory mode. In other words, when a society, or an organisation such as a business, or an individual, thinks ahead about how its actions are to be judged and performance measured, it will amend those intended actions to gain the largest amount of credit. Consequently, the connection (order) between action (activity) and audit (thought) is capable of being reversed – such that knowledge about the audit influences the activity, rather than (or alongside) knowledge about the activity influencing the audit.

'Action first, think about the audit afterwards' does not necessarily give the same result as 'think about the audit first, act afterwards'. Indeed, if the actor does not know what the auditor is going to pay attention to, then this is a situation of inherent uncertainty and potentially a stressful one. However, in so far as audit is thinking differently, anticipation is inevitably going to be difficult and the actor could be better placed by seeking to take the best actions in terms of their own judgement rather than by anticipating that of the auditor.

Whilst the future performativity of a current audit report depends on the extent to which it will generate future action, to the extent that the report has been anticipated and already acted upon 'in anticipation', then the audit report has already been performative; that is, it's performativity is in the past. If, perhaps as a consequence of thinking differently, the current audit report is difficult to anticipate, then its future performativity is likely to increase at the expense of its past performativity. Future performativity is also higher when the auditor has new, unanticipated information – for example, information relevant to a company's going concern status. In respect of an audit, an auditor's report should increase its future performativity when it contains new thinking and/or new information but will lose performativity over time as that thinking/information is superseded and no longer new.

The higher the performativity of a representation, the greater its influence upon society and the actions that society chooses, but whether such influence is 'good' or 'bad' depends upon the level of understanding derived from the representation. Performativity may be a 'bad thing' when the level of understanding provided by the representation is low or materially incomplete, but becomes a 'better thing' as the representation becomes more complete and the level of understanding improves. To take a simple example, suppose the Post Office decides to represent its performance by the number of letters delivered within two days of posting and incentivises its postal workers on this basis. As a consequence, letters that are not delivered within two days are neglected. In these circumstances, the choice of representation shapes the postal service (i.e., it is highly performative), but both the representation and the postal service are incomplete (a bad thing) unless the issue of undelivered mail is addressed, assuming, as seems likely, that undelivered mail is a material issue. To improve representation and the quality of its performativity, the representation must cover the mail not delivered within two days and lead to action in this regard.

MacKenzie pioneered the application of the idea of performativity to the role of financial models, notably the role of the Black-Scholes model in the development of markets trading in options at prices determined by the model. Mackenzie talked of such a model or representation as being an engine, not a camera (MacKenzie, 2006). The Black-Scholes model is an example of a self-fulfilling representation. It was developed from a model in physics of Brownian motion, which is the small random fluctuations of a particle suspended in a liquid or gas. In 1905, Einstein explained that Brownian motion was due to the random buffeting of the particle by the molecules of the fluid. Black-Scholes draws a direct comparison between commercial activity (in markets) and physical activity (of molecules), of how the world of physical movement and financial movement can become closer than we might think. In this case of markets in options, it is the prices that are derived from the model rather than the model being derived from the market prices. The key connection that comes from creative thinking is between physics (Brownian motion) and finance (option pricing). It is the acceptance of this connection (model) by both buyers and sellers that enables both to believe that the price is fair and thus enables the market to operate. In this case, there is a connection between the model and a sense of fairness, though this might not prevent the creation of a better model leading to a better sense of fairness. The model helps produce a market that is less about speculation and more about meeting the needs of its participants.

Pursuing the potential for similarity between audit and physics, it is interesting to speculate whether the idea of performativity in the human world has its counterpart in the world of physics. This can be discussed in the context of Schrodinger's box, a thought experiment in which a cat is placed in a closed box with some poison that the cat may or may not take. The box is opened later by an observer. To the human mind, prior to the opening of the box, the cat is either dead or alive but in one version of quantum theory, the dead cat and the alive cat are, prior to opening the box, in an interactive connection known as quantum interference.[3] It is possible to represent Schrodinger's box as a network of interactions between an alive cat, a dead cat and some poison, with the observer initially excluded from the network. The interactions are as follows: the alive cat has the potential to become a dead cat courtesy of the poison, whilst the (potentially) dead cat can become (or rather stay) an alive cat courtesy of not taking the poison. When the box lid is opened and the observer is no longer excluded from the network, the interaction between the dead and alive versions of the cat collapses since the cat is seen as either dead or alive. In this case, the inclusion of the observer (the auditor) in the network causes the network to collapse and, thus, the observation is 'performative'.

The coexistence or coincidence of the dead cat and the alive cat prior to the opening of the box is known as a 'superposition'. Superposition is a different way of imagining or representing reality. Instead of having either a dead cat **or** an alive cat, we have, before the box is opened, a dead cat **and** an alive cat; a cat that is dead and alive at the same time.[4] Thinking of 'or' is replaced by thinking of 'and'. In Schrodinger's experiment, the superposition is one of potential, being between a potentially dead cat and a potentially live cat; between the potential for sadness and joy. It sees the present (existence) as a superposition of potential futures (existences). It is a different way of thinking about the world.

Thinking differently is important to both physics and the audit but there remain many ways in which physics, at least in the form of the box experiment, and audit are different. What happens if the observer knows the cat and feels that the cat has too much experience to be tempted to take the bait? What happens if the observer can talk to the cat and persuade the cat not to take the bait? What happens if the observer knows the owner of the cat and can influence the owner to remove the cat from the situation it finds itself in? How does the experiment take into account time, for instance, if the cat gets hungrier as time goes by and becomes more likely to take the bait? What happens if there are multiple periodic observations by the observer? What happens if there is no box lid and the observation takes place in real time? What happens if the observer cannot open the box because it is not possible or permitted? Can we assume the observer can tell the difference between a dead and an alive cat? What is the significance of the difference; that is, how do subsequent actions differ (a dead cat is buried and an alive cat given food!)? What if the observer is an observer of many boxes in which some cats might be dead and others alive? What happens if the observer opens some boxes but others remain unopened? What if, in the process of opening boxes, the observer discovers or realises that the number of boxes is growing? The latter is getting close to an audit where the auditor is taken to open boxes but, in the process, comes to realise, or creates, further boxes that remain unopened.

Although the experiment does not fully resemble an audit, its introduction of the notion of a superposition is very important. As indicated by the above 'what if' questions, it provides the basis for very different thinking and understanding of the features of audit. Furthermore, Schrodinger's experiment influences the selection of our own (audit) thought experiments in Chapter 5 – experiments involving poison that may or may not be taken/fatal but incorporating many more 'audit-like' features than the box experiment itself.

Schrodinger's experiment reinforces the point that when an auditor is appointed and becomes an observer of a societal or corporate network, then the auditor inevitably becomes a part of that network. This new inclusion of the observer changes the network of connections and creates a pathway for performativity that has to be borne in mind when considering observation and measurement as a form of audit evidence. The influence of the observer who is joining the network has to be allowed for, as does the influence of the newly joined network on the observer.

What is clear is that an audit can either constitute or endorse a 'self-fulfilling' representation and consequently, to prevent this happening, it is imperative that (a) the audit both generates and is based upon the best possible current understanding of the entity subject to audit and (b) the audit does not inhibit but promotes better understanding in the future.

Materiality introduces a boundary

It is the idea of materiality that introduces a boundary between what the auditor pays attention to and what the auditor does not. A step in the societal audit network is for the auditor to identify where attention is to be given and this is done on the basis of what matters in relation to the purpose of the audit.

At this stage in the development of our arguments, we take the purpose of audit to be the representation to society of its reality so that society can move on and progress by way of a suitable response to what the audit reveals. If a boundary is placed upon the audit that does not allow the audit to fulfil its purpose, then the auditor should decline the appointment. The auditor searches for evidence on issues that matter, evaluates that evidence, leading to an understanding of how the society or organisation should be represented and communicates the findings of the audit. For now, we can think of the audit as a pathway – attention, evidence, understanding, communication– with identification of where to pay attention as the crucial first step requiring awareness of what matters (materiality).[5] But every step is crucial, including communication, since this should report the opportunities/actions for progression (making things better). This sequence is a flow that carries us around the left side of the outer ring of Figure 1.1, and as the audit unfolds, the flow changes from identifying key matters (attention) to gathering evidence (evidence), to making sense of the evidence (understanding) and finally to communication to society. Attention and all subsequent steps in the audit pathway are driven by the purpose of the audit, which, in general terms, as we have stated, is to represent the reality of the auditee's existence in order to promote and facilitate the auditee's progress.

The dynamic of audit, whether it be the individual audit (or new audit ideas in general), includes the search for a materially complete understanding and representation of the auditee's existence, an understanding and representation that is right hemisphere and holistic. Completeness and materiality are closely connected with the notion of evidence. When an audit is materially incomplete, there is a need for further evidence but once an audit is materially complete, there is judged to be no need for further evidence. Without the concept of materiality, the audit would be potentially endless. So, when faced with the possibility of obtaining evidence, the auditor internally might ask the following question: will this further evidence, even if the result is unanticipated, fail to overturn our understanding of the auditee or to otherwise disrupt the audit pathway? Or would it be a significant piece of the jigsaw, changing or completing the overall picture and requiring the auditor (and, in turn, people receiving the auditor's report) to think differently about the auditee? In this regard, the auditor will need to be contemplating how to respond to (unexpected) evidence but also assessing the likelihood of finding unexpected evidence.

The mantra of our book is that 'thinking differently is audit', whether at the level of the individual audit or at the level of the future of audit. An audit is valued or special because the auditor thinks differently and does so continuously – first, thinking differently, then seeking evidence to support or discount that thinking; and, in turn, considering whether this new evidence generates the need for further fresh thinking. If thinking differently is audit, then auditors need to think differently about: the purpose of the audit, what matters in relation to the purpose of the audit; what evidence is material (to this purpose); understanding (how we connect) the evidence; and how best to communicate to maximum effect? Thinking differently matters because it guides and inspires purposeful action.

But thinking differently cannot be endless. It is itself subject to a materiality test. The auditor has to ask the question whether the different thinking can provide a material advance in our understanding and representation of the auditee, before pursuing evidence to confirm or discount that thinking. We cannot have a society or economy in which an endless search for different thinking (creativity) displaces all other activity. There has to be a balance between different thinking and thinking the same way as before; of judging, ultimately, whether thinking differently will help, either by producing fresh insight or by reinforcing existing insight.

There is a conundrum in associating materiality with completeness. A materiality judgement introduces a boundary beyond which the auditor does not search. We do not know for sure what might have been found if the search had continued, and in that sense, the introduction of a boundary to produce completeness as closure also introduces incompleteness. There is also a relationship between judgement and scepticism, scepticism being a propensity to search for connections that do not readily present themselves. A more sceptical judge will push out the boundary. A less sceptical judge might do the opposite. The conundrum of simultaneous completeness and incompleteness is similar to the issue of establishing a boundary and extending or crossing the boundary at one and the same time: an issue raised in Chapter 2 and central to the coexistence of correspondence and progression audits. A progression audit has as its purpose thinking differently to achieve positive change, in contrast to a 'correspondence audit' where the purpose is to measure performance against established norms. Progression and correspondence audits are introduced in this chapter but discussed further in Chapter 4.

Figure 1.1 shows constituents of an audit pathway, such as attention, evidence, understanding and communication, and these can themselves be subject to audit (i.e., auditing the processes of audit); an internal reflection that potentially invites a sense of endless regress. Within an audit firm, such internal reflection normally takes place through supervision and review, and it is, of course, possible to review the reviews and so on. Indeed, government requirements for the governance of audit firms add yet another, this time external, layer of audit supervision and regulation. This potential for endless regress must be bounded through the judgement of materiality.

Whilst physical action may not be reversible, a human objective or purpose often requires thinking in reverse. In particular, planning is anticipatory and requires thinking from the end to the beginning as well as from the beginning to the end – i.e., planning connects the end and the beginning. In general, in society, cause and effect need to be considered in both directions. For example, it is generally argued that poverty is a cause of unhealthy behaviours (eating junk food, drug taking etc.) whilst at the same time unhealthy behaviours, rendering a person unemployable, are a cause of poverty. Cause and effect can thus play out in both directions, mutually supporting an undesirable situation.

To move away from the undesirable situation, a greater understanding is necessary. As previously noted, two 'things' (variables) might often be observed moving together, highlighting an 'association', but understanding the connection between them might require an evaluation of connections that each thing has with other things, and that those other things, in turn, have with each other.

Some arguments of this book are concerned with undesirable outcomes flowing from a materially incomplete understanding of the potentially endless complex of connections that are present in the construction of society or of an organisation (such as a business) operating within it. We, therefore, see audit as a constant drive for more completeness and understanding (albeit one that, in practice, is clearly not costless nor supported by unlimited funds), with the judgement of materiality essential in drawing a boundary between (albeit incomplete) understanding and what is (justifiably) not understood.

Nevertheless, an aspirational intent on each audit should be to strive to understand better, giving a key role to thinking differently, including thinking in different (or reverse) directions – inwards as well as outwards, forwards as well as backwards and from the anticipated to the unanticipated. As understanding improves, it is likely that the judgement of materiality will change to reflect the new understanding of the connections that form the society or organisation being audited. The role of audit is to continue the development of understanding 'what should matter' and to influence society (or other stakeholders in the audit) accordingly.

Incompleteness, endlessness and materiality are inextricably linked. To explore the potential for incomplete understanding, consider a web of three interactions (connections) AC, BC and BA with nodal classifications A, B and C as shown in Figure 3.1 (the original representation of roundaboutness was provided in Chapter 2).

If BC is observed but A and its connections are hidden, then a change in A may cause a change in BC that is observed but not understood. Understanding BC is holistic in the sense of requiring observation of BA and AC as well as BC. Incompleteness in the form of A being hidden (incomplete representation) is the cause of a lack of understanding if BA or AC are material.

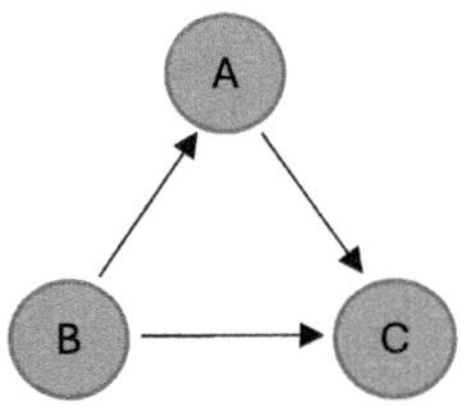

FIGURE 3.1 **Roundaboutness revisited.**

The flows between A, B and C form a network of three. This can become a network of 'n' by adding further nodes (classifications) to the web.

Understanding is holistic by nature. We might take something apart, but we really start to understand it when we also see how it was put together in a way that the whole is greater than the parts. The drive for understanding is a drive towards holism, for whilst the whole is connected to the parts (and through the parts to the outside world), it is also connected directly to the outside world and by providing that connection adds value to the sum of the parts. BC is the direct flow between B and C, whereas there is also the 'long way round' via A. Consequently, we cannot observe/measure the impact of B on C (and vice versa) without also observing/measuring indirect impacts via A. If the long way round takes significantly longer, then there is a measurement issue because any contemporaneous matching of changes in B and C is 'interfered' with by those 'long way round' impacts of B on C that started in a prior period.[6] It follows that roundaboutness introduces an element of obscurity or opacity.

To sum up, the number of indirect connections is potentially 'endless', highlighting the inevitability of incomplete measurement, evaluation and understanding and consequently the important role of materiality. 'Endlessness' is also an issue in physics. To quote Baggott (2012):

> If matter is endlessly divisible, then we would reach a point where the constituents themselves become rather ephemeral – to the point of non-existence. Then there would be no building blocks, and all we would be left with are interactions between indefinable, insubstantial phantoms which give rise to the appearance of substance.........To a large extent, this is precisely what modern physics has shown to be true......The physicists kept dividing, and in the end found nothing at all.
>
> (pp. 2–3)

The words 'to a large extent' are important here, because the work of Planck (and the discovery of Planck's 'constant') shows there may ultimately be a limit to endless divisibility and such endlessness ends with the quanta which lie at the heart of quantum theory.[7] Anything that is endlessly divisible (or infinitely expandable?) does not exist unless we revisit our quantum notion of what it is to exist.[8] Existence is associated with boundaries (however small they may be) rather than the infinite. It is, in essence, something that has to be viewed as discontinuous rather than continuous.

Judgement connects the left and right hemispheres of the brain but is itself a predominantly right hemisphere activity. Accordingly, materiality has to be treated as a judgement and serves a key role in both establishing the classifications upon which subsequent analysis depends and in determining when to stop analysing. Judgement is, or at least should be, in command of the analysis – highlighting the primacy of the right hemisphere. In practice, much judgement includes comparison of a current case with prior cases with which the auditor has experience. Thus, pattern recognition plays an important role, especially regarding issues such as future corporate collapse or success. Artificial intelligence can extend pattern recognition to encompass a far wider set of experiences than is possessed by a single individual. If pattern recognition by humans is regarded as a predominantly right hemisphere activity, then arguably, artificial intelligence captures and extends the right hemisphere of the brain, whereas traditional computational information technology extends the left hemisphere of the brain.[9] Digital advances, in whatever form, change the way in which the left and right hemispheres of the brain come together and this can have performative effects, changing the way in which work is seen and conducted (see, for example, Willems and Hafermalz, 2021).

To sum up this section, materiality requires us to pay attention to those connections, which are significant to our understanding. This selection is a judgement, a feeling, a sensation. It is like using the zoom and focus facilities on a camera. We zoom in or out to give us what we judge to be the required mix for our purpose, our field of vision and focus. In auditing, the exploration of the potentially endless web of connections is bounded by judgement – judgement being a sensation operated upon by experience and often made within, and because of, constraints of time and cost.

The auditor is, of practical necessity, a 'finitist' – an idea discussed in the last chapter in connection with classification and the introduction of boundaries. The finitist human judges when any potentially infinite regress has gone far enough and therefore introduces a boundary. Finitism is essentially the introduction of a practical or 'real world' necessity to a theoretically infinite collection or network of things and to a potentially infinite evidence/understanding of each individual thing in the network. Both understanding the collection of things and understanding each specific thing requires a boundary in practice. But if each thing only exists courtesy of its connection to other things, then the two requirements are convergent in the sense that what matters is understanding of the auditee's role in the overall network of connection. This is an understanding shaped by the audit's purpose. For instance, judging materiality for the purpose of a company audit (i.e., understanding the company) must relate to the company's role in its stakeholder network of connections and the auditor of the company must decide to what extent it is necessary to audit the company's stakeholders and their stakeholders in turn (potentially an infinite process). There has to be a boundary or limit on how far the auditor can audit the network of which the company is a part, yet the engagement and health of the stakeholders is a material consideration since it is the network of stakeholders that constitutes the existence of the company.

The point of any model/theory of auditing is to connect across the space-time continuum of the stakeholder network in order to provide integration and holistic understanding. This integration follows the way our minds work to give a progression of, but never complete, understanding. The potential for endlessness highlights that rational argument (reason) has its limits and 'sense' has to be applied to rational argument to establish a boundary.[10] However, we should at the same time be pushing (through a commitment to thinking differently) the established boundary in a search to extend our understanding. Materiality is the boundary that avoids endlessness and therefore determines 'substance' – but this boundary is a function of purpose, which belongs to its time and spatial circumstances (context). As we understand more, then the boundary formed by materiality changes and with it our notion of substance and existence, together with the focus of thinking differently and what that specifically comprises.

Audit as research

In this section, we discuss the nature of research and then argue that it resembles any audit that has progress as its purpose, with implications for the audit (and for research).

We might call that which lies beyond human imagination the hidden zone of radical uncertainty. It is research that explores this 'hidden zone' and, through creativity, moves its possibilities to a place in the human imagination and subsequently, through experiment and testing, to a place in 'reality for which we have evidential support'. Once an idea has evidential support, then it might be developed further with a view to demonstrating its potential (value) as a commercial or social product.

Thus, both research and development are boundary-crossing (and boundary-shifting) instruments, with research crossing the boundary from the 'hidden zone' into the imagination and on to evidential support, and development crossing into practical application. Research and development are crucial to the progress of both business and society and hence to any audit (a progression audit) that sees progress as its purpose. As stated earlier in the chapter, a progression audit has as its purpose thinking differently to achieve positive change, in contrast to a 'correspondence audit' where the purpose is to measure performance against established norms. The audit of research and development is crucial to a progression audit. Claims of progress need to be both challenged and confirmed. Confirmation might require the development of research norms, whereas challenge comes from thinking and possibly proceeding differently from the norm. Thus, the audit of research progress is likely to consider both correspondence and progression and to require the coexistence and coincidence of both as a source of new thinking.

Society, through universities, research institutes and commercial organisations must invest in research before the outcome of the research is known. Consequently, the researcher (and the investor in the research) holds parallel universes in mind – one in which research is deemed a success and one in which it is deemed a failure. However, the judgement as to what constitutes success may not be straightforward. Success and failure are both perceptually dependent since the research findings may matter more and be more acceptable to some than to others, and time dependent since the research may come to matter more in the future than in the present or near future. Consider Schrodinger's cat as a piece of research, albeit a thought experiment. If Schrodinger developed the experiment to highlight the absurdity of the idea of superposition as a description of reality, then, rather than closing off the idea of superposition, Schrodinger's cat has become famous by highlighting the issue of superposition and spurring further debate, with his experiment being interpreted in different ways. Research can and should spur different thinking and yield unanticipated outcomes. Research in the academic world is a search for reality but it is a search that contributes to the generality of human understanding and debate over time, and can contribute by pointing the direction of yet still further research and discussion rather than yielding immediate outcomes. Academe builds a 'body of research' that can be drawn upon, sometimes inappropriately, by those with more immediate needs for specific problem-solving.

Research by commercial organisations is not directly, or not typically, a search for reality but rather a search for a commercially successful product. Nevertheless, the identification of what to research is intimately bound up with the prejudices and hopes of the company. These not only shape the way research proposals are constructed and put forward but also how the results of the research are understood and communicated. Further, if the perceived success of the research depends upon its commercial success, then much also depends on how commercial success is represented (which brings into play all the accompanying issues of performativity in the company). Auditing an organisation's research commitment can be a key element of a progression audit, given its direct connection to the organisation's future prospects. Research, for instance, may have been oriented in the organisation to short-term scenario analysis or even have been curtailed itself to boost short-term profits – meaning that current profits might misrepresent the longer-term sustainability of the organisation. We could also look at development as a pathway whose purpose is the direct extension of existing products or disruption through new products.

Both an academic and a commercial research pathway resemble the audit's process of identifying what to investigate, generating and understanding evidence and communicating the findings. Research is predominantly, at least in its early identification stages, a right hemisphere activity involving imagination, and hence the research flow or pathway should not be highly specified but allowed to evolve as the research progresses (and potentially transforms into some form of product development). An initial creative research idea – the joining of 'dots' in ways not seen by others – is an 'aha' moment that can come from any quarter, at any point in an existing research programme, and from any specialism but is likely to involve experience across different quarters, research programmes and specialisms. Although the 'aha' moment might take place within a single human brain, it is the consequence of wide experience and connection with many other human brains and with the environment.

To the extent that research resembles audit, then research might be regarded as audit but equally audit might be regarded as research. Thinking differently is crucial to both research and audit and both in their way are searching for an understanding of reality. A progression auditor, as such, can be said to be searching or hoping for an 'aha' moment; to join the 'dots' in a manner not seen by others and to facilitate the delivery or development of something new. This is similar to the position of a researcher and the successful progression auditor, in particular, is likely to have experience across very different audit clients both directly and through interaction with colleagues. The outcome of research is a new network of connections, which, in the case of a commercial organisation, will impact its (market) valuation and overall standing. Auditors tasked with assessing an organisation's viability and long-term sustainability have to understand and evaluate the organisation's research both from a purely financial and a social/environmental viewpoint. When the progression auditor assesses what to pay attention to, research and development is right up there in their frames of thought.

Clockwise and anti-clockwise pathways

In terms of progress, audit is primarily concerned with two questions: (1) is the subject of the audit on the right /best possible pathway and (2) how far has there been progression along the pathway? Progress takes the form of finding better (or additional beneficial) pathways and progressing along them. The subject of the audit might be society as a whole, an organisation within society or an individual purposeful pathway such as research. The subject might also be the audit itself when the questions become whether the audit chose the best pathway(s) and how it has progressed. However, in each case, progress along the pathway, and hence the pathway itself, does not necessarily follow a clockwise sequence. Indeed, the societal audit network of Figure 1.1 has both clockwise and anti-clockwise pathways operating simultaneously, and so does a research pathway, where there is an issue as to whether understanding comes before or after observable evidence and whether the order of the observable evidence matters.

For instance, there were several decades, from 1964 to 2012, when we had Higgs' mathematical explanation of the Higgs boson but the boson had never been observed (Baggott, 2012). In so far as mathematics provides understanding and observation provides evidence, then understanding came before evidence. This is an illustration of how understanding and evidence (in the form of observation) do not necessarily progress together at the same rate and do not necessarily follow a set order, giving rise to the subtleties of existence. Did the boson only come into existence when it was observed? Did the boson exist before 1964 (when it was mathematically derived)? One answer is that it existed in some form the whole time, but the form or level of its existence 'relative to us' transitioned both when it was understood (understanding in the sense of knowing its mathematical derivation) and again later when it was observed (at CERN's Large Hydron Collider).

Alternatively, the mathematical derivation might be considered a form of evidence supporting the existence of the boson. In effect, evidence from the analytical left hemisphere in the form of mathematics did not and could not interact, until 2012, with evidence from the sensory right hemisphere in the form of observation. Looked at in this way, it is the ordering of the visibility of the evidence that causes our sense of the boson's existence to transition. Our perception of existence transitions as the audit pathway progresses but the pathway might not progress in a fixed order.

As societal audit pathways can operate in two directions, both directions must be considered. So, to consider the connection between audit and existence, we should reverse the direction of the pathway and ask what it means, for a period, or point in time, to have communication without understanding, understanding without evidence (as in the case of the boson) or evidence (such as observation) without identification.[11]

With regard to communication without understanding, it should be noted that communication typically implies a giver and a receiver. It is quite possible for the giver to have a much fuller understanding than the receiver, who, in this case, has an explanation but only a limited understanding. However, it is also possible that the giver's understanding is limited. This can happen when providing any 'standard' explanation based upon tick boxes and compliance. The so-called 'audit expectation gap' arises when the giver's (i.e., the auditor's) understanding, or even their willingness to communicate understanding, is limited, whilst the receiver (i.e., the user) may well imagine a level of existence above that assessed or substantiated through the audit process. It is a failure to develop joint cognition. Ultimately, an ever more detailed checklist can result in the auditor scarcely thinking at all, with such a superficial level of understanding discouraging substantive adaptation to the idiosyncrasies or context of the particular audit assignment.

Observation without identification implies an absence of, or deficiency in, a classification scheme. To identify is to classify (e.g., the Higgs boson was recognised as being different and given its own classification). Big data and other forms of collective experience are important to enable differences (and similarities) to be recognised, and hence for a classification scheme and identification of connections to develop. For an auditor, individual experience, including experience on the current audit, is also important for identification. In fact, recognition of the need to explore or pay attention to something different or unexpected can occur at any time on an audit, causing a disruption to the originally intended audit pathway; a pathway based on an initial appreciation or idea of existence – of what there is and what matters.

The original intended audit pathway is based upon an initial understanding of the world. The quality of an audit is dependent upon both this initial understanding and the audit pathway's ability to challenge, confirm and develop it. The thinking is two-way, both initially and throughout development. For example, we communicate what we can identify, but at the same time, we identify what we can explain and communicate. The initial thinking should be subject to challenge and development throughout the audit, and accordingly, the pathway design invites both confirming and disconfirming evidence in respect of the initial thinking. Disconfirming evidence disrupts the audit pathway and where this happens, the pathway evolves in response to its own findings.

Considering the audit pathway from both directions means that the audit reflects and explores existence as being between two opposites. It might be called a 'co-audit' in which we audit forwards and backwards, with thinking in both directions promoting deeper and more creative thought: right hemisphere activity. There may be events or findings during the audit that disrupt the orderly flow of the pathway (or disrupt its reverse ordering) – and require the audit to move in unanticipated directions as it responds to unexpected information (left hemisphere) and/or feelings (right hemisphere).

In any event, whether the order is disrupted or not, throughout the audit, the auditor conducts both left hemisphere and right hemisphere activity and holds both in the brain at once. For instance, identifying should include all material interactions (materiality is a judgement made by the right hemisphere) between the company and, say, its customers. This could involve identifying and reviewing individual transactions, such detail being processed by the left hemisphere and a more general overview of customer relations sensed by the right hemisphere. Moving on from identification to evaluation, evaluation involves bringing together observation provided by the senses residing in the right hemisphere with the measurement techniques and analysis of the left hemisphere. Understanding requires all the evidence to come together to give the overall picture that resides in the right hemisphere. Communication requires an appeal to both the left and right hemispheres of the recipient's brain; the two hemispheres then come together to give the recipient the bigger picture. This is discussed further in the next chapter.

Evidence and cognition

There are many ideas in cognitive science and philosophy as to how the mind works and develops, a good number of which are directly relevant to audit. Mautz and Sharaf (1961, p. 56) quote Immanuel Kant:

> Our knowledge springs from two main sources in the mind, the first of which is the faculty or power of receiving representations (receptivity of impressions); the second is the power of cognizing by means of these representations (spontaneity in the production of conceptions).
>
> (Kant translated by Meiklejohn, 1953, p. 44)

Given that evidence is a representation (of reality) and a representation is evidence (of reality), then the two main sources can also be regarded as the power to receive evidence and the power to cognise (to evaluate and understand) on the basis of evidence.

There are other, more recent philosophers whose work is relevant to the relation between evidence and cognition. For example, Foucault argues that minds work, often subconsciously, in response to power and historical conditioning in its various forms (summarised in the Little Book of Philosophy, 2018, p. 190). For the auditor, such conditioning might be a force for good, for example, in relation to professional duties, or a force for bad when it is consequent to pressures from directors. Gadamer says that behind every thought lies a whole body of assumptions and background beliefs, some of which should be retained because they represent knowledge (positive prejudice) but others which should be rejected because they represent prior prejudice in a negative sense (see Grayling 2020, p. 496).

These issues of prior belief and conditioning are recognised in the cognition literature in the form of belief perseverance and confirmation bias. Reisberg (2001, p. A2) describes belief bias as a "tendency, within logical reasoning, to endorse a conclusion if the conclusion happens to be something one believes is true anyhow". This may, of course, not be 'bias' in a pejorative sense but an appropriate coming together of the left (logical) and right (emotional) hemispheres of the brain. It is this coming together of sense as feeling and sense as logic that is central to audit. Reisberg (2001, p. A3) describes confirmation bias as a

> family of effects in which people seem more sensitive to evidence confirming their beliefs than they are to evidence challenging their beliefs. Thus, if given a choice about what sort of information they would like in order to evaluate their beliefs, they request information that is likely to confirm their beliefs.

According to Merleau-Ponty, what people perceive is, in significant part, conditioned by what they can do about it; to perceive is to see a range of possibilities in action (Grayling, 2020, p. 483). For Habermas (as explained in 'The Little Book of Philosophy', 2018, p. 194), reason and communication ('communicative reason') are about the need we have to justify ourselves to others. Like Merleau-Ponty, Habermas is thinking from the future to the present but not so much in terms of what is going to be possible but rather in terms of what is going to be acceptable (as justification). When thinking from the future, the (anticipatory) priors which influence our actions have to be found in the future.

Heidegger (as reported in Grayling, 2020, p. 495) argued that the possibility of understanding anything involves having 'to have already understood it' in the sense that the very basis of our being able to understand anything at all requires us to be in the world with that particular 'thing'. Rovelli makes a similar point in relation to the totality of things: he states

> If we imagine the totality of things, we are imagining being outside the universe......but there is no outside to the totality of things. The external point of view is a point of view that does not exist. Every description of the world is from inside it.
>
> (Rovelli, 2021, p. 152)

Consequently, an auditor cannot be a complete outsider and cannot come to an audit without forming priors. Priors form the basis on which judgements are made as to what the audit should pay attention to, but the audit should admit the possibility of alternative priors.

An appropriate balance, therefore, has to be struck between the search for confirming evidence that supports the initial judgement and the search for disconfirming evidence that supports feeling differently; that is, supports alternative possible priors. The original or initial priors are likely to come from experience gained on other audits (including the auditee's audit in previous years).[12] However, audit is not merely a process of confirmation, but also (perhaps more importantly) a process of learning, of revealing what we didn't expect. As Rovelli (2021) puts it, the 'relevant input is not that which confirms what we already know, but that which contradicts our expectations' (p. 163). Disruption is part of the learning process. We must avoid what has been called Occam's Broom, where contradictions are ignored in order to preserve the hypothesis behind our expectations (McGilchrist, 2021, p. 1077).

If the way our mind works can be conditioned by power, by prior 'prejudice' or by possibilities for action and acceptability, the auditor must recognise such influences as good or bad in the circumstances and respond appropriately, particularly at the identification and evaluation stages. This is not easy territory for the auditor who needs to be self-challenging and self-understanding. It takes us into another area of philosophy/psychology concerned with the self and managing oneself.

The ability to distinguish positive from negative conditioning is a vital skill for the auditor and relates to the traditional audit concepts of due care, independence, scepticism, objectivity and ethical conduct as well as experience. At the heart of audit is the auditor's interaction (connection) with the self. The construction of the 'auditing self' comes from the interaction and internal management of positive and negative conditioning. If feelings exist by reference to other feelings, then, in general, the auditor manages (baser level) feelings such as the desire to please management and the desire to make money, by appealing to (connecting with) higher level feelings such as the desire to do a good job and the desire to serve the community. These feelings all come together (synthesise) in the act of auditing by the individual.

It is conditioning that shapes both the auditor's beliefs and scepticism – and scepticism requires as much justification as belief does (See Grayling, 2020, p. 333). Management of conditioning is, in effect, an audit process requiring identification, evaluation, understanding and finally explanation (rather than justification) to the self; and as with any audit process materiality plays a key role. This self-explanation cannot be solely rationalisation but should appeal to both logic and feeling (be both rational and intuitive with intuition as the final judge, see McGilchrist, 2021, pp. 722–723).[13]

It is possible to classify an organisation's annual report and accounts prepared by its management as being a self-audit. The traditional justification for an outsider as an auditor is that management's commitment to what they are doing and their wish for it to be seen in the best light will impair their ability to distinguish positive from negative conditioning. The interesting question is just how much of an outsider should the auditor be? Addressing this question, philosophically, requires contemplation of what an auditor contributes through being an outsider and whether there is more to contribute by functioning in a different manner or more specifically, whether more can be gained compared to what might be lost by the auditor perceiving and pursuing their outsider responsibilities in a different fashion.

For example, currently, the external auditor is typically represented as a 'reporter' rather than a 'doer. Humphrey et al. (2021), however, argue that the audit should be more about 'doing' things than just 'reporting' on things. This issue is explored in more detail later in Chapter 4 when discussing 'performativity' and the 'progression audit'. In the progression audit, the 'external' auditor is a reporter but can report (communicate, explain) in a way which is influential on management as well as on other stakeholders. This can see an auditor as a reporter becoming a 'doer' (at least indirectly), but it certainly opens up the importance of viewing the auditor as an influencer.

Audit is valuable if it is influential, and maximising the value of audit through influence (implying perhaps a greater use of social media?) has to be a key driver of any 'claimed' auditing profession. In so far as the auditor is an influencer, then the audit can shape, as well as assess, the future. This type of reflection adds an additional dimension to the significance of the notion of 'thinking differently' in that an auditor, as an influencer, has to be continually thinking not just about doing the same function in different ways but of the potential benefits of developing or reframing the audit function itself so as to maximise its effect and overall (social) significance.

This gives audit its sense of dynamism – with output and effect driving the construction and reconstruction of audit rather than any standardised set of procedures or ways of representing what is or is not audit. In thinking differently, audit is a process of being and behaving differently when circumstances justify and merit such a development. This does not rule out a sense of consistency and comparability in audit but consistency and comparability now start to resemble a far from natural state of affairs for audit.

Summary and conclusion

Figure 1.1 in Chapter 1 identified two connections between the (rest of the) societal audit network and reality that help to shape reality. The first was the relationship between reality and society. Society takes action with the intention or purpose of impacting reality for the better. However, with inevitably incomplete knowledge of an inherently uncertain world, purposeful action at some stage leads to unintended consequences and disruption – such that reality can take the form of an unexpected (and even unwanted) impact on society and the organisations and individuals that comprise society. Society, as a channel, allows audit to have an indirect connection with reality through its impact on the actions of society, its organisations and individuals. This impact can be classified as the audit's performativity.

The second key connection was between reality and audit evidence. The auditor's perception of reality (following Kant) is of two kinds: that for which there is audit experience (evidence) and that which lies beyond experience (and, for which, therefore, no evidence is felt or seen to exist). Reality for which there is evidence is also of two kinds: that to which attention is given by the auditor and that to which attention is not given. This boundary is determined by the auditor's judgements of materiality. Reality for which there is no evidence divides into that within the human imagination (of the auditor) and that which lies beyond human imagination, with the boundary between the two following the limits of the auditor's imagination. The boundaries of human imagination are formed and crossed in significant part by the activities of research and development; activities, which, therefore, form a material focus for audit.

The chapter's discussion of evidence and cognition leads to a recognition of the limitations of people's cognitive powers and hence, the importance of seeking disconfirming evidence; evidence which, if found, can shift our initial thinking on materiality and, hence, the boundary of (auditor) attention. Through this chapter, it becomes possible to see that, as well as the nature of reality yielding evidence that influences the audit, the auditor's attention and imagination (reflecting an ability to think differently and consequently to change boundaries) are influential in shaping the nature and perception of reality. The chapter, accordingly, incorporated a discussion of materiality, imagination, and evidence and their roles in shaping reality as we see it.

From one perspective or viewpoint, audit can be seen in Figure 1.1 as the messenger of society's environmental reality and, in particular, an economic reality of scarce resources necessitating choice: the reality of 'or'. Should society choose consumption now or less consumption/more investment now, leading to greater consumption later? This choice relates to reality as a discipline. However, Figure 1.1 also implies that, through its engagement with society's values, audit can enthuse and infuse those values with the 'spirit' of promise, potential and progress. Imagination, thinking differently and the desire for progress uncover the reality of 'and', inspiring research and development to displace the discipline of 'or'. This perspective relates to reality as an opportunity. Functionally, this places audit as something that is continually in the position of becoming or contemplating becoming or contributing something different.

Thinking differently gives audit a persistently dynamic character as the mediator between the reality of discipline and the reality of opportunity and hope; reality as a 'superposition' of pessimism and optimism. Since audit is always trying to make sense of existence, to understand its nature and to contemplate how existence can be improved, then we can begin to think of audit as a philosophy of existence and its materiality; in terms of what exists and could exist, what matters and what matters more.

Notes

1 In Figure 1.1, audit and society are directly connected through values and indirectly via reality. Hence reality and values become connected with values shaping reality, or at least how we see reality, whilst reality shapes the values shared by society and the audit.

2 The auditor's going concern opinion is an example of high performativity since an opinion that the company is not a going concern is likely to be self-fulfilling. A problem with the going concern qualification is that it is too rare and too late, often appearing once the time for necessary action, on the part of the company and stakeholders, has passed. Not all representations are so self-fulfilling. Performativity exists to varying degrees across different circumstances (for an analysis of the conditions for performativity, see Marti and Gond, 2017).

3 Quantum interference, superpositions and Schrodinger's box are discussed by Rovelli (2021, pp. 44–49).
4 The superposition idea that a cat is dead and alive at the same time still relies on a dead cat and an alive cat being distinct things. In the network relations between the dead and alive cat, taking the poison would be an irreversible action since a dead cat cannot come alive again. If it could and the action of taking the poison was reversible, then, essentially, the distinction between a dead cat and alive cat would be lost and there is no superposition. Quantum superposition depends upon irreversible order effects – order matters (Rovelli, 2021, p. 94).
5 The audit as a linear sequence of events (audit as left hemisphere activity) will be challenged later in the chapter. In his discussion of linear versus circular progression, (McGilchrist, 2012, pp. 446–449) argues the merits of circularity. He states

> ... the shape that is suggested by the processing of the right hemisphere is that of the circle, and its movement is characteristically "in the round" – a phrase we use to describe something that is seen as a whole, and in depth. Circular motion accommodates, as rectilinearity does not, the coming together of opposites.
> (p. 447)

6 Much of accounting (e.g., the matching concept) is taken up with this issue, something recognised by the economist Friedrich Von Hayek when discussing capital (investment in long term assets) as 'roundaboutness' (see, for example, Steele, 2014, on Von Hayek's 'Pure Theory of Capital'). In the absence of borrowing, investment reduces cash flow in the present period but, if successful, it enhances cash flow in future periods. In such circumstances, the connection between investment and cash flow would be observed, evaluated and represented/interpreted as a negative unless the longer-term roundabout impacts on cash flow were also taken into account. This is dealt with through the introduction of new classifications and connections into the network of accounts – classifications such as assets, depreciation and profit that take us from a cash flow statement to a profit statement. Depreciation is the flow that connects cash spent on long-term assets with profit.
7 For an understanding of Planck and Planck's constant, see Kumar (2009, pp. 3–29).
8 Discussion of (in)divisibility has a long history going back to the ancient Greeks.
9 The question of whether artificial intelligence is thinking differently and therefore an activity that would otherwise be conducted by the right hemisphere reappears in later chapters.
10 This appears to be a reversal of Kant's ordering. Kant argued that the brain applied reason (in the form of a left hemisphere organising function) to the incoming sensory data received by the brain. Arguably, materiality applies 'sense' (in the form of 'common sense' – a right hemisphere function), to the 'logic' of endlessness. It is likely that both Kant's order and the reverse order should be applied by the auditor, with the reverse order having the final word if, as McGilchrist (2021) argues, the right hemisphere is taken as the 'master'.
11 A further question is what does it mean to imagine or conceive of a (potentially material) connection for which no evidence of its existence can be found? This implies that audit has to contemplate, and even challenge, notions of existence and what it means to exist or to be real. If reality in the form of existence 'exists', then unreality (non-existence) must also exist. Unreality may only exist in our imagination, but if it exists in our imagination, then, in a sense, it is also real. For

example, what do we make of a virtual digital reality that is not real (and we know it) but nevertheless feels real?

12 Following Hume, an idea can be preceded by an impression so that the audit's initial idea can be formed from and based upon an impression gained prior to the audit – or, often in practice, from prior audits or similar audits. For a discussion of Hume, see Kenny (2012), notably pp. 612–613.

13 This and other relevant issues are discussed in chapter 18 in McGilchrist (2021), entitled 'The untimely demise of intuition' (pp. 707–51). Intuition might be associated with experience and hence conditioning. In his conclusion to Chapter 17, McGilchrist (2021, p. 706) writes

> We inhabit a world in which reason is needed more than ever before, yet in which reason is so narrowly conceived that it drives out true understanding. For that we would have to learn respect for the power of intuition, not as opposed to reason, but as both grounding it, and the means for it to fulfil its potential in making judgments in life.

For audit, as for society, understanding the role of conditioning is a key challenge.

References

Austin, J.L., 1962, *How to Do Things with Words*, (Clarendon Press, Oxford).

Baggott, J., 2012, *Higgs: The Invention and Discovery of the 'God Particle'*, (Oxford University Press, Oxford).

Grayling, A.C., 2020, *The History of Philosophy: Three Millenia of Thought from the West and Beyond*, (Penguin, Random House, London).

Humphrey, C., Sonnerfeldt, A., Komori, N. and E. Curtis, 2021, 'Audit and the pursuit of dynamic repair', *European Accounting Review*, 30:3, pp. 445–471, https://doi.org/10.1080/09638180.2021.1919539.

Kant, I., (translated by Meiklejohn, J.M.D.), 1953, *Critique of Pure Reason*, (Wiley, New York, NY).

Kenny, A., 2012, *A New History of Western Philosophy*, (Oxford University Press, Oxford).

Kumar, M., 2009, *Quantum: Einstein, Bohr and the Great Debate about the Nature of Reality*, (Icon Books, London).

MacKenzie, D., 2006, *An Engine not a Camera: How Financial Models Shape Markets*, (MIT Press, Cambridge, MA).

Marti, E. and J-P. Gond, 2017, 'When do theories become self-fulfilling? Exploring the boundary conditions of performativity', *Academy of Management Review*, 48:3, pp. 487–508, https://doi.org/10.5465/amr.2016.0071.

Mautz, R. and H.A. Sharaf, 1961, *The Philosophy of Auditing*, (American Accounting Association, Sarasota, Florida).

McGilchrist, I., 2012, *The Master and his Emissary: The Divided Brain and the Making of the Western World*, (Yale University Press, New Haven).

McGilchrist, I., 2021, *The Matter with Things: Our Brains, Our Delusions, and the Unmaking of the World*, (Perspectiva Press, London).

Reisberg, D., 2001, *Cognition: Exploring the Science of the Mind*, (W.W. Norton, New York, NY).

Rovelli, C., 2021, *Helgoland*, (Allen Lane, London).

Steele, G., 2014, 'Hayek's pure theory of capital', in *The Elgar Companion to Hayekian Economics*, Garrison, R.W. and N. Barry (eds.), pp. 71–93, (Edward Elgar Publishing, Cheltenham), Ch. 4.

The Little Book of Philosophy, 2018, (Dorling Kindersley, London).

Willems, T. and E. Hafermalz, 2021, 'Distributed seeing: Algorithms and the reconfiguration of the workplace, a case of 'automated' trading', *Information and Organization*, 31:4, https://doi.org/10.1016/j.infoandorg.2021.100376.

4

AUDIT AS REPRESENTATION

With Chapter 3 having focused upon the connections between audit, society and reality within the context of the overall societal audit network, this chapter completes our study of this network by concentrating upon representation and its place in the network as a pervasive field, a channel and an entity.

A major role of representation is as a channel of communication, raising questions of what is to be communicated, how, to whom and for what purpose? Looking at Figure 1.1's clockwise flows and the conclusion of Chapter 3, we see that what is communicated through audit is based upon the understanding that the auditor has of society's reality, bringing together both reality as discipline and reality as 'real' opportunity. It is an understanding informed by the audit's insight and especially the insight gained from thinking differently. The communication is made to society as a whole and/or to particular stakeholders in society, including society's managers who are empowered to take purposeful action. The communication is made and framed (the 'how' and 'what' of communication) to induce appropriate purposeful action, including action intended to deliver on real opportunity. Looking at the anti-clockwise flows of Figure 1.1, it is society's purposeful actions and any (consequent) disruption that are communicated to the auditor in order that the auditor can think differently about what to pay attention to, how to reinterpret audit evidence and how to rethink, reframe and progress audit representations.

As an entity, representation is formed, in terms of Figure 1.1, by the coming together of clockwise and anti-clockwise flows. Ideally, these flows come together in a representation that is agreed upon by both the auditor and those responsible for running society – a case of joint cognition. The wider the distribution of the representation, the more the representation operates as a pervasive field influencing all stakeholders in society and the

DOI: 10.4324/9781032721293-4

audit and through them, reality. Representation should be both pervasive and persuasive. Chapter 1 highlighted the importance of society not being left or right hemisphere dominated and the role of audit in keeping or achieving this balance. This is of prime importance when it comes to framing representations of reality; that is, deciding the substance of the message, the medium for the message and its distribution.

A key message of this current chapter is that, in order to achieve or preserve balance, representation – the audit report – should not serve specifically as a representation of society or of reality or of the audit, but as a representation of the connections and flows between all of these. In other words, representation is a representation of the societal audit network, its connections, its flows, its values and ultimately yields the connection between representation and reality. The network is dynamic and accordingly, the chapter addresses an issue pertaining to the progression of the network over time: a study of the connection between time and representation.

The chapter proceeds as follows: the first section addresses the need for audit representation to be performative. To be performative and induce appropriate action, such representation needs to be persuasive and to offer persuasive evidence and understanding. We argue that the audit report needs to (1) demonstrate understanding and provide explanation, (2) reflect on the performativity of the audit (its influence), (3) make recommendations for further action and above all (4) provide an assessment of society's progress. Thus, there are four interwoven levels of communication, being explanation, reflection, recommendation and progress. These are studied in the section following performativity.

Currently, company audit reports focus on an explanation of what the auditor has given attention to and on this we are critical of the current (audit) reporting practice for limited companies. We consider that the reporting of what the auditor has paid attention to needs to be balanced by reporting of what the company has paid attention to, what the company needs to pay attention to and what the company has achieved or could achieve – its progress.

Next, the chapter looks at communication theory in the form of the work of Marshall McLuhan and the idea that 'the medium is the message'. This section generates a discussion of the relationship between the substance of the message and the medium chosen to distribute the message. If audit is considered a medium, then audit becomes the message – and the chapter explores what this means and signifies for audit.

The chapter then considers the case of joint cognition where the representation is agreed by the auditor and by those in the society or organisation subject to audit who decide upon and execute action. This highlights the reality of significant co-production and interdependence, as opposed to the 'unreality' of independence. Independence is not treated as a lack of involvement but as thinking differently and any need for distance from management rests in the need to maintain the ability to think differently from management.

There are, accordingly, different ideas of independence inherent in the cases of the progression and correspondence approaches to audit. Correspondence requires the development of norms or an agreed course of action and the audit becomes an examination of whether those norms or the agreed course of action have been applied or followed. Correspondence is compatible with independence of the audit mind from the mind of the audit subject but is not independent in the sense of thinking differently. The section on the progression and correspondence approaches to audit considers their coexistence and the implications of this coexistence for reporting and standard setting.

The final section of the chapter picks up on the dynamic nature of the societal audit network and considers the realities of the relationship between representation and time. We argue that a representation of this relationship is missing from conventional audit reports and we explain how and why this matters.

The performativity of representation

McGilchrist (2021, p. 1306) does not enthuse about maps and, by implication, other forms of representation. He states, "A map contains some truth but unless you can interpret it in the light of real-world experience it is useless. And although a map depends on the world, the world does not depend upon a map". Certainly, as in all representations, much has to be omitted in the interest of clarity. What is omitted should be that which is not material to the purpose for which the map is to be used.

The world is much more than what is shown on any given map and the value of a map in the hands of anyone who has no experience or idea of using a map is open to question. The process of inclusion and omission depends upon the mapmaker's understanding of the world, on the one hand, and of the map user's needs on the other.

A geological map or survey might, for instance, show rock formations associated with valuable minerals, following which the drillers move in and the world changes. In so far as the users of the map have an impact on the world, then the world is not independent of the map and, consequently, not independent of the mapmaker's judgements. If we see and act upon the world in accordance with the representations made of it, then those representations – reflecting the understanding of the representation maker(s) – are centre stage. To improve our world (and our relations with it), we need to improve, and continue improving, our representation of the world. Extending the above example, we could 'map' and develop understanding not just of the geology, but also the economic and environmental consequences of mineral extraction. Or using another example, a brain scan assists a brain surgeon by providing a range of important information in a fashion that he/she is able to interpret and determine where best to operate. In the example of the map, representation improves by creating a fuller picture (greater breadth). In the second example, representation improves through a higher resolution scan (greater depth/detail). In both cases, the representation enhances cognition and, hopefully, through this, improves performance.

In building on such examples, it is possible to see audit as the study of relations between the activity of society and the representation of that activity. Audit influences society through its role in the assessment and representation of society's performance (a clockwise flow in Figure 1.1). Such influence is achieved partly through management responding to specific recommendations for action made by the auditor but in particular through management's actions in anticipation of how the auditor assesses society's overall progress (anticipatory performativity). We suggest that the auditor reflects in the audit report upon the influence/impact that the audit has upon progress and how both the recommendations made (for action) and improving the representation of performance have led and will lead to improved understanding of progress, of how to progress and ultimately to its achievement. This reflection is challenging but focuses the auditor's thinking on the role and nature of the progression audit and its fulfilment in the circumstances of the company.

Society influences the auditor through representations from society's managers (an anti-clockwise flow in Figure 1.1). Their representations to the auditor are an important influence shaping the auditor's attention and, to this extent, are themselves performative. It is possible for the auditor's thinking on how to represent and achieve progress to be ahead of management but it is also possible for management's thinking to be ahead of the auditor, generating a potentially creative tension.

This chapter studies how progress in representation, progress in understanding, and progress in the undertaking of activities (towards a better society) can go hand in hand. In terms of Rovelli (2021, p. 87), this represents a 'dance of/for three' incorporating society's activity; understanding of the activity; and representation of that activity – representation that leads to further thinking and, through, action, to progression.

Four levels of communication

The two connections shown in Figure 1.1 as directly shaping the representation of reality are those with audit and with society. These two connections each involve a flow of understanding and a reciprocal flow of communication. Understanding and communication are reciprocal in so far as the act of communication both requires and stimulates understanding. Representation brings together understandings, drawing on the understanding of reality by audit and by society. In this sense, representation is itself a form of (i.e., it represents) understanding.

Communication can be the transmission of data or of data plus an explanation of the significance of the data. In the former case, the auditor's role is often limited to establishing the validity of the data in the sense of its correspondence to expectations or established norms. In the second case, the audit adds value by providing, endorsing or challenging an explanation of the data and its context.

An audit that has the explanation of representations as a primary requirement is a central focus of this book. We see audit as being directly associated with the development and communication of understanding, with our conceptual analysis extending to consideration of the value provided through, and the impact of, such communicated knowledge, insight and actions of the auditor. This introduces a further important role for audit in the communication of not just understanding and explanation and, based on this insight, recommended courses of action – but also the impact that the present and past audits have had on the actions taken and progress made. This ties in with the four interwoven levels of communication expressed previously in this chapter as: explanation, reflection (insight), recommendation, progress (impact).

Explanation at the end of an audit is closely tied to identification of where it was decided to pay attention at the beginning of the audit. As such, the auditor's role in the selection of data (and accompanying explanation) to be communicated is a vital consideration and should not be presumed to be outside the remit of audit. This type of presumption tends to occur because audit is so often framed purely as an information verification function – but the audit can also be more 'originating' in terms of identifying what information can be transmitted as part of a holistic representation of performance. Sir Donald Brydon, for example, very much opened the door for the development of origination when highlighting the need for auditors to provide decision-useful information to the users of audit reports – stressing that such information could (on occasion) include original information not produced by the auditee (Brydon, 2019, para 5.3.2).

The nature of understanding (including how it is arrived at) is an important topic in philosophy and it has a long history. Grayling (2020, p. 87) states that "what Aristotle wished to achieve was understanding – that is, he wished to give explanations of things and, ultimately, of the universe itself". The famous quantum physicist, Erwin Schrodinger, searched for an explanation of 'life' and there is an evidently close, reciprocal, connection between 'understanding' and 'explanation'. In essence, we need to explain our understanding but also to understand our explanations.

William of Ockham, who lived in the 13th and 14th centuries, is credited with the principle of Occam's Razor; that there is no need to invoke more things than are sufficient for an explanation of something.[1] To be able to do this is a sure test of understanding. For example, if we see business as a complex web of connections, then any explanation (representation, audit) needs to invoke (light up) those connections necessary to understand the business. Identifying the material (i.e., relevant) connections is a crucial step at the end of the audit (when there is greater understanding), but also at the beginning of the audit. The point is that greater understanding enables us to identify and turn off redundant connections as well as identify and turn on new ones. 'Progress' is about appreciating the importance of subtraction as well as addition. Explanation involves understanding and clarifying complexity and then using that understanding to deliver (communicate) a clear explanation, which involves appreciating what has been left out and why. Things should be left out if they are redundant. Things should not be left in simply because they were felt to be too difficult to explain or justify their exclusion.

To the extent that the auditor's understanding is based upon judgement coming from the right hemisphere, it may not be easy for the auditor to explain the audit work undertaken and judgements made. The auditor having tacit knowledge is a case of "we know more than we can tell" (Kay, 2011, chapter 17, pp. 143–149).[2] To a degree, therefore, it is necessary for the recipient or user of the audit representation to trust the auditor – with trust being a feeling based upon insight and experience, and another right hemisphere function, this time in the brain of the recipient. The recipient's understanding flows from what is explained in the representation (currently this tends to focus primarily on the auditor's left hemisphere activity) together with the recipient's trust in the auditor.

Spectacular audit failures have happened in limited company audits[3] and undermined trust in audits. However, if such trust is a right hemisphere feeling of the recipient, this is unlikely to be restored through a greater, more formal resort to regulatory 'standards' of practice, which largely operate on the left hemisphere activity of the giver. Audit failures are often a failure of judgement on the part of the auditor. Typically, the reaction of society and its agents to such failure has been to pursue and implement more standards and codes, more regulation and supposedly 'stronger' regulators. This boost to left hemisphere activity does little to deal with a problem which resides in the auditor's right hemisphere. If such an increase in the auditor's left hemisphere activity does result in greater trust in the auditor, then it is probably only going to be short-lived and illusory.

The key to appropriate communication between auditor and users is that it should be 'whole' brain to 'whole' brain and therefore engage not only the left but also the right hemispheres of both the auditor and the recipient user. The involvement in communication of the right hemispheres of both the auditor and the stakeholder recipient (the potential user) of the audit report means that the understanding of the recipient and of the auditor is unlikely to be precisely the same. We all sense things slightly differently and this difference cannot be generative or productive if there is no open and effective form of communication between auditors and recipients (users) (see Minutti-Meza, 2021). Without the opportunity for auditors and users to work together, joint cognition between them does not develop and some degree of understanding or 'judgement' gap is likely. Again, it can be argued that such judgement gaps cannot be addressed through standards that encourage the conformity of left hemisphere activity. Nevertheless, there is a risk that too much openness and accountability, particularly if associated with financial and reputational damage when things go wrong, might inhibit the risk-taking that goes with thinking differently and instead promote a flight to conformity, and compliance with standards. There is a need for society to address this and ensure that accountability is framed in a way that supports constructive action (and does not inhibit progress).

When the time comes for the issuance of the audit report, the complex of findings and feelings brought together in the auditor's right hemisphere may be simplified for the representation (report) to be understandable to the stakeholder who receives it. This may result in a largely sequential linear explanation (representation) to provide an accessible logic and apparently left-hemisphere explanation. The disadvantage here is that the extent of judgement that led to the linear presentation is not readily visible. The report might only appeal to the recipient's left hemisphere, with their right hemisphere not being engaged. If so, the recipient will not be able to see the 'big picture'. Whilst 'left hemisphere' to 'left hemisphere' communication avoids conflicting judgements and emotions, 'right hemisphere' to 'right hemisphere' communication, based upon common judgement and emotions, avoids contact with details that might not support those common emotions. However, such single hemisphere communication, though deficient, and possible seriously so, may appear easier in many contexts than a more balanced and holistic dual hemisphere (or 'whole brain' to 'whole brain') mode of communication. If this is the case, then too much pressure for accountability may run the risk that 'whole brain' to 'whole brain' communication is abandoned in favour of one of the seemingly easier options (such as establishing new rules and targets in a manner that may lack imagination and serve to accentuate the underlying problems).

The imbalance in the company audit report

Although an open conversation might be an effective form of communication between auditors and users of company financial reports (see Minutti-Meza, 2021), such conversations only take place on a limited basis. Indeed, shareholder presentations by management can be without any auditor contribution. In the statutory communications, the 'contribution' of the auditor is to be found in the audit report – for example, with a listing of 'key audit matters' and the explanation of the auditor's choice of materiality being the current dominant attempt to explain what the audit has focused upon (see Wilson, 2021). In so far as key audit matters reflect the nature of the company, then they also play a role in representing the company as well as the audit. But, we suggest, this is not an appropriate way to represent either the company or the audit.

Looking at a typical company audit report, such as that of Rolls-Royce (2022, pp. 197–205), it can be seen that each key audit matter identified is investigated and evaluated through audit activity (procedures), starting with one of a variety of 'action' words. In the case of Rolls-Royce, these include "we focused, we attended, we obtained and read, we assessed, we challenged, we re-performed, we compared, we verified, we validated, we considered, we tested, we evaluated, we read and understood, we sampled, we created an independent expectation, we agreed". These are 'action' words but refer not to actions which the auditor is inviting or recommending management or other stakeholders to take (as would be the case in performative speech) but to actions taken by the auditor.

They are words associated with a list of audit activities that we can recall from our days of audit practice. Identifying, evaluating and understanding the key audit matters involves substantial judgement and the danger is that because we cannot easily explain judgement, we try to explain judgement through detailing procedures – a predominantly left hemisphere activity.

Ultimately, at the end of all these procedures, there is a statement of concurrence with management. However, we know that because they are essentially right hemisphere activities, the judgement of management and of the auditor will not, and arguably should not, be identical. If so, what is required is not so much a long list of procedures/investigations carried out by the auditor but an explanation of the different feelings (judgement) of management and of the auditor and, if there is an unqualified report, how they were brought together. In a limited company audit, the opportunity for the audit to develop a joint cognition with company management is much greater than the opportunity to work and develop joint cognition with other stakeholders, including investors. Consequently, company management is likely to be more influential than other stakeholders with whom the auditor communicates but only at a distance.

We consider that the reporting of what the auditor has paid attention to needs to be balanced by reporting of what company management and society needs to pay attention to. Our conclusion is that current audit reports are too introspective and defensive – reflecting a limited concept of what an audit is and demonstrating a lack of imagination as to what an audit could be.

The medium is the message

According to McGilchrist, history represents or exhibits periods of left hemisphere dominance in society, followed by collapse and periods of right hemisphere dominance and vice versa. A second possibility is that the divided brain leads to neither a predominantly left or right hemisphere oriented society but produces an increasingly divided society – divided into those who engage with the world through their left hemisphere and those who engage using their right hemisphere.

This opens up two ways of viewing the role of the auditor within society. One is to see the auditor as an influencer (e.g., influencing the reversal of a persistent tendency or direction taken by society towards engaging with the world through a single hemisphere). The other is of the auditor as a healer (or unifier), bringing together, in a divided society, thinking that predominantly engages with the world through the left hemisphere, with thinking that engages through the right hemisphere – thinking that brings together, for instance, analysis and imagination. The two roles of influencer and healer are not mutually exclusive but the importance of each depends upon the state of society, which in turn depends upon the audit's success in progressing society. At certain moments in time, an audit's progressive intent could rest more in the developmental challenges it poses to society while, at others, it can rest in how the actions of the auditor facilitate connection across or unify perspectives across different elements of society.

Progress here can mean increasing society's capacity for new ideas – for imagination, innovation and creativity – as well as a capacity to exploit systematically the ideas it already has. This in turn requires a healthy coincidence of opposites, of left and right hemisphere engagement – a coincidence that the auditor should ensure results in progress rather than a potentially damaging division. To determine the balance of the audit roles, therefore, the key step taken by the auditor is to understand the state of an organisation or society and subsequently to use that understanding as a platform for improvement. Audit is about understanding and such audit cognition requires an understanding of the nature and state of social cognition taking place within society.

Social cognition is profoundly influenced by the development of new media and this invites a discussion of the work of Marshall McLuhan (1964), who died in 1980, but is best known for his still current, attention-grabbing, dictum 'The medium is the message'. What is the relationship between the message and the medium that is carrying the message? Initially, any medium constitutes a medium without a message – being, for instance, a platform without content. However, once populated by content, the receipt of the content (the message) is shaped by the form of the medium. Each medium has its own set of attributes that leads to the message being sensed and processed differently. Each medium appeals to different human senses or activates different hemispheres of the brain. So, the message and the medium are very much not separate but are intertwined. Given the entanglement between 'the medium and the message', the development of auditor assessments, such as a 'true and fair' representation of society or of an organisation within society, must consider the media used to communicate such a representation.

Harold Innis (1951) wrote about the role of media in building or creating society and its role in sustaining a society amidst the challenges it faced. Society needs a balanced connection between (1) media which enable it to be creative and (2) media which provide it with continuity or sustainability over time. Continuity is associated with the handing down of tradition and culture in a society through the media of myth, folk song, legend and religion. However, continuity also requires, on a quite different dimension, the ability to respond creatively to discontinuity; that is, to respond to challenges and disruption created, for example, by new media brought about through technological development. With regard to the world of accounting and auditing practice, there is, it could be argued, too little left of a professional community that can communicate through the generations the culture and tradition of being a professional, with its necessary emphasis on judgement, truth and fairness. Instead, what increasingly seems to be being handed down is an expanding set of detailed, technical accounting and auditing standards that are dominated by left hemisphere characteristics. It is these standards that have become the dominant medium for communication and leave the practice environment arguably stripped of a sense of professional tradition and a limited capacity to handle disruption.

McLuhan (adopting Innis) argued that you can tell much more about a society or civilisation from the media it uses than you can from the total of the messages conveyed by that media. In his book *Understanding Media: The Extensions of Man*, McLuhan (1964) suggests that the medium affects the society in which it plays a role mainly by the characteristics of the medium rather than any associated content. In so far as audit is a medium, then society might be judged by its mode of audit: compliance or progression.

Drawing on Innis and McLuhan, there are two closely related aspects to whether the media's representation of society, or of an organisation or profession within society, is in balance. First, following Innis, is there a balance between the use of media supporting, respectively, creativity and sustainability? Second, following McLuhan, is there a balance between media suitable for left hemisphere transmission and media suitable for right hemisphere characteristics?

Understanding the use of media by society or by a societal organisation is a key part of the auditor's understanding of the nature and state of society. If the auditee is an organisation within society, then the use of media to connect the organisation with society is key to the auditor's understanding of what society knows about the organisation and vice versa. This understanding is, in turn, a crucial part of the auditor's initial (prior) assessment of the society or organisation and consequently of where to give attention during the audit.[4] Society's choice of media comes to represent or provide evidence of society itself. An organisation's choice or society's choice of media represents, in part, the nature of the organisation or society itself – and evaluating society or an organisation can start with an exploration of how the organisation or society employs auditing (for example, a progressive society or organisation could see audit as a medium through which to promote improvement).

McLuhan's work is not only relevant to the auditor's identification of where to pay attention during the audit; it is also relevant to the form of communication by the auditor to stakeholders at the end of the audit. Since there has traditionally been relatively little person-to-person communication between auditors and stakeholders beyond management, communication by the auditor with non-management stakeholders is, currently, largely dependent upon the audit report. The audit report becomes the medium for the auditor's message. However, much of today's audit reporting is taken up with explaining (representing) the audit rather than the auditee. We have seen, for instance, that the written company audit report may be appropriate for communicating the formal, essentially left hemisphere, characteristics such as compliance with accounting and auditing standards but not so effective at communicating or transmitting informal, right hemisphere, activity such as a holistic judgement of the company's performance. Arguably, judgement is better explained in a 'to' and 'fro' discussion and might require media that supports open conversation. Generally, very little 'to' and 'fro' involving the auditor takes place at a company's Annual General Meeting (AGM). It is necessary to consider the possibility of meetings directly between auditors and key stakeholders and this could involve the use of online meeting technology.

McLuhan was fond of saying that those who failed to understand him failed because they were using their 'left brain', whereas he was using the right hemisphere of his own brain. Communication should be 'whole brain' to 'whole brain' and to achieve this, a variety of communication media might need to be employed. McLuhan was identifying a breakdown of social (joint) cognition (i.e., the way understanding is explained and developed between members of a society or organisation) – a breakdown fostered by an imbalance in the communication media employed (in our case, between auditors and audit stakeholders).

Joint cognition, co-production and interdependence

Representation is shown in Figure 1.1 as an exercise in social cognition; that is, the joint development of cognition (understanding) by the auditor and by society or its representatives.[5] If a single representation is to speak to (communicate with) both the auditor and to (the rest of) society, then both the auditor and relevant members of society need to be involved and work together in its preparation. Thus, representation is a coming together or synthesis of understanding emerging from a discourse between auditors and society, between their respective experiences and value judgements – essentially, a discourse as to what is true, what is valuable and how it should be valued. How this discourse operates in practice is likely to be a function of the audit arrangements that determine the timing, the responsibility and nature of involvement of each party.

Suppose the audit arrangements are similar to those for the audit of a company's financial statements. Such statements, though influenced by the auditor's involvement, are the responsibility of the directors. The role of the auditor is, through the audit report, to endorse (or otherwise) the financial statements prepared by the directors. Although, through endorsement, the statements can come to be seen as those of the auditor, arguably it is the directors, as the original preparers, who have the major influence on what goes into the financial statements and, in particular, their connection, expressed through the directors' accompanying narrative, to the financial and other 'realities' of the company. The role of the auditor is, in the case of the current form of a company audit, to provide assurance that the directors' statements (representations) are true and fair and can be trusted. With the growth of accounting and auditing standards, this role of judging truth and fairness has become much closer to a compliance audit (assessing correspondence with the standards) and the auditor's influence on the financial statements, let alone the company's actions, may have declined. Influence only survives in the narrow sense of influencing the company to follow norms.

As an example of a different audit arrangement, consider value for money reports prepared by public sector auditors. Although such reports use evidence from the organisation itself, including discussions with management, they are prepared by and represent the auditor's judgement as to whether the public sector activity is delivering value for money. It is likely that the auditors, being the preparers, are the major influence on the value for money report, which is more likely (than say the company audit report) to be performative and to have an influence on society's actions. Because they are prepared by the auditors, the auditors are in a better position to deliver their insight and can more directly call forth action to create a better society. The value for money report is more likely to challenge norms than is, say, a conventional audit report on financial statements.

Whilst both auditors and management are in each case involved, the audit arrangements and what they imply for the order/balance of involvement may be important in determining influence and consequently impact. Order matters. Typically, for instance, in a financial statement audit, the financial statements are initially prepared by the organisation's management with assistance from the auditor when management deems it helpful. On the other hand, the value for money report, whilst paying attention to management's views, is initially prepared by, and remains the responsibility of, the value for money auditor.

We argue that to be influential and performative, audit arrangements should enable the auditor to think differently, be insightful and make recommendations for action. Audit needs to move beyond its confirmatory role to be an originator and instigator; to move beyond trust and assurance to embrace more directly the challenging dynamic of making society better.[6]

Nevertheless, whatever the audit arrangements, the auditors and the management will both have a level of involvement, although that level might differ. Thus, there is always a degree of co-production and joint cognition. In respect of a business, the element of co-production of financial statements between the auditor and preparers, being management, is discussed in a paper by Knechel et al. (2020), who centre on the importance of understanding audit from a service perspective that is responsive to the idiosyncrasies of the audited company. In accordance with the service science literature, the audit can be viewed as the result of a co-production between the auditor and relevant actors in the audited company. This implies a more rewarding and engaged role for both auditors and the audited in the generation of financial information that connects with the business and its environment. To the extent that there is co-production, audit may be seen as an example of joint action cognition (Tollefsen and Dale, 2018). In this regard, the true nature of 'joint auditing' is the co-operation between management and auditor in the joint action of producing the financial report. The service perspective is important because it challenges conventional views on things such as the role of audit standards, demands to limit non-audit services, allocation of blame for audit failures and the existence of audit and financial reporting as independent activities.

There is also an important temporal aspect here. The service perspective modifies a sequential ordering of the production of financial statements in which the audit comes late, by requiring the auditor to be continually involved from an early stage. In practice, co-production is a key element of how good audits are produced but this necessity is inadequately recognised by conventional thinking/arrangements that see the financial statements and their audit as separate – with the financials being produced by management and the audit framed as an assessment of the truth and fairness of those financial statements. A combination of the service and conventional production perspectives recognises the complexity and reality of the modern company audit and highlights the need to rethink the conventional framework. However, it can be argued that the service perspective is not something totally novel, but more a case of audit's conceptual framework catching up with practice? As such, improving correspondence between the practice of audit and its representation (in the conventional framework) does not of itself constitute progression.

In cognitive terms, co-production highlights that the Chief Financial Officer (CFO) and the audit partner (AP) are not just independent individuals but also interdependent individuals. Froese (2018, p. 173) states,

> in principle there is nothing mysterious about the theoretical shift from treating an interaction as an external affordance for independent individuals to conceiving their interaction as an opportunity for the establishment of an internal relation between interdependent individuals.

An interaction between two individuals is an affordance when, for example, the interaction enables one individual to learn from the other and vice versa (the interaction affords mutual learning). Increasing the degree of interaction results in interdependence and might ultimately result in 'inter-being' (Varela, 2000), where the two individuals become mutually coupled in a single holistic 'brain–body–environment–body–brain' system (as represented diagrammatically in Froese, 2018, p. 175). It is then a case of two brains operating as one. Froese describes Varela's idea of inter-being as genuine inter-subjectivity, "i.e., an interaction in which we constitute a shared awareness in contrast to an interaction that remains external input to independent individuals..." (p. 171).

Arguably, it might be helpful if the conventional framework of auditing was constructed around interdependence rather than independence. In practice, relations between the audit staff and the client's staff can never be fully independent. As David Hatherly recalls regarding an experience from his time in audit practice:

> When I qualified as an accountant, I was put in charge of the field audit team for the UK subsidiary of a large US based corporation. For various reasons it was a complex client and the audited numbers had to be in Chicago twenty days after the year end. I had worked on the audit as a junior and knew there were likely to be three particularly difficult issues being the calculation of deferred tax, the reconciliation of book stock with the physical stock from the stocktake and the provision for bad debts and warranty claims. The client struggled with deferred tax and so did I. I sat down with them, we went through the principles and we calculated the deferred tax number together. This was close to a case of inter-being?
>
> Next, I was handed the client's stock reconciliation, went through it, and it reconciled! Short of time, I moved on to prepare my arguments for the negotiations on bad debts and on warranties which were closely related and taken together had the potential to turn the profit of the UK subsidiary into a loss. The provision, prepared by me according to my own arguments, was independent but during the negotiation I had to listen to

and accommodate, to an extent, the client's arguments. The outcome was, arguably, a case of moderated independence.

At the eleventh hour, during the partner review, a member of the client's staff interrupted the meeting to explain that they had discovered a material error on the stock reconciliation. A reconciling item that should have been added had been subtracted and I had failed to notice! This was a case of inter-dependence. I had relied on the client and the fact that the reconciliation appeared to reconcile whilst the client had relied on the fact that it reconciled and that I was happy with it. This might be considered a case of interdependence as a bad thing!

Overall, the above experience comprises three different forms of relationship and associated cognitive processes – in the form of 'inter-being', 'moderated independence' and 'interdependence'. Rather than assuming that the dominant characteristic of an audit is independence, we can see that an audit is capable conceptually of being characterised by a plurality of interactive cognitive processes.

The progression and correspondence roles of audit

We saw from the discussion of performativity in Chapter 3 that performative reporting encourages society, or organisations within society, to take action that brings reality and the representation of reality closer together (convergence) but that such convergence does not necessarily mean there is progression. In Figure 4.1, two things are happening at the same time: first through performativity there is a pull towards the 'line of audit' where representation and reality converge (correspond). Second, if there is positive performativity, there is a pull along the line of audit in an upward direction (progression), towards better representation and a better organisation.

Picking up the example of the postal service given in Chapter 3, the representation of postal performance in terms of delivery within two days encourages and 'corresponds with' post office activity that prioritises such a delivery time-scale – even if the post office ignores mail that has failed to make the two-day deadline. However, it is clear that a better and more holistic (more complete) representation of postal performance would include consideration of the lateness of mail that failed the two-day target. Such a more holistic representation would encourage a better postal service (activity) 'in the round'. The objective, therefore, is not just to achieve 'correspondence' but to achieve a better postal service through a better (less partial) representation of its performance. To achieve this, the audit needs to be more insightful and influential than just reporting on the 'two-day' target. In Figure 4.1, movement upwards along the 'line of audit' reflects, and is reflected in, better representation and better societal or business activity (the X and Y axes). In particular, after setting a target, it is important that

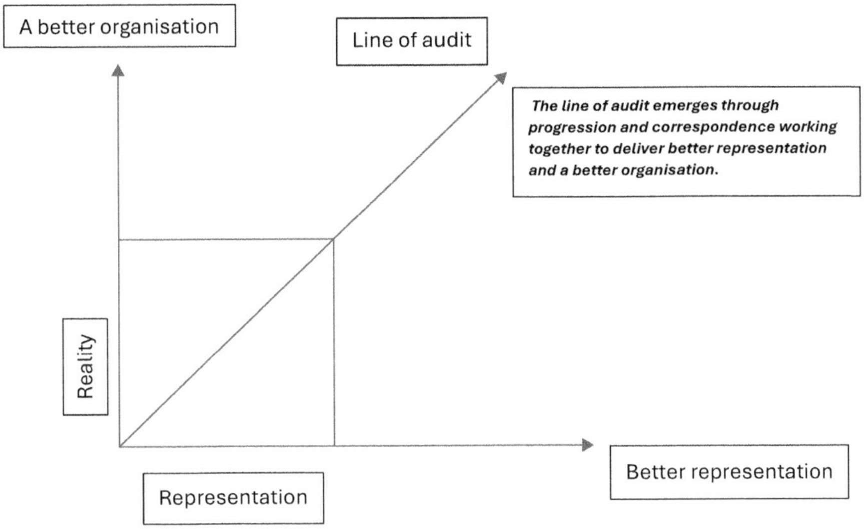

FIGURE 4.1 **The line of audit.**

its negative consequences are monitored and, through representation, included in any assessment of whether performance 'in the round' is better.[7]

The lesson is that inadequate (partial) representation must be addressed by an audit. Partial, distorted or retarded performance will follow from audits that fail to highlight inadequate performance assessment (a progression issue) or fail to see when appropriate performance measures, though agreed, are not implemented or given attention (a correspondence issue). In general, an audit that fails to address a material correspondence or progression issue impacts performance negatively (negative performativity).

We can refer to the two dimensions of audit as comprising (a) correspondence (concerned with convergence: that is, moving closer to the 'line of audit') and (b) progression (concerned with moving upwards along the line). In relation to Figure 4.1, the progression audit focuses on greater insight and better representation, whilst correspondence considers whether that greater insight has been followed by action, leading in reality to a better organisation. A doctrine of continual audit improvement is the challenge faced by auditing, especially in relation to auditing the future and the increasing scope of audit activities to include, for example, environmental impact.[8]

Arguably, correspondence and progression are akin to a conjugate pair and two dimensions of the same thing. In physics, the classic conjugate pair (introduced by Heisenberg as discussed by Rovelli, 2021, pp. 92–95) is position and speed. If we measure position and then speed, by the time we have a measure for speed, the position has moved on. If we have an accurate position, there is uncertainty as to speed and vice versa. There are many other such conjugate pairs in physics. Returning to correspondence and progression, if we assess correspondence, then by the time that dimension of the audit is completed, in an environment of continual improvement, which is the ambition, progress has moved the position of society (or societal organisation) towards betterment along both axes and the original assessment of correspondence no longer holds. In such cases, correspondence and progression must be assessed together (simultaneously). If the auditor focuses on one, then it creates uncertainty for the other.[9] The auditor cannot talk about (report on) one without talking about the other. Correspondence and progression are not separate audits but different aspects of the same audit. We are talking here of correspondence with a previously decided course of action, such as to deliver mail within two days. In a dynamic environment, by the time such correspondence is established, new preferred courses of action (such as delivery in one day) may have emerged. And so, the audit sees the reporting of progress both in terms of correspondence with courses of action (pathways) previously decided and in terms of new, improved courses of action. This connects the audit's representation to both the past and the future and the reverberation between them. Hence, the important connection between representation and time, a connection that is discussed in the next section and arises again in subsequent chapters.

The idea of correspondence can also be applied to compliance with standards, such as accounting and auditing standards. Whilst the audit of correspondence with a pathway to improvement is part of the dynamic of progress, correspondence (compliance) with (auditing and accounting) standards is, in essence, promoting the stasis of conformity, unless there is a constant rethinking of standards by standard setters to promote progress. When this is not the case, then correspondence and progression move apart. They are no longer a conjugate pair and it becomes possible to talk of, and report on, each separately.

In terms of conception and practice, there is a major difference between the traditional audit based upon generally accepted standards and an audit approach, which sees audit as thinking differently. If standards are not going to stand in the way of progress, then they need to establish thinking differently as a core part of auditing. In effect, auditing the performance of standards in terms of progress should be a routine, integral and regular part of standard setting.

Standard setting as such can be viewed as involving a confrontation of acceptance and challenge, a contrasting case of the thesis (each auditor thinks the same) and the antithesis (each auditor thinks differently). The idea of thesis and antithesis is taken from Hegel.[10] Following Hegel, once new thinking is absorbed into a higher standard of thinking, different thinking again arises to challenge the new standard and so on. In his view, a synthesis emerging from an antagonism of thesis and antithesis itself becomes a new thesis, which generates its own antithesis – which in turn gives birth to another synthesis. This dialectical process is one in which the human spirit comes to ever more accurate understandings of itself. In our case, the initial antagonism or contradiction is between standards, as thinking the same and thinking differently, the synthesis of which leads to a higher level of understanding.

In asserting that 'thinking differently is audit' (Humphrey, 2020), audit, by definition, has to challenge generally accepted thinking. Viewed in this light, thinking differently is the driver of progress, the universal 'spirit of auditing' in search of better organisations and a better society. This overarching audit 'standard' could be supported by a set of ever-developing 'illustrations' of auditors (and audits) thinking differently – showing how such thinking raises levels (sets 'new standards') of understanding. The 'illustrations' might be updated online by the audit firms themselves, in effect becoming a public illustration of that firm's (and collectively the profession's) insight and creativity – insightful illustrations that serve to inspire ever deeper insights.

In 'Thinking not ticking', Jonathan Hayward (2003) proposed a second audit report, arguing that each public interest company should have a second audit firm acting as an 'evaluator'. The second firm's responsibilities were to be limited to the consolidated accounts and the evaluator would rely upon the conventional audit's findings in respect of the detailed checking of operations, systems and accounting records. The idea is that the second firm could be a smaller group of experienced professionals without the need for a global network and an army of staff – with the hope that this would transform the opportunities for new entrants to the audit marketplace, at least at the level of the overall audit judgement. However, Hayward's proposal was for a second opinion rather than any other fundamental change to the conventional audit framework.

Now might be a good time to revisit Hayward's proposal but with a fresh conceptual emphasis. For instance, the second auditor, applying the audit spirit of 'thinking differently', could be functionally required to conduct a very different styled audit compared to the approach taken by the first auditor. Rather than being a smaller version of, and perhaps aspiring to be, a big firm, the second auditor could be structured in a more agile, integrated fashion, that readily allows its auditors to benefit from a cross-fertilisation of ideas, perspectives and experiences in order to provide fresh insights ('progression-oriented' assessments) of the organisation subject to audit.

Timely representation and the representation of time

In pursuing dynamic progress, representation not only needs to be dynamic but also of a timely form. In this section, we first discuss the importance of timely representation and communication using the limited company audit report as an illustration of the issues at stake. Later, the discussion turns from timely representation to the representation of time. The audit report can be regarded as representing audit time (i.e., in the case of the financial audit, the time between the date of the financial year end and the date of the audit report) but the audit report traditionally makes no reference to the significance of timeliness (i.e., the necessary balance between timely representation and the representation of (audit) time is not addressed). Such a crucial audit judgement is not explained in the audit report and is a notable absence – especially for a progression audit where time is clearly of the essence. There is, for instance, no point in making recommendations for improvement that were once relevant but no longer are.

With regard to timely representation, the understanding and explanation provided by the audit arrive a while after the point or period of time to which the understanding (that is, the representation by the directors) relates. In practice, understanding the recent past is taken to give an understanding of the current situation but there is an uncertainty similar to Heisenberg's uncertainty.[11] Namely, by the time the understanding is achieved, the business has moved on. Consequently, time is a crucial element in the impact that any audit report or recommendation is likely to have on progression. Time is of the essence not only for dynamic societies and businesses but also for stable ones (who, paradoxically, may only be able to remain stable by embracing progress).

We can define audit time as the time between the business event and (endorsement of) its representation by the auditor. In the case of balance sheet items, this might be taken to be the time between the financial year-end and the date of the audit report. There is a balance to be struck between the importance of minimising audit time and having enough time to keep down the risk of audit failure; audit failure in practice is taken to be a material misrepresentation rather than a material delay in reporting. There is a tension between the materiality of audit time and the materiality of misrepresentation. The risk of audit failure depends on the availability of quality evidence within the audit time.

This trade-off and, in particular, the importance of audit time (the dating of the audit report), is seldom, if ever, discussed in the auditor's report. Auditors are often under pressure from management and investors to report quickly after the year-end and such pressure can be a source of judgement error due to a lack of a stand-back opportunity. In this regard, Jones (2022) argues that current practice is biased towards audit times being too short, especially given the proliferation of regulations and standards often issued without regard to their impact on audit time or upon judgement. He proposes that we revisit the balance between professional judgement (professionalism) and regulation, a viewpoint supported by Humphrey et al. (2024), who see an excess of regulation as a barrier to innovation and the progression of audit.

An issue regarding time is the difference between the actual (physical) audit time and the human perception of time taken to complete the audit. Given our limited life span, time is of major importance to humans and a fundamental variable of the human world, at least from an individual's perspective. Time is something we all share and yet we all experience it differently, depending upon how we use and respond to it. Consequently, with time, we all have our own perspective and emotional connection and the human's perception of time is not identical to 'actual' time in the physical world. Time can seem to move slowly, for example, whilst waiting for any result that really matters. Hence, human time has a strong connection with the materiality of audit time, whilst the time necessary to obtain evidence that avoids the risk of audit failure determines the actual audit time.[12]

Einstein used the contrast of physical (actual) and human (perception of) time to give a simple explanation of relativity. He reflected that an "hour sitting on a park bench with a pretty girl passes like a minute, but a minute sitting on a hot stove seems like an hour" (Quoted in Baggott, 2012, p. 196). Clearly, circumstances matter, in turn, highlighting the similarity of materiality and relativity.[13] Circumstances transform the exchange rate between actual time and perceived (human) time. On the park bench, it could be 60 to 1, whilst on the hot stove, it could be closer to 1 to 60. We are dealing with three related transfers or exchanges: (1) from the park bench to the stove, (2) between cold and hot and (3) from actual time to perceived time. Einstein's reflection highlights the distinction between human physical time and (actual) time.

To represent Einstein's reflection as an audit story, we must identify a purpose, say to keep warm, and recognise two alternative pathways (actions) to this end, being (1) to move a sensible distance from the hot stove or (2) to move closer to the 'pretty girl' in order to keep each other warm. The choice is between two pathways and the auditor might recommend a sensible distance from the hot stove, explaining that moving closer to the girl would not be socially acceptable. In terms of getting warm quickly, the relationship with the stove might be more effective in terms of physical (actual) time, but the other option might be more effective in terms of the human experience of time. This might change the recommendation but the auditor would have to evaluate the relationship between the two people on the park bench. Consequently, what matters is not just where we are and who we are with, but what we are trying to do and the availability and acceptability of actions to achieve that purpose. This framing of materiality is a form of 'conditioning' of choice and an important part of a holistic audit that embraces both future action and social acceptance.

The human perception of time might be considered in relation to imaginary time. The concept of 'imaginary' time, as introduced by Stephen Hawking (1988, p. 134; 1993, p. 82), can be used to connect with many of the ideas covered so far in our book. Hawking introduced imaginary time to allow the universe to be unbounded, without a beginning or an end. In imaginary time, the curvature of time causes the beginning and end of time to join up. Thus, there is no big bang to begin the universe and no big crunch to end it. Space-time is thought of as a sphere rather than a straight line and, in that sense, is endless. There is no boundary and therefore no order.

If we were to apply Hawking's idea to audit, then the (imaginary) audit would be endless (continuous) and the potential biases of anchoring/adjustment and recency effects (Kahneman, 2012), associated with the beginning and the end of the audit respectively, would be avoided. In anchoring and adjustment, cognition is anchored at the beginning of the audit (and the first audit experiences), whereas with recency, it is dominated by evidence from the end of the audit (and the last audit experiences). With no beginning and no end, there would be no such cognitive biases and no constraint of time or cost; the gathering of evidence and the use of the human imagination would have no boundaries and without boundaries, there is no order.

However, auditing is not identical to the physical universe since human judgement plays a key role in audit. In real-world auditing, materiality judgements are made as to when to start and finish the audit. The judgement of materiality is an ordering of priorities (something matters more than or relative to something else). Thus, materiality introduces order and, in particular, the order of there being a beginning and an end, so that the audit is not endless. The key materiality judgement is whether continuing the audit (seeking out or constructing more evidence and/or applying more imagination) would be beneficial, set against the audit's requirement to be both timely and acceptable in terms of cost. Thus, introducing human judgement avoids endlessness and provides order but at the price of introducing uncertainty, in terms of what further evidence and/or imagination would have revealed if there were no closure.

Nevertheless, we have stressed the importance of reverberation. Conceptually, reverberation connects the beginning and end of an audit by thinking continuously in two directions: from the beginning to the end and vice versa, and in that sense, introduces endlessness. It is thinking from the future to the present that starts with imagination, an imagination that drives thinking differently and progress. It seems audit must embrace materiality and order together with imagination and endlessness at one and the same time. Audit is seen as a superposition or coincidence of opposites – of order and endlessness, of continuity and discontinuity, of evidence and imagination. And, we argue, what is needed to bring these opposites together, to create and cross the boundaries between them, is to think differently.

Summary and conclusion

A representation exists courtesy of its connections, through understanding and communication, with the audit and with society. Representation matters because it is performative. If there is to be a single representation of society or an organisation within society, then the auditor and those members of society responsible for the preparation of the representation must work together to co-produce it. This requires a level of joint cognition, although this common understanding will differ across different contexts. Representation serves as a vehicle for communication between preparers and auditors in order to develop such a common understanding. The position of the auditor varies between those situations where the auditor is the originator of representations and those where the auditor endorses the representations of the preparers (management). Where the auditor is the originator, the auditor must still work closely with the management, who will be required to accept or contest the findings. Where the audit 'signs off' on management's representations, then the auditor is accepting those representations as their own. In both cases, the management and the auditor work together. This has implications for the idea of independence and audit should be thought of as a fundamentally interdependent activity between management and auditor.

The role of representation is not so much to serve as a channel of communication between the auditor and preparers/management but to communicate with those stakeholders in society, or in organisations within society, who are not involved in management or preparation of the representation. In general, the auditor has tended to have less regular informal contact with these stakeholders and the transmission of understanding relies on the explanatory power of the representation. The dictum 'the medium is the message' is relevant here. The message is not independent of the medium that carries the message. We see that a written, typical audit report is capable of transmitting details of where audit attention has been given and what procedures have been carried out but is not so effective at transmitting the feelings and judgements of the auditor and where those feelings come from. Audit judgement failures are often dealt with by the authorities through more detailed and extensive procedural requirements, but we should recognise that right hemisphere failures of judgement cannot be compensated for by more extensive reliance upon left hemisphere logics. Similarly, a dearth of procedures cannot be compensated by ever more reliance on judgement, judgement that can be subject to cognitive bias. Auditors (and their regulators) must be concerned with balance.

We are in a world of extensive, we would argue inappropriately extensive, standards and procedural requirements with which companies, for instance, must comply. The financial audit has become first and foremost a compliance audit. We need to restore the balance between compliance and progression. The representation of progress is discussed further in Chapters 6–9 of the book using the limited company as an illustration. There, we explore further what it means to think differently, demonstrating the progression audit as the 'playing field of progress'.

The final section of this current chapter addressed the need for the timely communication of representation to be in balance with the materiality of audit failure. This is arguably the most important judgement made by the auditor but it is one that is not represented in the audit report – a representational absence that may not matter so much from a compliance viewpoint. But for progression, time is of the essence and the significance of this message is reinforced in Chapter 5.

Notes

1 According to Kenny (2012, p. 326), William Ockham is best remembered for something he never said, namely 'Entities are not to be multiplied beyond necessity'. In any event the principle named after him appears to be adopted by the human brain. According to Carl Zimmer (https://carlzimmer.com/the-dark-matter-of-the-human-brain-361/, most of the brain consists not of neurons that connect to form the neural network (which is thought to do most of the brain's processing) but of dark matter or glia (glue). Glia cells are versatile multitaskers guiding the brain's development and sustaining it throughout our lives. Einstein, whose brain was left for medical research, was found to have far more glia than normal. One kind of glia – microglia – prunes away extra branches on neurons to help fine tune their developing connections. These pruned branches are those that are not found necessary for the brain's processing or understanding. Hence the connection to Occam's razor. There may be a case for seeing audit as a kind of glia that maintains and develops the neural networks of society.

2 Kay (2011) and Kay and King (2020, p. 268) make detailed reference to David Beckham's dramatic last minute equalising, free kick against Greece in England's final 2002 World Cup qualifying match in order to highlight the difficulty that experts have of explaining activity that is significantly right hemisphere. In a chapter entitled 'Bend it like Beckham: How we know more than we can tell', Kay (2011, p. 147) notes:

> People spend inordinate amounts of time asking experts like Beckham what is the secret of their success. They don't come away much the wiser...The message is the same when you read the biographies or autobiographies of successful businessmen...like Beckham, they describe their achievements rather than explain them.

3 Significant cases of audit failure have been with us for decades. Enron's demise in 2002 proved to be a harbinger of the global financial crisis of 2007/8 which arguably set it apart from other failures but also raises questions as to how we define audit 'failure'. For instance, if economies have continued to struggle since the 2007/8 financial crisis, does this highlight the importance of an audit profession giving greater consideration to broader-based notions of economic and social well-being?

4 A society or organisation dominated by social media might require an auditor to reflect on whether such media is camouflaging a concordant lack of (non-media) innovation and creativity. For example, there might be much highly creative advertising and innovative promotion of products that are fundamentally the same and not advancing.

5 According to Google's English dictionary, provided by Oxford Languages, cognition is the mental action or process of acquiring knowledge and understanding through thought, experience and the senses. Social cognition in our audit context is concerned with how two or more members of society develop a common understanding by reference to each others' thoughts, experiences and senses.
6 Progression audits can be traced to the notion of 'learning audits' (Hatherly, 1988); Also see Bhaskar and Sellars' (2025, chapter 7) call for more proactive auditing.
7 You can set a performance criterion for a postal service such as guaranteed delivery within two days but this cannot ignore the impact on other issues such as undelivered mail or postal costs. Improvement in representation and understanding can lead to an improved service without additional expense, but it might require additional investment including extra monitoring activity. Consideration of performance is incomplete without consideration of (opportunity) cost. Cost therefore needs consideration alongside the other performance criteria.
8 The need for continual improvement was part of a submission to the then named UK Government department of Business, Energy and Industrial Strategy (BEIS) by academics at the Alliance Manchester Business School. It included the recommendation "…. we encourage BEIS to shift its role to one of creating a space for innovation and to facilitating a 'market for actioned-ideas' in which competition is focused on delivering a new audit future". (see https://committees.parliament.uk/writtenevidence/10755/html/). It is also possible to claim that the auditor should be exposed to a dynamic, self-imposed expectation gap – with continual improvement being referred to as 'perpetual beta' and the basis of 'super-auditing' (Hatherly, 2022).
9 Rovelli (2021, p. 23) reports that both Einstein and Schrodinger were passionate about the philosophy of Schopenhauer and his interpretation of the world as 'representation'. Arguably, Figure 4.1 follows Schopenhauer's notion of 'will' as being the inner nature of all phenomena. According to Schopenhauer, 'will' is universal and represented in both our thoughts and actions. In Figure 4.1, the line of audit (as a vector) might be taken to be 'will' and the X and Y axes to be the respective 'representation of will' as thoughts ('representation') and actions ('reality'). In Figure 4.1, 'will' might be taken as the 'will to learn' or the 'will to improve' driving the auditor upwards along the line of audit.
10 For a concise exposition of Hegel's view of how the world develops see *The Little Book of Philosophy*, pp. 112–114.
11 Heisenberg's uncertainty principle is explained well by Kumar (2009, pp. 225–249).
12 Although not considered here space, like time, also has both actual and perceptual (sensual) dimensions. The sensual or notional distance between a business and its financial statements is reduced given strong evidence rather like the 'distance' between two towns is notionally reduced when a fast new road is built between them.
13 Einstein was taking a certain male vantage point that would not be universally acceptable today.

References

Baggott, J., 2012, *Higgs: The Invention and Discovery of the 'God Particle'*, (Oxford University Press, Oxford).

Bhaskar, K. and R. Sellars, 2025, *Reflections on the Case for Audit Reform: Seeking to Avoid Future Financial Scandals*, (Routledge, Abingdon).

Brydon, D., 2019, *Assess, Assure and Inform: Improving Audit Quality and Effectiveness, Report of the Independent Review into the Quality and Effectiveness of Audit*, https://assets.publishing.service.gov.uk/media/5df8edfced915d0938597e1f/brydon-review-final-report.pdf

Froese, T., 'Searching for the conditions of genuine intersubjectivity: From agent-based models to perceptual crossing experiments', in *The Oxford Handbook of 4E Cognition*, Newen, A., De Bruin, L and S. Gallagher (eds.), pp. 261–280, (Oxford University Press, Oxford).

Grayling, A.C., 2020, *The History of Philosophy: Three Millenia of Thought from the West and Beyond*, (Penguin, Random House, London).

Hatherly, D., 1988, 'Learning audits', *Accountancy* (November, pp. 164–165).

Hatherly, D., 2022, 'The super-auditor, perpetual beta and pervasive performativity', *International Journal of Auditing*, 26, 23–26, https://doi.org/10.1111/ijau.12263.

Hawking, S.W., 1988, *A Brief History of Time: From the Big Bang to Black Holes*, (Bantam Press, London).

Hawking, S.W., 1993, *Black Holes and Baby Universes and other essays*, (BCA by arrangement with Bantam Press, London).

Hayward, J., 2003, *Thinking not Ticking: Bringing Competition to the Public Interest Audit*, Centre for the Study of Financial Innovation (CSFI). https://assets.publishing.service.gov.uk/media/5329dbc0ed915d0e5d0000bd/130516_independent_audit_ltd_monograph.pdf.

Humphrey, C., 2020, *Thinking Differently is 'Audit'*, (Audit Futures, ICAEW, London), https://icaew.access.preservica.com/portal/asset/sdb%3AIO%7C3c14db66-e5bb-4aa0-b043-90c3a0b3f472.

Humphrey, C., O'Dwyer, B. and M. Martinoff, 2024, 'Escaping Groundhog Day: the transformative possibilities of reconceptualising audit', *Accounting and Business Research*, 55: 6, pp. 668–692, https://doi.org/10.1080/00014788.2024.2375713.

Innis, H.A., 1951, *The Bias of Communication*, (University of Toronto Press, Toronto).

Jones, M.E., 2022, 'Opinion: Time for more 'stand back' rather than more standards', *ICAEW Insights*, www.icaew.com/insights/viewpoints-on-the-news/2022/feb-2022/time-for-more-stand-back-not-more-standards.

Kahneman, D., 2012, *Thinking Fast and Slow*, (Penguin Books, London).

Kay, J., 2011, *Obliquity*, (Profile Books, London).

Kay, J. and M. King, 2020, *Radical Uncertainty: Decision Making for an Unknowable Future*, (Bridge Street Press, London).

Kenny, A., 2012, *A New History of Western Philosophy*, (Oxford University Press, Oxford).

Knechel, W.R., Thomas, E. and M. Driskill, 2020, 'Understanding financial auditing from a service perspective', Accounting, Organizations and Society, 81, February, https://doi.org/10.1016/j.aos.2019.101080.

Kumar, M., 2009, *Quantum: Einstein, Bohr and the Great Debate about the Nature of Reality*, (Icon Books, London).

McGilchrist, I., 2021, *The Matter with Things: Our Brains, Our Delusions, and the Unmaking of the World*, (Perspectiva Press, London).

McLuhan, M., 1964, *Understanding Media: The Extensions of Man*, https://designopendata.wordpress.com/wp-content/uploads/2014/05/understanding-media-mcluhan.pdf.

Minutti-Meza, M., 2021, 'The art of conversation: The expanded audit report', *Accounting and Business Research*, 51:5, pp. 548–581, https://www.tandfonline.com/doi/pdf/10.1080/00014788.2021.1932264.

Rolls-Royce, 2022, Annual Report, accessible at: www.rolls-royce.com/~/media/Files/R/Rolls-Royce/documents/annual-report/2022/2022-full-annual-report.pdf.

Rovelli, C., 2021, *Helgoland*, (Allen Lane, London).

The Little Book of Philosophy, 2018, (Dorling Kindersley, London).

Tollefsen, D. and R. Dale, 2018, 'Joint action and 4E cognition', in *The Oxford Handbook of 4E Cognition*, Newen, A., De Bruin, L. and S. Gallagher (eds.), pp. 261–280, (Oxford University Press, Oxford).

Varela, F.J., 2000, 'Steps to a science of inter-being: Unfolding the Dharma implicit in modern cognitive science', in *The Psychology of Awakening Buddhism, Science and Our Day to Day Lives*, Watson, G., Batchelor, S. and G. Claxton (eds.), pp. 71–89, (Weiser Books, Boston).

Wilson, A., 2021, "The art of conversation: The expanded audit report' – a practitioner view', *Accounting and Business Research*, 51:5, pp. 582–584, https://doi.org/10.1080/00014788.2021.1932269.

5

AUDIT AS A LENS ON LIFE

Two thought experiments

In society and business individual choices (preferences) are aggregated through the mechanisms of politics and markets to generate purposeful action. In broad terms, society and its organisations connect individuals with the purpose of making those individuals better whilst those individuals should act with the purpose of making society and its organisations better. Both society and its organisations (and their politics and finances) are in essence the aggregation and interaction of many individuals' purposes, preferences, feelings and values. The relations, studied in this chapter, are between audit and the individual and become the starting point for developing understanding, in later chapters, of audit in the context of society, its organisations and their betterment. Thus, this chapter does not consider business or society directly but stays at the level of the individual and his/her network. It illustrates the ideas covered in the previous chapters using 'snakebite stories' that are, to a significant extent, removed from the worlds of business and society. They have a similarity with Schrodinger's cat in that they concern poison, life and death!

The stories show how life of the individual can be looked at through the lens of audit but also how our understanding of audit can come through the lens of life's experiences. This chapter is pivotal in taking the reader from the more philosophical thinking of the first four chapters through to the more practical illustrations of our thinking in a wider business and societal context in the chapters that follow.

The stories are thought experiments that concern actions taken by, and on behalf of, an individual in relation to the preservation of that individual's life. Since life is threatened, the experiments are not concerned with the individual's purposes and preferences on the assumption that an individual will choose to preserve his/her own life and, in this regard, choice and purpose are taken as

DOI: 10.4324/9781032721293-5

given.[1] By focusing the experiments in this way we are able to study audit, and in particular audit evidence, in terms of the tensions between visibility and time, and between individual and collective ('big') data. This leads, in later chapters, to consideration of audit as the connection between the individual and the collective (society and its organisations).

In each experiment or story, the purpose of the individual is clear. In the first story it is to seek assurance that a received snakebite will not be fatal and in the second it is to seek assurance that a fatal snakebite will be avoided. Both stories serve to highlight the connections shown in Figure 1.1 featuring purposeful action and disruption, attention and evidence, and communication and understanding – raising interesting questions and implications as to what constitutes audit and what constitutes society. In each story there is a network temporarily connected for the express purpose of providing assurance regarding a snakebite or potential snakebite. We call this the audit production network; that is the network that produces the representation, being in this case a representation of assurance. There is another (overlapping) network of those with an emotional stake in the continuing life of the (potential) victim. This emotionally committed network, which naturally includes the potential victim, receives the representation and, for our thought experiments, it is the stakeholders in this network that constitute society.

However, in the experiments there is considerable overlap between the subject of the audit (the well-being of the potential victim), the production of the audit and the beneficiaries. This might suggest, for instance, that a principal-agent setting where there is clear distinction between the auditor, the principal (the beneficiary) and the agent's behaviour (the subject of the audit) is not crucial to the concept of audit. Indeed, the chapter demonstrates the general point that audit production (the auditor), the subject of the audit (the auditee) and the recipient (the beneficiary) can all be networks that overlap and connect. The audit, accordingly, can be seen as a network of overlapping (connected) networks.

As they follow Figure 1.1, the two thought experiments are in essence audit stories. There are similarities between the two, the most significant being that the purposeful action is to deal with poisonous snakes, but also differences, the most significant being that one is dealing with a snakebite that has happened and the other with a potential snakebite. The two stories take place respectively in Florida and in the Adelaide Hills of South Australia. Both stories concern the representation of reality through the medium of 'assurance', provision of which is often taken to be a prime audit function or purpose. However, as the chapter develops, we shall argue that the audit should provide more than assurance. It should give help and provide assistance in the form of advice, insights, original and alternative thought; and through these insights audit itself is part of a wider process of delivering confidence.

In general terms, any audit explanation is formed from an understanding of the connection between what exists and what matters and the audit progresses by progressing this understanding. As Grayling (2020, p. 583) says in his concluding remarks, philosophy rests on two deep and fundamental questions. The first is what is there? The second is what matters? Audit exists as a connection between these two fundamental questions of philosophy. The first requires the audit to understand matter through its material existence (in potentially varying forms). The second requires audit to understand matter as something that is material in the sense of significance or importance.

It will be shown that an audit requires the connection or 'coincidence' of the two 'materialities' – existence and significance. As such, 'materiality' can be thought of as a single concept that bridges the two questions of what is there and what matters? It is audit that supplies the bridge.

In effect, this chapter, through the snakebite stories, investigates the operation of audit when the ultimate question of what matters (staying alive) is not in dispute but needs to connect with the availability of evidence. The focus therefore, at least initially, is on the availability of evidence and which of the evidence available matters in helping to answer the ultimate question.

Whilst visibility connects to the question of what there is (to see), materiality in an audit sense relates to the question of what matters. Audit can be regarded as the matching of visibility and materiality. We shall see that visibility and materiality are matched on timeliness and on reliability. While visibility flows from the reliability and timeliness of evidence, materiality determines the timeliness and reliability that is required.

The Florida story

Rick is a keen ornithologist. On holiday in Florida whilst out walking Rick saw an unusual bird sitting on a post, grabbed his camera, stepped off the path to get a better picture and was bitten by a snake he had not seen in the grass. Instead of the bird he took a picture of the snake! This was a piece of quick thinking. His wife, who was with him, 'googled' on her phone to find the nearest hospital, called to check they could deal with snake bites and they sped off, arriving 30 minutes later. Unfortunately, the hospital could not identify the snake and so the picture was sent to the Snake Centre in Georgia for identification. Some minutes later the Centre came back with its report. There were two possible visual matches with the snake in the photo. Both options, let's call them X and Y, were rare in Florida but Y was extremely rare. X, though painful, was not serious, whilst Y was deadly. The Centre advised that if it had been Y, Rick would already be dead! Since he was still alive, the snake was identified as X. The relative prior probabilities of X and Y did not matter in this case, though both being rare was in part why the hospital could not make the identification. 'Big data' can provide a 'statistical visibility' in terms of probabilities but in this instance, there was no need to rely on the comparative rarity of Y.[2] It is a story with a good outcome at least in terms of staying alive. Of course, the original objective of getting a close up of a rare bird was not fulfilled. Rick got a close up of a rare snake instead and that outcome was not the originally intended one.

Rick's purposeful action was to visit Florida to photograph rare birds and the disruption was the snakebite causing Rick to embark on a different set of actions in order to discover the seriousness (materiality) of the bite. The 'Florida' story is a useful one for exploring the concepts of materiality (flowing from the bite), and visibility (flowing from the accumulation of evidence in response to materiality). Materiality and visibility are dynamic in the sense of unfolding over time and space.

In the beginning what mattered was photographing the rare bird, being a purposeful action of the kind that Rick planned. This was not achieved but this failure did not matter as soon as the snake had bitten him. At this point what mattered was to stay alive and this in turn meant that it mattered to locate, and get to, the hospital. Purposeful activity is not fixed but responds to experience. Attention is given to what matters. On getting to the hospital, what became material was obtaining the identification from the Snake Centre, who duly narrowed the alternatives down to two. What then mattered was to find a basis for separating the two possibilities. It came through a comparison between the time for which you can stay alive following a bite from Y and the time since the snakebite. Observation that Rick was still alive allowed an explanation and firm conclusion that the bite was not from the deadly snake. Naturally, this was the assurance Rick was hoping for. Once this message was communicated and explained, what mattered to Rick was not just that he was staying alive but that he also now had the option of continuing his holiday. He could resume the original purpose he intended to follow before the disruption, continuing to seek out rare birds but presumably with greater vigilance regarding snakes!

Rick's Florida story is, for the most part, a story of disruption, of survival – but, ultimately, it is a story of reversion to continuity informed by the experience of the snake bite. By adding to Rick's experience, the 'audit' (of the snake bite) is performative and shapes future action. The actions taken between the disruption and potential resumption of the holiday are identifying what matters and needs attention, accumulating and evaluating the evidence that provides visibility, developing a thorough understanding of Rick's situation and communicating this understanding to Rick. These are the activities, the constituents, of audit as shown in Figure 1.1 and they form a pathway between the reality of disruption and the representation of that disruption in terms of staying alive with an option of resuming his holiday.

The plan of action or audit pathway starts with the snakebite and Rick's anxiety (respectively, a physical/natural and an emotional property). It ends with assurance relevant to longevity and the option to continue the holiday (respectively, an emotional feeling and a physical activity). Audit connects the two over the physical time taken to complete the audit. Given the circumstances, Rick's perception of the time taken by the audit is likely to be longer than the actual time. That is, due to anxiety, the human perception of time taken is greater than the physical time.

The sequence of events and actions is searching for visibility and, ultimately, the provision of assurance, with the sequence planned (directed) through the materiality of each event to that ultimate assurance. The audit is planned by thinking in both directions; from the end to the beginning in terms of materiality and from the beginning to the end in terms of what is visible. Materiality, leading to the identification of where to give attention, flows backwards from the future (the end desire for understanding the consequences of the bite) whilst visibility, coming from the acquisition and evaluation of evidence, flows forwards from the beginning. The materiality of the assurance is a function of both the importance of staying alive and the possible threat to life posed by the snakebite. If there was no possible threat then the snake bite wouldn't matter (or would matter far less) and nor would the assurance (the audit) have such high value.

The plan of action starts basically as one of getting Rick to a hospital with the necessary skills. The photo is taken instinctively and so becomes part of the context for planning rather than being in the plan itself. The initial plan is just to get to a hospital with the necessary knowledge of snakes and the plan evolves into (ultimately) the comparison of two durations. So, the plan (course of action, intended pathway) is evolutionary and responds to a new discovery such as finding that the hospital cannot give an answer. The progression audit evaluates the (latest) plan to assess if it is/continues to be the best option. The correspondence audit is concerned with whether the (revised) plan is being followed but also whether conduct of the revised plan is throwing up new evidence that requires new thinking. Ultimately, timely assurance incorporates: choosing (or having the confidence that you have chosen) the best option; making appropriate/pertinent revisions at all stages; and carrying out the plan including revisions. Assurance, therefore, follows from a combination and interaction of progression and correspondence.

The contribution of the environment

There are many aspects of the environment – human, physical/natural and technological – that come together to contribute to the Florida story. The importance of staying alive is an ever present which is triggered to a higher level of attention by the threat to life posed by the snakebite. There is the interaction between two fields. One is the field of human behaviour and the other is the field of the natural environment with both the human and the snake exhibiting the will to live. When the two fields bump against each other we have the disruptive event (the snakebite). Thus, the disruption arises because of the space-time contiguity of Rick and the snake. The will to live, as a feature of the natural and human environments, is taken to be universal in space-time and is the driver of the ordered actions that follow.[3]

The picture of the snake is facilitated by a combination of technology (the camera) and human response (quick thinking). The location of the hospital is accessed through technology (Google). The identification of the snake is based upon resemblances with snakes in the Snake Centre's data base, a crucial part of the technological environment for the story. For each of the two possible snakes, cause and effect data gives the life expectancies. The data base has been built from reported (human) experience. The outcome (i.e., the assurance of survival) is based upon human observation of Rick's current condition and a logical relation between two durations and, hence, is dependent upon the human power of reasoning. The duration from the snakebite is a particularity observed by Rick's wife and is compared with life expectancy following a bite for each of the candidate snakes. The audit transforms (connects) the fear felt by Rick immediately after the bite, to the comfort (i.e., assurance or relief) felt by Rick once the audit is complete and its insights/findings communicated to him. These two emotional spaces, separate in time, are connected by a logical mental operation applied to empirical snake data for both the universal and the particular.

The human ability to exercise observation and access experience, both fostered by technology, to apply logical reasoning and to embrace emotions/preferences are all key elements of the audit story. It should be noted that in the world of commerce and the world of politics, human preferences, unlike in the snakebite example, are seldom universal in space-time; that is the human preferences are not as clear as in the snakebite case but are revealed in aggregate, either through market or political processes or some combination of both.

Completion of the audit and the completion of steps in the audit

The materiality of each individual action (audit step) is derived from the materiality of the assurance provided through the audit process. Thus, because (early) assurance matters, it then matters to have the Snake Centre's opinion and, since access to the Centre is through the hospital, it matters to get to the hospital, which means that googling to find out where it is also matters – and since the hospital and Snake Centre need to identify the snake, it means the photographing of the snake matters. And through this chain of derivation (derived materiality) we can conclude that the snakebite matters because staying alive matters.

Each action in the audit pathway is material until completed – at which point, materiality passes to the next action. Materiality cannot dictate the outcome of any action but, assuming the action delivers visibility that matches the materiality of the action, attention is then directed towards what matters next. Ultimately, we reach the final act in the sequence of actions (that form the audit pathway) to deal with the disruption – and this is the giving of assurance to Rick that he is going to live. Even this, though, loses its materiality if/when Rick resumes his holiday (his original pathway). However, for that instant in time when assurance can first be given, we have both, visibility derived from the cumulative evidence, and a materiality that is not derived but comes directly from Rick; visibility and materiality in equal measure, matching each other.

This is the final moment of the pathway, when visible existence and materiality connect (coincide) and, consequently, because audit is the connection or co-incidence between what exists and what matters, this is also the moment when the audit as a whole is completed by the report to Rick. Assurance flows from this communication and it needs to be timely, a point discussed later. At the conclusion of the audit, the reality of the snakebite and the representation of it as 'not life threatening' connect to each other and the audit is completed. Once the pathway is finished and the assurance given, no further progression in this audit story is necessary or possible, but there is the option to progress the holiday, and if the holiday goes ahead the audit story becomes part of the story of the holiday. The wider significance of this is that every audit results in a representation that is potentially connected to another larger story, and this potential connection is an important consideration for the conduct of the audit.

Visibility and materiality, though connected and brought together by the audit pathway, are also different concepts. There is much that is potentially visible which is not material and much that is potentially material but not currently visible. Materiality helps to determine the choice of audit evidence and, hence, what becomes visible. However, the availability of evidence should not determine materiality, while a lack of visibility does not mean a lack of materiality. As long as materiality exceeds visibility, then there is incompleteness and the drive to progress the audit. In our story, the visibility of the outcome remains low right up until the story ends with the report from the Snake Centre – but right from the start the importance of the outcome to Rick is huge and this drives progress. Neither cost nor a lack of necessary evidence is an issue in this particular story. That said, in other circumstances, a lack of available evidence and/or the cost/difficulty of obtaining new evidence or understanding can operate to place limits on the speed at which progress is possible or desirable. This is an issue which will be addressed later.

There can also be a performativity 'trap' whereby more attention is given to the visible than is deserved and less than deserved attention is given to that which is out of sight. Materiality should not be biased towards the visible if to do so detracts from the momentum of the search for new visibility, understanding and purposeful action contributing to progress. In commerce, for instance, that which we presently can't see (or don't understand) is likely to constitute the majority of the commercial universe and yet it matters because it is through new visibility, understanding and action that progress comes.

Visibility, but not materiality, is directly a function of audit evidence. Outcome visibility comes at the end of our story as a consequence of case knowledge (the picture of the snake, the time lapse before it is processed by the Snake Centre), access to big data and technology (the snake data base and its recognition software) which ultimately gives the survival times for the two alternative snakes, the current condition of the victim (still alive), and logic allowing the elimination of the deadly alternative. It is audit that connects the pieces of evidence together. The assurance it provides flows from the visibility of the conclusion that the victim will continue to stay alive; being an assessment of the future, the product of logic and all the other factors coming together and supporting each other.

As such, in this story there is little or no visibility and little assurance that can be given until all pieces of the jigsaw, all the pieces of evidence, are in place. The whole provides the complete picture and is much larger than the disconnected pieces. Assurance depends upon the connectivity of the pieces of evidence which, in turn, serves to connect the event (snakebite) with the prospects for staying alive.

Furthermore, identifying and understanding the connectivity of the pieces requires expertise – a term that covers knowledge, experience and judgement, including the instinctive, the intuitive and the calculative. Rick had the instinctive reaction to take a picture and his wife knew how to locate and access a suitable hospital with the necessary experience of treating bites. The hospital, in turn, recognised its diagnostic limitations in this case and knew to consult with, and had access to, the Snake Centre and its wider knowledge base.

The hospital had knowledge of the condition of the patient and the time to get to hospital was provided by Rick's wife, allowing the Snake Centre to apply a calculative logic. The logic and its conclusion were passed to the hospital and then to Rick. All of the actors – Rick, his wife, the hospital and the Snake Centre – contributed expertise, which came together to complete the jigsaw. The audit is a boundary crossing instrument to assist in achieving this completion. Also necessary were the camera and the car and, from the natural world, the snake. Although, as objects, the camera and the car adopt as their purpose the role given to them by the human actors. In effect, there is a physical, natural and human collective (i.e., a stakeholder network, a collective of expertise and trust) that parallels the evidence collective. The human, natural and technological environments shape both.

The importance of trust

The connectivity of the evidence is intimately connected with the connectivity of the participants' expertise, a concept that includes the trust the participants have in each other. Without trust, an essentially human feeling, the visibility provided by evidence is much reduced. If, for instance Rick did not initially trust the Snake Centre, he might search for a ratings and review site to see the experiences of others and, if he was still unsure, he might ask for a separate analysis by another Centre.[4] As it happens, Rick was happy with the fact that the hospital worked with and trusted the Snake Centre in Georgia and, hence, he felt any further evidence was unnecessary.

Trust is enhanced when those in the expertise collective, the audit production network, share a common purpose (i.e., to help Rick) and the participants explain to each other, their actions and conclusions, demonstrating their concern for each other and creating a collective cognition. The expertise collective includes the subject of the audit (Rick) who took the photograph, Rick's wife who found the hospital and recorded the time taken to get there, the hospital who knew to contact the Snake Centre, and the Snake Centre. Rick's wife is the audit entrepreneur in the sense that she takes command of the situation and makes the audit happen. An important element of the audit is the willingness of members of the collective to share their expertise, or at least the benefits of their expertise, with other members of the network. Trust might be regarded as a form of social cognition but one where those involved do not have equal expertise, experience, access or understanding. If they did, then trust would be less necessary.

We give two current real world audit examples where trust is a big issue. The first is where there is conflict between stakeholders because they have very different experiences and perceptions of the evidence. In these circumstances, where both parties have relevant experience, any audit and audit judgement cannot be trusted until those differences have been understood and resolved. The Great British Post Office scandal (Wallis, 2021) represents an audit failure since conflicting evidence from numerous sub-postmasters on the one hand and the Post Office/Fujitsu management on the other was not resolved. Instead, the sub-postmasters were taken to court individually, and the audit failure became a massive injustice, with trust placed in a computer system and those who developed it rather than in the sub-postmasters who experienced its operation.

The second concerns trust in big data driven internet activities such as those of Facebook, Apple, Amazon, Netflix and Google. These were once known as the FAANGs, the acronym providing a coincidental connection to snakebites! To a lesser or greater extent, these organisations and others like them provide the ability to connect (free connection services) through which the individual, perhaps without realising, provides data, aggregated as 'big data' to which machine intelligence is applied to generate behavioural profiles of individuals; with the profiles being sold to interested third parties such as advertisers. Here, the participants do not share a common purpose and do not share explanations, such sharing being vital to an audit collective. Zuboff (2019) argued that such organisations should not be trusted, and if so, it has significant implications for their audit. It is interesting to conjecture the extent to which individual profiling (that is a representation of the individual) is performative over time – for instance, is the profiling activity, backed by advertising, shaping the individual to fit the profile rather than developing the profile to fit the individual? Power (2022) discussed the implications of these activities, which Zuboff called 'surveillance capitalism', for his idea of the Audit Society. He noted how surveillance capitalism tends to develop humans into 'cyborgs' (part machine, part human) and such cyborgs may not have the full range of human feelings including trust; instead, trust might be placed in the machine intelligence constituted of algorithms that may only be auditable by other algorithms. If so, trust goes digital, and the assessment/creation of trust through the left and right hemispheres of the human brain working together is disrupted.

Evaluating trust and its basis is an important element in the audit of any societal network. An audit relies on trust between members of the societal audit network and when the evaluation and experience of the network shows that such trust is not misplaced, then the audit will over time develop, as well as rely upon, trust. This includes trust in the auditor's ability to think differently as necessary to secure progress. Trust must be put to work as a basis for progress.

It should be noted that there are two stakeholder networks at play in the Florida case. First, as explained, there is the audit production network, and second there is the network (the 'emotional network') of those who are deeply impacted if Rick lost his life and who therefore need (re)assurance. The latter network includes primarily Rick himself, his wife, family and friends. Rick and his wife are key members of both networks which, therefore, intersect – ensuring that each network is a stakeholder in the other. In effect, Rick's wife is developing and executing the audit pathway on behalf of Rick's emotionally involved network, whose members place their trust in her. She does, when time permits, keep family and friends informed, reporting to them how the pathway is performing. She is managing two networks, operating as both controller of the emotional network and controller of the action-oriented, audit network. The distinction between management and auditor that normally applies for instance in a limited company audit does not apply in the Florida story. Here, the audit activity is the business of promoting action and giving assurance, and hence business and audit have, to a significant extent, become one. The audit pathway and business pathway are essentially one and the same. In a sense Rick's wife becomes manager and auditor all in one person.

Rick's wife trusted the audit network, including trust in herself, to think through the necessary audit steps in a situation she had not faced before. In her case, 'thinking differently' is thinking for the first time in a dynamic situation different to any she had faced before. Since Rick's wife is, in effect, both auditor and manager there are none of the trust issues between manager and auditor that may be experienced on a limited company audit (where the manager equates trust with confidentiality but the auditor has a duty to the public interest).

Audit as the evaluation of time; time as the auditor

The relation between audit and time is explored through the removal of a piece of evidence at a time; that is, the systematic introduction of incompleteness. If Rick had not taken the photograph and had been unable to give a clear description of the snake (the absence of case specific data) then the prognosis would have had to rely on the 'bigger data' held by the Snake Centre. As time passed and the victim stayed alive, then each deadly snake could be eliminated systematically with the fastest acting poisons being dismissed first. Each dismissal would cause an increase in visibility of outcome with the dismissal of the most common deadly snakes giving the largest visibility boost. In this case, the visibility profile over time would resemble a series of large and small jumps until all possible deadly snakes could be eliminated.

The time taken to reach a conclusive outcome would be longer and possibly much longer given the absence of specific data. The speed with which the audit provides assurance (and/or stimulates or recommends action resulting in assurance) is an important factor in the utility and value of the audit process. Naturally, Rick and his emotional network would want assurance as soon as possible. Assurance has a time value linked to the materiality of the outcome. Rick's case can be compared with Schrodinger's box. In Schrodinger's box, the cat may be considered dead and alive until the very moment that the box is opened. In Rick's case, the outcome is in the future and Rick may be going to live or going to die until the time that the evidence becomes conclusive. If Rick were to contemplate his existence during his trip to the hospital, he might consider himself in a superposition just like the famous cat. Rick is in a superposition of two connections, one being to life and the other to death, until the box is 'opened' by the audit.

If Rick did have a picture of the snake but what was missing was access to the Snake Centre then, although logic would suggest that the longer the victim stayed alive the better the prognosis (the more snakes that the hospital was familiar with could be eliminated), there is very little from which to develop any firm visibility profile for the outcome – and, potentially, there would be a lingering uncertainty for quite some time.

As such, the missing evidence examples reiterate that time essentially is the 'auditor of last resort', while the role of (other) evidence, including in the Florida case comparative durations, is to foreshorten the time taken to reach a conclusion on assurance. There is a distinction between time (duration) as a form of evidence, which like other evidence can enable a conclusion on assurance, and time as the timeliness of that assurance.

In general, the passage of time tends to increase assurance due to improved visibility and reliability, but reduces the timeliness of assurance in so far as that assurance is much more valuable if delivered quickly. Making the trade-off between visibility and timeliness is a matter of judgement. In many circumstances, it will be worth waiting for further evidence to confirm or build upon the evidence that is initially available.[5]

In the Florida story, for example, it is necessary to wait for the report from the Snake Centre to get meaningful assurance. However, if the centre had reported that the snake could be either X or Y (that is, the duration did not allow Y to be eliminated), waiting further to allow death to decide between the two, would not be an attractive option to Rick! In this case, the best course of action would be immediately to give Rick any available antidote for Y as a precaution. The underlying purpose of the audit is not solely to establish whether the bite corresponds to one from X or Y, but to help Rick. And this would suggest that in the Florida case the purpose might be seen not so much in terms of assurance but in helping Rick stay alive and progress his life; hence our concept of audit is not based solely upon assurance but also on promoting action – in ways that deliver an audit (pathway) that works for Rick whether the snake is X or Y. The ultimate purpose of the snakebite audit is not detective in orientation but preventative, albeit to prevent the consequences of a past event. It is to prevent Rick from death (if Y) or to prevent him from unnecessary worry (if X). The search for the type of snakebite (detection) is a necessary step on the route to prevention. The audit only looks backwards in time (detection) in order to look forwards more clearly (prevention).

Audit in the Florida case is detection and prevention working together. In a similar way, the purpose of a going concern audit of a company could be framed as helping to prevent the company from ceasing to be a going concern. This would add a preventative emphasis to the audit function – transforming what, currently, is primarily a detection activity and requiring the auditor to recommend actions that would enable the company to preserve (and even improve) its going concern status.

This section has demonstrated how time as the auditor of last resort is improved upon through knowledge, including evidence of, and provided by, time durations. Time is of the essence in audit and in particular in a dynamic context such as the Florida experience. However, time as the auditor or provider of audit evidence can be a slippery notion in the sense that assurance comes through the lens of human preferences, attitudes etc., at whatever time the evidence is evaluated or assurance is given. In the snakebite example, these preferences are considered not to change (the will to live is considered to be universal) but if they do change over space-time then the audit 'case file' is never closed as preferences/attitudes in the future or across different groups might be different to those of today. It follows that a time reference (a date stamp) has to be built into the audit explanation and the user or user group identified (a space stamp), as is the case with most current audit reports.

The underlying issue here (i.e., one of endless regress such that the last resort is never reached) is similar to that which McTaggart explored when claiming that time is unreal.[6] If the auditor leaves the audit open so that the future becomes the present and, hence, more visible, then, at that point, there is a new future whose uncertainty can only be resolved by once more leaving the new future to become the present and so on, endlessly.

Uncertainty generated by the snakebite (a disruptive event) can manifest itself in one of three different visibility-time profiles. We can call these profiles A, B and C. Each profile relates to a different future and, hence, to a different notion of existence.

First consider profile A. When we have access to all the pieces of the jigsaw, but no single piece of evidence is, by itself, conclusive, then the time covered by the profile is the time it takes for all the pieces to come together. There is little visibility until the final piece is in place but, if this can be done quickly, then the profile is a short period of low visibility followed by high visibility (providing the assurance). There is a sudden big step upwards in visibility. This visibility-time profile (profile A) is associated with relative early completeness compared to visibility time profiles (to be labelled B and C) where evidence pieces are missing; profile A readily and clearly points to a future in which Rick will not die from his snakebite.

If case data are missing then a similar ultimate outcome in terms of reliable assurance is achieved by a series of upward jumps in visibility over a longer time period, with the jumps corresponding to the elimination of dangerous snakes as time elapses. Such a visibility-time profile is labelled profile B. It points to a future in which there will be a series of step changes in the assurance that can be given to Rick.

If it is the big data held by the snake centre that is missing, a similar level (reliability) of assurance can only be achieved over an even longer period and (movement in) visibility over this time period is fuzzy. This visibility-time profile is labelled C. It points to a future with a lengthy period of considerable uncertainty. This fuzziness may be equated with blurring. Rovelli (2019, p. 123) states that 'temporality is profoundly linked to blurring' and that 'blurring is due to the fact that we are ignorant of the microscopic details of the world'. In the case of C, the absence of any detailed knowledge of the relations between different snake bites and death, leads to blurring.

To sum up, each category of visibility-time profile points to a different (emotional) future for Rick and these differences will be reflected in Rick's own sense of his present existence. In profile A we have all the evidence needed to form a strong conclusion and to give both reliable and (relatively) timely assurance. In A, the time frame is relatively short, in C it is long, and profile B is in between. With missing evidence, the time frame lengthens whilst, particularly with C where big data is missing, the outcome loses focus. Thus (in the context of the Florida experiment), with missing evidence the time necessary to provide the level of assurance required by Rick is extended (the assurance is less timely) and, particularly for C, the assurance is less reliable as well.

To help Rick, the audit needs to connect the snakebite (the past) with the future. The ability to do this depends upon the availability of quality evidence and the quality of the auditor's insight. Thus, the ability to audit in a timely fashion depends upon the timeliness and quality of both evidence and insight. Whether quality is more material (i.e., matters more) than timeliness depends upon the circumstances but in the case of Rick's snakebite the seriousness of the circumstances ensures that both high quality and timeliness would be welcome. Time moves slowly for Rick whilst waiting for an important report and this human perception of time adds to the importance of timeliness.

The Florida story has explored the connection between evidence (giving visibility) and (material) assurance, not by building evidence and assurance, but by reducing evidence and exploring the resulting impact on the timeliness and quality (reliability/insightfulness) of assurance. Where the evidence available results in a visibility-time profile such as A, it gives a more comprehensive audit than either profile B or C in the sense that it does better on both quality and timeliness. Across all three profiles, the evidence seeks to connect two emotional spaces being the anxiety of Rick immediately after the snakebite and the (re)assurance Rick feels once the 'audit' is over. The audit carries Rick across this emotional space in the time taken to perform the audit. Much of this 'audit time' is the time it takes to place (essentially a spatial activity) Rick's experience of the snake bite (case data) in the far wider experience (big data) of all recorded snake bites. This placement connects two different evidential spaces – case data and big data. Thus, an audit crosses both (evidential and emotional) space and time to connect the evidence obtained and assurance given. What allows the audit to make this connection is the duality of space and time, each existing in a physical sense but also as a human perception. This perception may differ from individual to individual and differ as a consequence of thinking differently – with the ability to think differently and to respond appropriately to such thoughts capable of varying across auditors. Rovelli (2019, pp. 115–124) discusses time as the changing state of ignorance. Rovelli is talking about the physical world and physical time but in the audit world the collection of evidence and the associated increase in understanding is similarly associated with the flow of time and space. Arguably, if we had complete knowledge and understanding of everything then there would be no ignorance and, by implication, human time and space would stand still and there would be no need for assurance since there would be no uncertainty or anxiety.[7]

The Florida story is a thought experiment (albeit one inspired by a real-life event) in which there is initially evidence to permit completeness giving closure but also then the opportunity to consider the relationship or connection between space-time and the uncertainty or loss of assurance introduced by reducing evidence. Once assurance has been received by Rick, he can decide whether or not to continue the holiday. Assuming he does continue (but probably with greater vigilance regarding snakes) then the audit has been restorative since he returns to his original purpose of photographing rare birds. In effect, the disruption has been reversionary and the audit serves to allow the original intentions to progress – the audit facilitates this progress. If, however, he is now too scared to continue then the snakebite is a game-changer. In either case, the original purpose and pathway is interrupted by the new purpose, and a new pathway is brought about through, or as, the audit. For the period of the interruption, staying alive remains the dominant purpose and for that period Rick's pathway becomes the audit pathway, since he has to find out about the snakebite before continuing.

A second snake story

In a second story, one of us (David Hatherly) describes his walk with an Australian friend, Lee, in the Adelaide Hills:

> The walk had taken longer than expected and we were keen to get back to the centre of Adelaide for an appointment. Lee suggested we take a short cut, leaving the recognised path and pioneering our own pathway across a grassy field. As we stepped away from the path he said 'be sure to look out for brown snakes, they are deadly poisonous and if bitten you must get to hospital within forty minutes.' 'Is there a hospital within forty minutes of here?', I enquired, recognising from our remoteness that it did not seem likely. 'No' Lee replied, 'That's why we have to look out for the brown snakes!'. It is not the exactitude of the 40 minutes that matters here but rather the emphasis it gives to the message that we could not get to a hospital in time. Lee knew the Adelaide Hills and I was happy to follow his lead but my eyes never left the grass. Only the paranoid survive![8] Nevertheless, I was somewhat reliant on (trusting of) Lee who had seen brown snakes before and knew how visible they would be in the grass. Visibility is significantly a function of expertise and experience. Happily, we negotiated the field without trauma and it became a story with a good outcome. In fact, two good outcomes, since the objective of making the appointment in time was also realised.

In the Adelaide story, thinking differently is represented by the idea of departing from the original planned pathway and crossing the field whilst looking out for poisonous snakes. Without the opportunity for observation, the idea of crossing the field might be considered unreasonably high risk. The audit includes prudent observation of the grass by both David and Lee to see that it is free of snakes. Lee is the more experienced in this regard. The progression audit, thinking of and assessing the idea to cross the field (with prudent observation), and the correspondence audit (of monitoring that activity), come together in the audit story and allow the appointment to be met.

The Adelaide story is also one of detection and prevention working together. It is the ability to see (detect) that the grass ahead is snake free that avoids (prevents) a snakebite. There is no separate pathway for the 'business' of crossing the field to make the appointment and the 'audit' is conducted with the intention of helping David and Lee meet the appointment safely. In a sense, David and Lee are both enacting the activity and auditing it at the same time, so it could be said that the activity (the business of crossing the field) is audited in real time. David and Lee as auditors help guide David and Lee as beneficiaries of the audit across the field. Auditors and the beneficiaries of the audit are one and the same, and so the audit is not only 'real time' but also a 'self-audit' by David and Lee. It is also worth noting that David and Lee's pathway is not the same as it would have been if the option of the (self) audit had not been available.

The Adelaide and Florida stories have much in common. Both concern deadly poisonous snakes, their visibility in the grass, the survival time without treatment, and the access to a hospital. Both stories highlight two key fundamentals of auditing, namely visibility and materiality. In both stories, the outcome most especially in terms of 'staying alive' matters (to the individuals concerned but also their friends and relatives) and both 'audit' stories might be thought a success in this regard.

However, the performance of the audit in each case might not be judged by whether the individuals concerned stayed alive but by what the audit did to help them to stay alive and/or to live better. An assessment of performance has to relate to purpose and the purpose of the audit in each case could be expressed in terms of helping the individuals to progress their lives quickly and with peace of mind. The audit should not be restricted to giving assurance but should be instrumental in helping the subject(s) achieve a good outcome. Thus, it is through the audit, that insight, assurance and assistance come together to provide or enable progress. Indeed, it could be said that the audit, which through its functioning can change original pathways, can be classified as having at its core 'the progression of purpose' and that its impactful(ness) has to be assessed not just in terms of what it does (through its provision of insight, assurance and assistance) but what it enables.

Both the Florida and Adelaide audit stories are part of a longer/larger story each with their own purpose and original pathway. These stories also have their own individual performance goals or measures – such as the number of rare birds photographed or whether the appointment is kept.[9] The original Florida purpose was to visit the Nature Reserve and then photograph rare birds. The trip to the hospital is an addition to the original pathway. Once the audit is complete, Rick has the option of continuing the original pathway with peace of mind regarding the original snakebite. This option exists because of the audit. Whether it is taken depends upon Rick's assessment of the risk of further snakebites relative to the rewards. However, it should be noted that the audit outcome, though one of peace of mind, might change Rick's feelings toward his original purpose, and that his decision on continuing will be a matter of judgement influenced by these new feelings.[10] The audit might have changed Rick's thinking (his assessment of the risk of another snakebite} and his feelings (his risk tolerance).

Risk tolerance is an issue for choosing courses of action (pathways). In the Adelaide case, Lee and David's risk tolerance did not allow them to cross the path without taking great care to observe what was in front, but was sufficient to allow them to cross with careful observation. In the Florida case Rick's risk tolerance did not allow him to shrug off the snakebite and without investigating it, continue with the holiday.[11]

The original Adelaide purpose was to undertake the walk and then make the appointment. The short cut represents an amendment to the original pathway. The short cut is the only option if the appointment is to be kept and this option exists because of the availability of the audit as an exercise in prudent observation, to facilitate a safe crossing of the field. Once again it is the audit that gives the option and whether the option (the short cut) is taken depends upon the assessment of risks and rewards. In both the Florida and Adelaide cases, it is the audit that provides the option to progress to the achievement of the original purpose. Generalising from the cases, we can say the auditor should search for and make known all available audit options (that is, options made available through audit), granting the opportunity for the subjects of the audit to achieve or progress their original purpose.

Since in both stories the participants survive, the disruption impact was not life-ending (but could have been). A negative disruption can prove intrusive but still permit reversion to the initial state (a reversionary disruption) or be fundamentally, 'game changing'. Similarly, a positive disruptive event can give either a temporary boost or change the game to a sustainably higher level. In business, a positive disruptive event is often preceded by a pathway of research and development whose purpose is to create a disruptive product. Such a pathway is an 'Adelaide' – but with the intention not of avoiding a disruptive event but of creating one.[12]

What differs between the two stories is the visibility of the outcomes over time – the visibility profile. In the first story, the snakebite is not anticipated and the outcome remains uncertain (it lacks clear visibility) all the way from the initial impulsive decision to step off the path through to the report received back from the Snake Centre. In the second story, each footstep in the pathway is a repeat of earlier steps, with each step carrying the risk of a snakebite. Confidence in a safe outcome rises (becomes more visible) as progress is made across the field and, with the final steps, the outcome becomes virtually certain.

These are the characteristics of a fourth type of visibility-time profile (profile S for smooth) where outcome visibility, although not conclusive until the path is completed, steadily or smoothly increases over time as the pathway (the distance across the field) is undertaken without incident. Of course, the increase would not be steady if the snakes were unevenly spread across the field and were known to congregate in one part, or if terrain was uneven rendering visibility more difficult in some areas. In this case any knowledge of the location of the snakes or difficult terrain would influence the chosen path across the field and the visibility-time profile.

Indeed, if such difficulties were known in advance, then the intended pathway would not be a straight line across the field but, in an attempt to avoid the difficulty, it would zig zag – developing the characteristics of a stepped or partially stepped profile. If the difficulties were known but their location could not be specified, then the pathway would, at the outset at least, be fuzzy and would respond to experiences encountered along the way. Instead of profile S the pathway would be closer to profile B or C. The pathway and its visibility-time profile might always be revised in the light of unexpected encounters along the way. If two parts of the pathway exhibit distinctly different characteristics, especially risk characteristics, then depending upon the circumstances they might be dealt with as separate pathways or as two sections of the same pathway or as two pathways combining to give a continuous pathway. Chapter 6 will give further consideration as to what makes a pathway distinct.

In the context of a conventional audit pathway, the auditor seeks out errors (snakes). Any knowledge of where the errors are likely to be is helpful here. The pathway is the inverse of our Adelaide story where the purpose is to avoid snakes. When errors (snakes) are found, the next step is to find out how significant (dangerous) those errors are. This step is equivalent to a Florida. These are steps in the pathway of a conventional audit consistent with the auditor's traditional role in giving an opinion on management's financial statements. It is arguable that the conventional audit is viewed too much in terms of detection and correction rather than prevention. Considering the Adelaide and Florida stories together we suggest that the audit should promote the ability to anticipate and prepare for disruption as much as respond, where possible avoiding negative disruption and promoting positive disruption in the form of innovative new products and services.

The Florida story is about reaction to an unforeseen risk and the Adelaide story takes a calculated risk so as to make the appointment on time. In terms of 'values', the Florida story places a higher value on getting Rick assurance that all is well rather than continuing the photo shoot. In the Adelaide story, a value judgement is made that the 'value' of making the appointment outweighs the risk of being bitten. Moreover, if Rick resumes his Florida holiday, he is likely to be extremely vigilant in respect of snakes. The disruption of the snakebite might be regarded as a one-off if the holiday is resumed with hopefully little risk of further snake bites.

However, we should also note that by Rick becoming ever more vigilant, he behaves more like David in the Adelaide story. Also, if when crossing the Adelaide field, a snake had bitten David or Lee, then the Adelaide story would become the Florida story. Thus, an Adelaide, given a disruptive event, can morph into a Florida and a Florida, given survival of the disruptive event, can subsequently adopt characteristics associated with an Adelaide.

This highlights an important point. Namely, that over time a disruption can generate (become) a pathway to purpose and purpose can generate a pathway to disruption – allowing us to frame the future in terms of the interplay between continuity (purpose) and discontinuity (disruption). Pathways become the connection, in both directions, between purpose and disruption.

Business activity, for instance, moves along a pathway guided by a purpose until the purpose is achieved or the pathway is disrupted in which case the business activity jumps (i.e., makes 'a quantum leap') to a new purpose and/or pathway. The progression audit has the purpose of helping business by focusing on disruptions, anticipating them, dealing with them, avoiding them and creating them.... through innovative new ideas, such as coming up with better pathways that avoid potential disruptions.

So, the two stories illustrate the close association of purposeful pathways and disruptions. The Florida story is a disruption followed by a purposeful pathway to deal with it. In the Adelaide story, the pathway amendment exposed Lee and David to a potential disruption (the risk of a snake bite). The Adelaide amendment is a revised purposeful pathway with exposure to a possible disruption but the revised pathway is conducted with risk control in mind (extra alertness and visibility!).

In the Florida case the snakebite (the experience) comes before the thinking (how to deal with it). In the Adelaide case the thinking comes before any potential snakebite experience. In both cases, the relevant phenomenon is the snakebite being experienced directly or tangibly in the Florida case and indirectly or intangibly in the Adelaide case. For the human mind, order comes with purpose, disorder with disruption, and actions (pathways) connect the two in both directions. Every purposeful pathway has a visibility-time profile corresponding to profiles A, B, C or S depending upon the circumstances. The visibility time profile is the coded instruction (A, B, C or S) or route map sent by 'progression' to 'correspondence'. It is progression that takes the lead and is in charge of correspondence. As the circumstances change over time then the pathways can change their profile, in effect forming a new instruction.

Summary and lessons learned

In accord with Figure 1.1, that shows audit as the channel between reality and representation, the audit story for each of the thought experiments considered in this chapter is a representation in narrative form of the realities of what happened; but with the audit also helping to shape those realities, by identifying and anticipating disruptions and offering or encouraging the pursuit of new pathways that deal with, avoid or prepare for those disruptions.

It is the role of the progression audit to engage with disruption; its core spirit is to provide (or stimulate) the (different) thinking necessary for progress. It asks whether we have chosen or are on the best pathway. It should always be switched on to the environment, its disruptions and the need and opportunity for new/different thinking. Correspondence audit is the activity that asks whether we are following the chosen pathway. It detects whether the pathway is taking us where we thought it would and can report back on the rate of progress (i.e., the degree/level of 'progression'), even pinpointing where new thinking maybe necessary. Progression, in some respects, could be thought of as a staircase or ladder, with correspondence being rungs on the ladder.

So, correspondence follows the pathway that leads between disruptions. It needs to understand and follow the visibility-time profile of the pathway or it will get 'lost'. The visibility-time profile can be thought of as a route map produced by the progression audit for the correspondence audit. Progression responds to past disruption, but preferably anticipates, avoids and also creates future (positive/progressive) disruption through thinking differently and crafting the required pathway as a visibility-time profile based upon the timings and evidence available.

In each case the audit introduces and enables a new option (of continuing the holiday, making the appointment) and is, in a sense, itself disruptive, highlighting that the audit is part of the story. The audit story narrative covers not just the original purpose of the individuals concerned and whether progress has been made along the intended pathway (part of the correspondence audit), but also includes the (progression audit's) response to a disruption or potential disruption to that pathway. Thus, the audit story is a crucial part of the representation of the whole story that includes the circumstances of the original purpose and pathway and how the disruptions and potential disruptions, including the attention given to them by audit, came about.

Translating to a business setting, the implication is that the audit story cannot be separated from the story of the business undergoing an audit. The audit story is an integral part of the business story as a whole and hence the progression audit in particular is an integral part of the representation of the business, helping the business to achieve its purpose, whilst at the same time helping to shape and re-shape that purpose and associated pathways in the light of new circumstances and understanding. In the two thought experiments, audit is not a formal position but is identified as a quality of mind and thought that is able to promptly, yet calmly, identify and (re)assess the purpose/pathway options. In a business setting this identification and assessment is the responsibility of management, who must, therefore, possess an 'audit' quality of mind/thought. The role of the auditor is not only to (re) assure stakeholders regarding management's assessments but also to challenge and influence management thinking so as to help improve and progress the business.

This invites the conceptual representation of audit as the progression of purpose. This includes progression along a pathway to a given purpose but, as the thought experiments indicate, where there is unexpected disruption or potential disruption, both a revised pathway and a higher priority purpose are introduced. Here, 'progression of purpose' will have a different connotation – being the development of purpose (and pathway) in tune with changing circumstances.

The circumstances leading to or invoking an audit are different in the two stories, one being a response to an actual snakebite and the other to a potential snakebite. Accordingly, the two audit stories differ in respect of order (that is, whether the audit comes before or after any snakebite) and in respect of their time profiles. They also require different uses of the brain. In Florida, there is a crucial initial role for quick thinking (instinct) and a closing role for logical thinking. In Adelaide, the focus is on concentration throughout. The implication is that audit as cognition adapts to its environmental circumstances creating a diversity of audits corresponding to the variety of environmental circumstances. Audit activity is diverse rather than uniform and, therefore, ultimately there is no 'standard' audit, but rather each audit is a unique representation. That diversity extends to the proportion of the audit that is a Florida rather than an Adelaide; that is, the extent to which it is detective rather than preventative, provides assistance as well as assurance and the impact this has on the roles played by progression and correspondence. Both correspondence and progression audits are valuable but it is the progression audit (i.e., the progressive role and spirit of audit) that deals with the bigger picture and we argue is the future of auditing. Nevertheless, the correspondence audit makes a significant contribution especially when highlighting what has been promised or intended but not delivered, and thus indicating where new thinking is required.

Notwithstanding the diversity of audits, the two stories highlight what is common to all audits and that is the necessary coincidence of what matters (materiality) and what is visible as a consequence of audit evidence. The audit activity of making things visible is driven by the audit activity of judging materiality, a judgment that takes into account the purpose and circumstances of the audit. There may be much that is visible without the need for audit work and this creates the risk of unnecessary (immaterial audit work) and of judgements that are biased in favour of what is visible.

There may also be circumstances where an issue is material but there is insufficient evidence to resolve it even after audit work intended to increase visibility. Here there is a gap ('an expectations gap') between what is hoped or wanted from an audit and what an audit can deliver. Such an expectations gap needs to be carefully explained as part of the audit story but it is a good thing if it drives the audit to discover new ways of improving visibility. Far less desirable is to close the gap by reducing expectations. We might say that when visibility exceeds materiality the danger is that the supply of audit exceeds the demand for it. However, when materiality exceeds visibility, demand for audit is likely to be most pressing (and may exceed supply). The 'balanced' audit comes into existence when visibility matches materiality – but both visibility and materiality are sensual notions and so their equivalence is inevitably a matter of audit judgement.

The matching of visibility and materiality also applies to each step of the audit (evidence acquisition) process. Thus, each step is a 'mini-audit'. Indeed, each piece of evidence is a representation and each representation is a piece of evidence. So, for instance, the photograph of the snake in the Florida story is both a representation of the snake and a piece of evidence in the larger audit story. The final assurance given to Rick is both a representation of his good health and a piece of evidence that Rick uses as the basis for his action of continuing his holiday. In the next few chapters, we show how both narrative and financial representations of a business serve as evidence that comes together to shape additional understanding and representation of the business – and, ultimately, helps to determine the (future) actions of the business and its stakeholders.

In conclusion, the chapter demonstrates that life through an audit lens resembles a network of disruptions connected by a series of purposeful pathways each with a visibility-time profile that reflects the timing and availability of evidence. In effect any activity – individual, business or societal – is represented by its purposeful pathways and disruptions together with the dynamics of the pathway encoding (A, B, C, S); a dynamic created by the search for the understanding and delivery of progress in an environment that is changing not least because our interpretation and representation of progress is changing.

We now move on from the life of the individual to the life of a business. A limited company audit illustration is utilised in subsequent chapters as a vehicle for appreciating how the audit captures, and consequently influences, the dynamics of business life. Through understanding these dynamics, the auditor highlights the need and opportunity for new purposeful pathways.

In our two stories the activity and audit pathways are one and the same. In a company audit the audit pathway and the business activity pathway are not the same but a most valued contribution of the audit is highlighting new purposeful pathways for the business that emerge from the audit and its forever developing representation of the business.

Notes

1 We do recognise that in some cases, such as suicide, the assumption does not hold.
2 Laplace, a giant of statistical and mathematical thought, looked upon probability as an instrument for repairing defects in knowledge (see https://en.wikipedia.org/wiki/Pierre-Simon_Laplace). In Rick's particular case, the initial defects in knowledge were remedied through other means so that the prior probabilities (base rates) for X and Y were not required.
3 Space, time and order are universal throughout Figure 1.1. That is, they are concepts that apply to audit, to society, to representation and to reality and each has both a physical and a human dimension. Order is important because of its association with direction – and, without direction, there cannot be any sense of progress.
4 Ratings and rankings can be regarded as one particular form of audit (Jeacle and Carter, 2011). Rankings and ratings are performative in so far as they pressure business to adopt the same criteria as the ratings agencies – demonstrating that audit can construct as well as reflect.
5 Although, technically, an individual audit could be regarded as 'completed' when the anticipated advantages of delay (enabling access to further reliable evidence) are matched or offset by the disadvantage of a loss of timeliness. This 'equilibrium point' depends upon the nature and circumstances of the audit and it does not necessarily follow that such an equilibrium point provides high assurance.
6 See Grayling (2020, p.326) for a helpful discussion of McTaggart's arguments on the unreality of time.
7 Given the seriousness of the situation for Rick, his 'human time' is likely to feel much longer than 'audit time'. The auditor in contemplating audit representations and recommended actions engages an entanglement of the human perception of time, physical time, the human perception of space and physical space – in ways that mean each audit will come to have its own (relative) space-time.
8 'Only the Paranoid Survive' is the title of a book by Andrew Grove (Grove, 1996), one of the founders of Intel, in which he talks of Strategic Inflection Points (these are game changing disruptions) that can be either threats or opportunities largely depending upon management's behavioural response. He described his business as long periods of equilibrium punctuated by game changing disruptions. Grove argued that in order to see these disruptions coming it is necessary constantly to scan the business horizon. Paranoia about game-changing disruptive events is

necessary to keep the business alive just as, in the Adelaide story, paranoia about brown snakes can be necessary to stay alive.

9 A known problem with such measures is that they do not capture the quality of the experience but focus on quantities. Such measures are a 'partial' form of performance measurement potentially giving a partial (possibly distorted) form of understanding which in turn, following the idea of performativity, leads to partial (and possibly distorted) performance.

10 The audit connects what we see (visibility) with what we feel (materiality), and after the snakebite experience what matters to Rick may no longer be photographing rare birds, at least not in the presence of rare snakes. It is illustrative of a connection between the purpose of the audit and the purpose of the holiday, the latter purpose being potentially influenced by the outcome of the audit even when the outcome of the audit has been good.

11 Rick's closeness to his wife means she as auditor has first-hand experience of Rick's risk tolerance both through communication at the time of the incident and through past experiences. Such proximity does not apply to company audits where the auditor has to be trusted to make the risk tolerance judgement (and the timeliness versus quality judgement) on behalf of stakeholders. However, recommended governance arrangements in Chapter 8, involving lateral communication between auditors and committed stakeholders, should be able to help.

12 Rick's original pathway seeking rare birds was an example of such an 'Adelaide' in the sense of seeking rather than avoiding. After the bite has been survived, it becomes dual purpose – seek rare birds, avoid rare snakes!

References

Grayling, A.C., 2020, *The History of Philosophy: Three Millenia of Thought from the West and Beyond*, (Penguin, Random House, London).

Grove, A.S., 1996, *Only the Paranoid Survive*, (Currency Doubleday, New York).

Jeacle, I., and C. Carter, 2011, 'In TripAdvisor we trust: Rankings, calculative regimes and abstract systems', *Accounting, Organizations and Society*, 36:4–5, pp. 293–309, https://doi.org/10.1016/j.aos.2011.04.002.

Power, M., 2022, 'Theorizing the economy of traces: From audit society to surveillance capitalism', *Organization Theory*, 3, pp. 1–19, https://doi.org/10.1177/26317877211052296.

Rovelli, C., 2019, *The Order of Time*, (Penguin, London).

Wallis, N., 2021, *The Great Post Office Scandal: The Fight to Expose a Multimillion Pound IT Disaster Which Put Innocent People in Jail*, (Bath Publishing, Bath).

Zuboff, S., 2019, *The Age of Surveillence Capitalism: The Fight for a Human Future at the New Frontier of Power*, (Profile Books, London).

6

AUDIT AS A LENS ON BUSINESS AND ACCOUNTING

In this chapter, whilst we talk a lot about business (and also some accounting), it is still very much a chapter about audit. It is the start of a journey (that continues through Chapters 7–9), demonstrating how looking at business through an audit lens necessitates and promotes thinking differently so as to (a) understand business better and (b) have a positive influence upon its conduct and performance. In this chapter, we move from what is, for the audit literature, the unfamiliar territory of snakebites towards the more familiar setting of the audit of a quoted company and demonstrate the potential power of our reconfigured conceptualisation of the purpose and functionality of audit.

Chapter 5 demonstrated how, when we apply an audit lens to events in life that have nothing to do with business, what we see or visualise (i.e., the audit 'story') can be represented and told in terms of purposeful pathways and disruptions. In this chapter, we apply the same lens to look at business and, then later, accounting to see both in terms of purposeful pathways, disruptions and the other related ideas brought out in Chapter 5.

Turning first to business, just as for the thought experiments, its dynamics are reflected in progress along purposeful pathways, together with the interactions between the pathways and disruption. In Chapter 5, we saw that the audit lens recognised the audit as part of larger stories – whether concerned with photographing rare birds or enjoying a recreational walk before a significant meeting. Similarly, the story of a business as seen through the audit lens is part of a much larger story of society, its progression in terms of its values and its connection to technologies, economy and natural and physical resources. The audit lens must keep this larger story in its field of vision, especially as a

DOI: 10.4324/9781032721293-6

potential source of both positive and negative disruption. The way that the audit is a part of this much larger story is addressed in more detail in Chapter 7.

However, it is important at the outset of this current chapter to recognise that no lens is perfect or fixed. As Rovelli (2019, pp. 29–32) observes, order is in the eye of the beholder. An eye (lens) that is sensitive to colour will see order and arrangement in terms of coloured patterns. An eye that is colour blind but sensitive to size will see order and arrangement in terms of whether there is a pattern based on size. Similarly, the 'audit eye' will see order and arrangement in terms of the (changing) pattern of purposeful pathways and disruptions.[1] Business architecture is seen as pathways arranged to meet the purpose of the business, a purpose that can change in response to, or to avoid, disruption. We do not claim that the two thought experiments (Florida and Adelaide) upon which our audit lens has been trained will give a perfect and undisputed vision of a business. However, it is a sufficiently insightful lens to set us on a journey that is beneficial to the business, its management and performance – with the accompanying recognition that there is always room for more thought and experimentation and for business to develop from influences not yet recognised through the current audit lens. More training or sharpening of the audit lens should continue to set the audit on its own pathway towards a wider and clearer vision.

Dynamics of business seen through an audit lens

So far in our analysis, two (business) dynamics have been revealed by the audit lens. The first is the dynamic between purposeful pathways and disruption. The second is the dynamic of movement along the purposeful pathway to completion when its purpose is either achieved or disrupted. In business, the understanding of the company by stakeholders, including management, comes through an understanding of these dynamics and provides the medium through which audit influences the performance and conduct of the company.

Turning first to the dynamic between purposeful pathways and disruption, the architecture of a business is seen through an audit lens as an arrangement of purposeful pathways intercepted by actual and potential disruptions. That is to say the overall visibility profile of the business is determined by many purposeful pathways and disruptions – many 'Floridas' and 'Adelaides' – being played out at the same time or one after the other, some being nested within a bigger purpose and pathway, some being one-offs, many being repeated through time or space, and some morphing from Florida to Adelaide or vice versa as a consequence of disruptions.

Ensuring that the pathways combine to form a coherent business and are not at cross purposes is a major organising function of senior management. It ensures that whilst any business can be decomposed into its constituent Floridas and Adelaides, the business must be viewed as a holistic, single pathway with an overriding purpose to which all the constituent pathways contribute, and which is more than its many parts. Both the holistic and the constituent purposeful pathways will be reconfigured as the business evolves.

A report from the Big Innovation Centre (2017) stressed the importance of corporate purpose, from which constituent purposeful pathways are derived. By 'corporate purpose', the report did not mean profit per se but purpose as a route to profit ('profit through purpose') and so there is a coincidence of profit and purpose. Whilst there is much of interest in this report, it gives too little consideration to the associated disruptions, both positive and negative, that flow from following a pathway – especially when knowledge and understanding of its limitations is incomplete and, therefore, partial. Companies need to think about and anticipate the unexpected (opportunities as well as threats) and have a continuing awareness of the need for, and importance of, repurposing. If there is entropy or disorder (in the sense of an organisation's tendency over time to lose direction), this could indicate the need to rediscover its original purpose or the need for a new purpose to be identified in order that the company is sustainable. Signals of the need to repurpose can come through a market process or through a political process reflecting changing consumer preferences or changing political priorities. Thus, loss of profit implies repurpose whenever that loss of profit follows a changing consumer or political environment.

Mayer (2021, p. 889) suggests that profit is about "ways of solving problems profitably where profits are defined net of costs of avoiding and remedying problems", problems that cause 'harm' to stakeholders. He went on to claim that far from causing harm, business should provide others (i.e., its stakeholders) with the capacity and capabilities to fulfil their purposes: "One should encourage as many flowers as possible to bloom and promote innovation and experimentation in corporate purpose" (p. 894). Such diversity and flexibility might allow purpose to connect with disruption but the nature and consequence of the relations between purpose and disruption are not covered explicitly. As an example of innovation in purpose, Mayer cited the pharmaceutical company Novo Nordisk who recognised that their purpose was not just to manufacture insulin for the treatment of diabetes but to understand the lifestyles that promoted diabetes and to work towards prevention.[2] Whilst this might have prejudiced the sales of insulin, Mayer stressed that the work on prevention made Novo Nordisk a trusted and respected health service supplier for pharmaceuticals. Novo Nordisk moved to a higher purpose that embraces prevention as well as cure.

Entropy: order, time and space

Purpose and order, which can be taken to include arrangements or patterns, are closely interlinked. Purpose instructs ordering and ordering requires a purpose. The issue of purpose versus lack of purpose connects to the issue of order versus disorder and is relevant to management both within and between pathways. Within a purposeful pathway, an incurred disruption shifts the pathway from order to disorder, whilst a remedial pathway resolves or responds to the disruption in a way that establishes a new purposeful pathway (that is, a new order). Thus, individual business activities (pathways) can be viewed as capable of going from either order to disorder as a consequence of a disruption, or from disorder to order as a response to a disruption. Ultimately, any purposeful pathway might suffer a game-changing disruption for which there is no remedy.

Holistically, a set of coherent purposeful pathways, focused on an overall purpose, represents order – but, with the passing of time, entropy suggests a tendency towards disorder (less coherence), perhaps because that original purpose is fulfilled or seen differently or because the company loses its focus or meets a game-changing disruption.

A 'successful' company will, however, over a sufficient portfolio of purposeful pathways and a sufficient time span, create net order. On balance, a company that is being successful converts the future (either disorder or unknown order) into the past (order), and hence the invisible into the visible. Whilst value starts in the future, its creation depends on thinking about the future now. This is the reverse of the physical world that, on balance, associates the passage of time with the conversion of order (low entropy) into disorder (high entropy). A company exists simultaneously in several worlds, including, but not limited to, the physical, and does not follow the physical world in all respects. Nevertheless, over time, few companies are continuously successful and may cease altogether either through liquidation or acquisition (both of which can be associated with game-changing disruption); in being run down or wearing out, they follow the tendency for things to become disordered (Koch, 2001, p. 279). Koch argues that "It is entirely possible to counter entropy ... but it requires constant innovation and improved use of the energy that is available".[3] This invites consideration of the similarities and differences between the commercial and physical worlds, particularly in relation to continuity versus discontinuity, and convergence versus divergence.

It is shown in physics that the past, present and future can be symbolised by the sequence >.< where the dot is the present. Every present is preceded by its cone (>) of past events. This cone symbolises all the possible sequences of past events (convergent pathways) that could have resulted in the present. In turn, every present is followed by its cone (<) of future events.[4] This symbolises all possible future routes (divergent pathways) that can be taken from the particular present. The sequence is one of convergence followed by divergence. The past converges on the present and the future diverges from the present.

However, a company is not necessarily open ended but can be discontinuous in the sense of having a start 'a' and ultimately a finish 'b'. Discontinuity creates the opposite sequence, where divergence is followed by convergence. In this case, the past, present and future might be symbolised as a<!>b where '!' represents the spatial cross-section of purposeful pathways currently in process; that is, the present activity of the company. In this presentation, the cone of past events has changed direction from (>) in the previous paragraph to (<) and now symbolises the pathways (and portions of pathways) actually undertaken since the company began at point 'a', with the result that the company now has in play the cross-section of pathways symbolised by '!'. The cone of future events (>) has also changed direction from the previous paragraph and symbolises the purposeful pathways (and portions of pathways) to be completed in the future in order to achieve the corporate purpose or future corporate objective by point 'b'.

At point 'a', all value is in the future. In contrast, at point 'b', all values can be deemed to be in the past if it is assumed that the company has fulfilled its purpose. To avoid reaching this 'natural' conclusion at point 'b', a company needs to innovate, to restart or repurpose itself. A company can extend its life by acting in this way before point 'b' is reached and, in principle, could extend its life indefinitely.

Accordingly, it can be argued that a successful company does not wait for point 'b' to arrive but innovates, appropriately repurposing itself whilst continuing to follow through on its original purpose. It needs both to close out (see through) the current purposeful pathways in process and open up new possibilities for the future. In this way, the company seeks both continuity and discontinuity simultaneously, creating a coincidence of opposites. This is a theme that will be taken up in Chapter 8, where it is argued that an investor is investing simultaneously in continuity and discontinuity.

A coincidence of opposites also manifests itself through the two sequences that symbolise the 'present'. One is for the 'present' to be symbolised by the dot in the sequence >.< and the other is for the present to be symbolised as the exclamation mark in the sequence <!>. This implies the relationship between the past, present and future could be a simultaneous moving apart, having previously come together (in the first sequence: convergence is the past and divergence is the future) and a coming together having moved apart (in the second sequence: divergence is the past and convergence is the future). The coincidence of opposite views or sequences for the relationship between the past, present and future is an issue returned to towards the end of Chapter 9 in relation to creativity.

The dynamics of the purposeful pathway

The first dynamic has been the relationship between purposeful pathways and disruption. A second dynamic revealed by the audit lens is the progress (movement) along the purposeful pathway towards completion (the purpose is fulfilled) or until the pathway is interrupted/terminated by disruption. The audit lens classifies pathways into Floridas that respond to disruption and Adelaides that seek to anticipate and avoid disruption. For a Florida, depending upon the evidence, the pathway's visibility-time profile is either fuzzy (profile C), stepped (profile B) or end-loaded (profile A). An 'end-loaded' profile is one where visibility only arises when all pieces of evidence are considered together. Consequently, visibility does not come until all the evidence is in and the pathway's purpose is achieved by taking all the evidence together. Progress along a fuzzy pathway is difficult to identify because visibility over time remains poor, until and unless unexpected evidence becomes available, allowing the profile to change. Progress along a continuing smooth (profile S), Adelaide pathway, on the other hand, can be detected so long as the profile does not change; progress then corresponds to the proportion of the pathway completed. Progress along a stepped profile can be identified in terms of the steps successfully accomplished, each step contributing to visibility. Progress along individual pathways should be coordinated by management to avoid any lack of progress on one pathway from disrupting another. With outsourcing and offshoring, fewer of the necessary pathways are directly under the control of company managers and the audit lens needs to be trained on progress by other stakeholders (such as suppliers and subcontractors) who can be potential sources of disruption.

In so far as the audit assesses progress as being 'progress along the business pathway(s)', then to evaluate progress, the auditor needs to know the profile of the pathway(s) the business is following. And is the pathway completed? Or has the pathway changed its profile during the year? Have new, progressive, pathways opened up or been created as a response to, or in anticipation of disruption?

Business as purposeful pathways and disruptions

The auditor needs to identify and assess all the different pathways that come together to create the business and serve/deliver its purpose. This section illustrates (some of) the different pathways and issues (disruptions) that an auditor faces. The issues and their assessment connect with the visibility profile associated with the business' overall pathway.

To illustrate the notion of business as connected pathways, let us consider Rolls-Royce's civil aviation division in the years immediately prior to the outbreak of Covid-19, a potentially game-changing disruption. Until then, Rolls-Royce's background story had been one of clear and steady growth in air travel. Rolls-Royce sees itself as delivering complex power solutions. According to its Annual Report 2019 (cover page), the company's purpose is to pioneer "cutting-edge technologies that deliver clean, safe and competitive solutions to meet our planet's vital power needs". This can be taken as its established, overall purpose prior to Covid. The contributing pathway that we shall be concerned with is the development and sale, pre-Covid, of the Trent aero engine – with its associated purpose of accelerating market share for long-haul jets, primarily through the, then, new version of the Trent 1000 engine.[5]

There are, in turn, many supporting purposeful pathways. The 'product development pathway' of the Trent engine has been preceded by 'a research pathway', and is followed by a 'sales and production pathway' (in order to generate profits). A long-term sales and production pathway is formed of annual sales and production pathways, which together generate an annual profit that comes steadily into view as the year progresses, and each annual pathway is considered to be completed at the year-end. These annual pathways exist to facilitate annual reporting ('reporting pathways') and form a vital link or connection between the business, accounting profit and accountability, evaluation of this connection being a primary function of the traditional audit. Annual reporting pathways, in turn, comprise an accumulation of 'micro-reporting pathways' that connect individual transactions to their records in the books.[6]

Thus, the core pathways of business are research, development, production, including supply, sales and reporting, with a response to the latter generating new or amended pathways. Turning to research and development, the visibility profile at any point in time depends upon the evidence to support its successful conclusion. Most research projects start as an idea but with many details missing and hard evidence yet to be obtained. At this point, the pathway for the project in terms of visibility has profile C-fuzzy. From there, if the early research is successful, prototypes are developed and tested across an increasing variety of conditions. The project pathway becomes a development pathway with profile B-stepped – since testing leads to step changes in supporting evidence for the success of the project. When testing is complete and the product is ready to launch, the project resembles profile A in the sense that all the evidence is in, but it has yet to face the ultimate test in the marketplace. The ultimate test is the sales and production pathway. Given a smooth advance in sales and production, then this pathway has an S profile, whereas if advances in sales are a series of step changes, then the sales and production pathway is more appropriately regarded as a B profile. In effect, a project, if treated as a single pathway, changes its visibility profile through time as it moves from concept formulation, to development and testing, to product launch, to sales and production. In its early years in service, there are likely to be problems to fix with a new engine and further testing required, making the sales pathway during this time more uncertain. However, some projects may not get beyond the research stage or beyond the development stage, at which point the pathway is disrupted without leading to a further pathway.

The new version of the Trent 1000 was billed as a star performer in terms of fuel efficiency and CO_2 emissions and consequently had disruptive potential. This disruption had both negative and positive implications for the company. It would make earlier, less efficient versions of the Trent more difficult to sell whilst increasing overall engine sales because the new level of engine efficiency provided an opportunity for airlines, both incumbent and challenger, to accelerate purchases to maintain or enhance their relative competitiveness.

However, any such story of, on balance, positive disruption was itself disrupted by a story of unanticipated problems with the longevity of parts in the new engine (a problem which would be persistent if excessive wear was a function of the engine's design). Measures to rectify the problem formed a 'remedial' pathway, with responsive actions including the use of sensors and the building of a database. Rolls-Royce had, in common with its competitors, seized the opportunity for sensors to provide early observation of the wear on an engine (case data). This use of sensors, an example of what has been referred to as the 'internet of things', helped Rolls-Royce to collate, over time, experience and data on engine wear, necessary responsive design changes, and the cost of repairs across the engine population. In time, such ('big') data helped to advance the visibility of the outcome of the engine wear disruption, with future cost estimates being revised as a consequence and cost visibility increased. This engine problem proved to be a serious disruption but in its 2019 Annual Report (p. 8), Rolls-Royce claimed to have designed fixes for all but one of the significant challenges it had faced and to have a clear pathway for resolving the final issue.

The excessive engine wear was a serious problem for the company and for the auditor in terms of assessing its materiality. To gain visibility of such a situation, the auditor needs (or needs to be) an engineering specialist with aero-engine knowledge. A remedial pathway is akin to a Florida with a B profile in so far as visibility and cost estimates tend to step change over time, but it is completed once all the issues have been resolved. Other pathways likely to have a step change or B profile are those concerning derivatives, deferred tax and defined benefit pensions. Such profiles refer to an outstanding financial contract or 'promise' that requires its own pathway to deal with it. For example, Rolls-Royce dealt with one of its major defined benefit pension schemes by agreeing a pathway with Legal and General, who would, at a cost, insure against future disruptive increases in liabilities, thus (for Rolls-Royce) changing the nature of the pensions promise from profile B (liable to step change) to profile S (smooth).

A further story of this pre-Covid period relates to Rolls-Royce's cost reduction exercise, billed as the removal of layers of bureaucracy. In untroubled times, this might be expected to lead to a sustainable improvement in financial performance but not necessarily in troubled times when extra management could be required. Much also depends here upon the skills and experience of the departed management. The cost reduction exercise could start as steady progress towards improvement in terms of cost efficiency but troubles with the new engine could prove difficult to contain with major staff shortages, so that the remedial pathway and the cost reduction pathway would potentially be working at cross purposes. There can be a trade-off between cost reduction and resilience. Any cost reduction exercise often starts with ambitious targets but some uncertainty as to its eventual outcome. However, as it gets underway the impact on profit becomes clearer and, if sustainable (or unavoidable if the impact is bad news!), it might then be treated as having an S profile.

Another consideration is the fines at the time imposed on Rolls-Royce in relation to bribery allegations. These required their own 'negotiating pathway' to settle the amounts with the relevant authorities. Until the negotiation is completed, the outcome is fuzzy and hence the negotiating pathway has a C profile and the possible fines are excluded by Rolls-Royce from its calculation of profit. A further issue is the note to the accounts covering the contingent liability in respect of amounts lent by Rolls-Royce (and other assistance provided) to customers to enable them to purchase engines. It should be noted that even before Covid-19 not all of Rolls-Royce's airline customers were in the best of financial shape. There was a potential loss which had not been evaluated and charged but had been disclosed as a contingent liability. In effect, this is another pathway with a C profile since the (negative) value can take a long time to become clearly visible. Dealing with both the bribery allegations and the contingent liability represent significant disruptions to the larger sales promotion pathway.

During the period covered by the above business story, important research and development pathways currently then in progress included the development of a hybrid engine, engines capable of running on low-carbon (sustainable) fuel, and the development of an all-electric plane. Rolls-Royce's intentions here were signalled by the acquisition of Siemens e-aircraft business. Potential future disruption related not only to the impact of electrification but also to changing human appetites for air travel and the prospects for the world economy. It is hard to anticipate and evaluate the long-term impact on air travel and engine demand if the world were to shift from globalisation to localisation as part of a human desire to protect local suppliers (thus, helping to secure supply chains), to 'save the planet' or to 'pandemic-proof'. Environmentally friendly travel makes an impact on climate change but, when combined with less travel, it makes a greater impact.

The unanticipated Covid-19 pandemic arrived with immediate consequences for airlines and air travel. This was a major disruption but, since the pandemic, the airline industry and Rolls-Royce's order book have bounced back and so, in that sense, the pandemic looks like a substantial but reversionary disruption. Nevertheless, the audit needs to consider the risk that, in the longer term, the profitability of the airline industry as a whole (not just Rolls-Royce) cannot provide sufficient resilience funding to cover future disruptions and/or sufficient research and development funding for new aircraft and engines that satisfy climate requirements. The audit assessment on this needs to be communicated to all stakeholders and will impact the auditor's judgement regarding deserved confidence and, consequently, where appropriate, any valuation or assessment of the valuation of Rolls-Royce by stakeholders and by the auditor.

Appointment of a new chief executive

A new chief executive (CE), Tufan Erginbilgic, was appointed by Rolls-Royce to serve from January 2023. This was promised to be a disruptive event.[7] In the 2022 Annual Report, Erginbilgic wrote (p. 4):

> We are capable of moving faster, aiming higher and delivering stronger returns for all our stakeholders. That potential needs to be realised in an external environment that is changing rapidly ...... If the past few years have taught the business community anything it is that uncertainty and change are the norm ......Further shocks cannot be ruled out and Rolls-Royce must be able to face them in a stronger position than it has in the past. This requires a stronger balance sheet to build resilience and to underpin profitable growth opportunities ......Our total shareholder return over the last five years is negative. Cash generation is unsatisfactory. Our debt is too high.

According to Erginbilgic, a major objective (purpose) for Rolls-Royce was to improve resilience by reducing debt and, in the process, restore an investment-grade credit rating, thus reducing the cost of debt. The pathway for achieving this included robust pricing (no longer selling engines at a loss in the hope of profitable maintenance), disposals, and a cost reduction programme that includes redundancies. This could, of course, be seen as a pathway replacing negative returns for shareholders with negative returns for customers and employees. But the new CE argued that improved finances will open up growth opportunities such as new engines for narrow-bodied, single-aisle aircraft, with benefits for both future employees and customers (though these may accrue to different employees and customers than those impacted negatively).

Erginbilgic was keen to change the corporate culture from a strong engineering focus to one that also has a financial focus and instigated a number of measures constituting a pathway to achieve this. Its purpose was to change the thinking and the balance of emotional attachment for employees and managers. It had to be done carefully so as to build upon and not lose the company's traditional engineering expertise. The new CE was keen on performance measures and targets, but performance measures have to be flexible if uncertainty and change are the norm for the firm's external environment. Otherwise, targets and performance measures could be a source of misdirection and disruption. In its 2022 Annual Report, the firm listed six financial performance measures but only three non-financial (p. 9 and pp. 13–14), with all nine being linked to remuneration. Aspects of performance that lie outside these performance measures could be neglected, and the auditor would need to be satisfied that this is not a problem and not something likely to impact on the auditor's assessment of deserved confidence.

It is notable that, in the three years following the appointment of its new CE, Rolls-Royce became a star performer on the UK stock market, with its share price rising more than ten fold. Clearly, market confidence in Rolls-Royce grew enormously but under current audit reporting regulations there is no requirement for its external auditor to indicate formally whether, in their opinion, the company was deserving of (such) confidence. In subsequent chapters, we will show how any such audit assessment of deserved confidence would need to take into account performance across different dimensions of activity, financial and non-financial and whether visibly measured or not.

The past, present and future

The Annual Reports of Rolls-Royce show that the company's business arrangements with suppliers and customers are highly complex. It has not been our purpose to detail these. Rather, it has been our purpose in general terms to reflect on how business could be viewed through our reconfigured audit lens; to illustrate the role played by purposeful pathways and disruptions in developing understanding of the business' past, present and future – and their significance to the audit. At any point in time, there are pathways that are completed, those that have started but have some way to run, and pathways and disruptions that are visible or envisioned for the future but have not yet started. Moreover, there are pathways and disruptions which simply cannot be conceived at the present time and are, therefore, over the horizon. We cannot eliminate these radical uncertainties (King, 2016, pp. 120–155) or 'unknown unknowns'.[8] It was ever thus. When Mr Rolls and Mr Royce started their motor business in 1904, they and their investors could not have conceived that the company would, twelve decades later, be making jet engines for wide-bodied aeroplanes and even, in another division, small-scale nuclear power plants. In this regard, what lies over the 'horizon' is radically or fundamentally uncertain and not fixed. Indeed, efforts to make it more visible and understandable could serve to expand perceptions of the scale and significance of the fundamentally unknown – as captured by the phrase 'the more we know the more (we realise) we don't know!'.

The essential role of research and development could be specified as being to unlock a piece of this zone of (fundamental) uncertainty and bring it within our understanding and, thereby, stimulate or justify the development of new products, which could well be radically different from what has gone before. The direction of travel for commercial development is, accordingly, one that sees value being unlocked (or accessed) from the commercial world's zone of radical uncertainty. If so, this is a process through which, in learning about various dimensions of the future, we essentially move the future (for us) towards the present. It is the future as a set of ideas (based upon thinking differently) that gives rise to the notion of the future coming towards the present. Ideas describe and envision the future, a future that can become the present through implementation of a series of directed actions.

What is over the horizon clearly does matter. The physical and natural environment, society, the economy and technology may be thought of as the 'force fields' which pervade the commercial universe, including its zone of radical uncertainty, but interact in complex ways.[9] Likewise, a crucial role of audit, as part of the business story, is to understand how the connections between these fields construct both positive and negative disruptions, which in turn provide purpose for the pathways that constitute the business. The connections that remain hidden provide future opportunities and threats – but trying to unlock 'unknown unknowns' is a major motivating force for entrepreneurial businesses.

Kay and King (2020, p. 15) restate Knight's belief "that it was radical uncertainty that created profit opportunities for entrepreneurs and that it was their skill and luck in navigating radical uncertainty which drove technical and economic progress". Positive and negative disruption as well as new and original purposeful pathways flow from what was previously unknown and inconceivable. This is the nature of creativity and discovery. Helping to unlock these new (positive) disruptions are expenditure commitments to both research and development – pathways with the purpose of creating a new disruptive product and later a sales pathway with associated marketing and promotional expenditure.

Audit as a lens on accounting

Just as the business arrangements of Rolls-Royce are complex, so are the accounting consequences of those arrangements. We have not dwelt on such complexities, as the intent of this section is to demonstrate (through two simple examples) how accounting treatment and the numbers so produced can be matched up with the view of business as connected pathways and disruptions. This matching process introduces five issues for consideration when matching a pathway and its accounting treatment. They are (i) timing, (ii) the visibility-time profile, (iii) purpose and disruption, (iv) pathway identification and (v) mutual dependencies between pathways. It is the consideration of these issues in particular that brings about an understanding of how business and conventional accounting connect.

The first consideration is time. Accounting can be viewed as being designed around a three 'time'-dimensional framework, the dimensions being the present, the past and the future. There is a reporting period taken to be the present, a past that ends with the beginning of the reporting period and a future that starts with the end of the reporting period. Accounting has traditionally concentrated on reporting performance in the present accounting period. This has typically taken the form of a profit statement (in financial terms) and a balance sheet or statement of financial position that reports at a point in time on the financial relations with stakeholders, including shareholders. The reporting of financial performance during the reporting period connects the opening and closing financial positions.

Representation of a pathway in the accounts depends upon its start and completion relative to the reporting period (taken here to be the 'present'). Thus, pathways at a point in time may be classified as (1) future pathways that have not started by the end of the reporting period, (2) pathways started during the accounting period that are still ongoing at the end of the reporting period, (3) pathways that are started and completed during the reporting period, (4) pathways started before and completed during the accounting period, (5) pathways started before the reporting period but still on-going at the end of the reporting period and (6) a history of pathways completed before the start of the reporting period.

To connect pathways with the framework of accounting, it is necessary to map the above six categories onto the past, present (accounting period) and the future. The financial numbers (for example, associated revenues and/or expenses) for all pathways completed during the reporting period (categories 3 and 4) belong to the present. All pathways and their financial numbers completed before the reporting period (category 6) belong to the past and all pathways not started by the end of the reporting period (category 1) belong to the future.

The challenges mostly arise with pathways that are still ongoing at the end of the reporting period (categories 2 and 5). A simple example of category 5 is the pathway for the company's fixed assets, where they exist before, during and after the accounting period. Financial statements allocate the cost of the assets between these three periods, being the opening balance, the depreciation charge for the year and the closing balance. Depreciation will typically be charged applying a smooth (S) profile to the wearing out of assets on the basis of time or usage.

In the event of a disruption such as unanticipated obsolescence or a change in purpose for the use of the asset, then the visibility profile would change and the assumption of an S profile would probably no longer hold. For example, if there is clear evidence of obsolescence (a disruption) and a need for immediate replacement, then the evidence and the life of the asset are complete, it now has profile A, and the asset is written off. However, if the asset continues to be used after it is fully depreciated and the life expectancy is now unclear, then the profile becomes fuzzy, and in practice, no accounting action might be taken. In both cases, there is new evidence (obsolescence /continuing use) disrupting the original assumption of the useful life of the asset, changing its expected visibility-time profile and possibly the accounting treatment. In both cases, if material, the change in circumstances and the accounting response and effect should be reported as a narrative note to give understanding to the user.

This simple example illustrates how both disruption and the expected visibility profile impact accounting. The fixed asset pathway is a subsidiary pathway of production. It starts when the asset is first used and finishes when the asset ceases to contribute to production.

As shown in Chapter 5, disruption plays a major role in generating and terminating pathways and consequently disruption, its existence and potential, is a major issue for audit. However, in business, disruption can be difficult to identify or recognise, especially in anticipation. As a result, it can be difficult to identify when one pathway ends and another begins. This has been of particular relevance to Rolls-Royce when, before a change in policy brought in by the new CE, it was willing to sell an engine at a small loss or margin and make up for the loss with profitable maintenance.

One possibility is to view the sale and the maintenance as a single continuous pathway. The accounting treatment that matches up with this view is to combine the small profit (or loss) from the engine sale with the expected profit from maintenance, and spread the combined profit over the expected useful life of the engine. The alternative is to view the engine sale (to the aircraft manufacturer) as one pathway and the engine maintenance (for the airline) as a separate pathway. This has the effect, if the engine sale makes a loss, of recognising losses sooner and profits (coming from maintenance) later. Before they were prohibited from doing so by a change in the accounting standards, Rolls-Royce would treat the engine sale and maintenance as a single pathway, but in recent years, following the change in the accounting standards, the company has treated the engine sale and maintenance as separate pathways, giving a more conservative statement of profit. In our terms, the current accounting standard treats the engine sale as a disruptive event that ended the production/sale pathway and started the maintenance pathway.[10]

There is an argument for treating them as separate pathways if they have different profiles. In so far as the sale of the engine is a single event, then it is best represented by profile A, where evidence in the form of order, delivery, and invoice all come together to convince that a sale has taken place at a point in time. Maintenance, however, is an ongoing event during the life of the engine (a kind of anti-depreciation that discourages the engine from wearing out) and might be treated as having a smooth profile where higher expected costs towards the end of the contract are added to smaller costs towards the beginning and the total sum spread evenly as an annual charge.

Nevertheless, it is important that the connection between the sale and maintenance pathways is represented and understood as mutually supportive. The subtlety of such connections needs to be explained through narratives, which therefore serve an important role. We can take the view that maintenance, where Rolls makes most of its profit, gives the business continuity and that the sale of another (replacement) engine is to avoid a discontinuity in maintenance income. Alternatively, we can consider that the business is about keeping engine sales up (a continuity of engine sales) and that maintenance is necessary to support this continuity. In terms of growth, it is difficult to increase maintenance income without increasing engine sales and also to increase engine sales without increasing maintenance. The two pathways support each other. If instead of investigating the mutual dependence, the auditor simply adopts the accounting standard, then the auditor's understanding of the business is liable to be limited. In effect, the auditor applying the standard would be performing a compliance audit that is not concerned with developing an understanding of the connection between pathways necessary for progression.

Similar issues relate to other mutually dependent pathways, notably production and sales. In this instance, production is regarded (by accounting) as a non-profit making pathway whilst all profit is attributed to the sales, but in order to calculate profit, production (cost) is connected to (matched with) sales. The identification of profit with sales rather than production does not recognise mutual dependencies; mutual dependencies that need to be part of the understanding that emerges when considering purposeful pathways and disruption and how to match them up with the financial statements. Sales continuity needs continuity of production and vice versa. Thus, mutual dependency allows each to form evidence of the other.

Disruption, both experienced and anticipated, also plays a key role in the accounting treatment of promises such as pension promises to employees, warranty promises to customers, deferred taxation and foreign exchange hedges, all of which are contracts with stakeholders and part of the stakeholder engagement pathway. They are contractual promises (often long term), the value of which is going to be dependent upon future conditions that are difficult to assess. The financial values of these contracts may have been recognised in the opening statement of financial position but may need to be revalued for the closing statement as a consequence of new information or evidence that disrupts the assumptions upon which previous valuations have been based. If possible, pathways need to be put in place to deal with the source of any disruption (for example, to improve product performance in respect of warranties) whilst the financial consequences of the revaluations are recognised in the financial statements.

An audit, which is concerned with matching the pathways and disruptions of the business with the financial statements, is in essence a form of correspondence audit – assessing the correspondence between the company's financial statements and the business, but without a clear audit focus on the health of the business and its prospects. The current audit lens is centred on the accounting rather than the underlying company, whilst the accounting lens is only capable of a partial view of the company (impaired vision). This impairment is because, in the search for a better truth and fairer society (Chapter 1, Figure 1.1), accounting struggles to address the values (other than financial values) that sit at the heart of, and are the core currency for, the audit (societal) network.

Summary and conclusion

This chapter has shown, using Rolls-Royce's aero engine division as an illustration, how both business and its financial statements can be seen as purposeful pathways, disruptions and visibility-time profiles. In terms of business, audit focuses upon two dynamics: (1) the dynamic between purpose, pathway and disruption, and (2) movement along a pathway towards either completion or disruption. In terms of the financial statements, the traditional limited company audit has been concerned with whether such statements match up with the business activity. Using two specific accounting illustrations, this chapter has shown how this match-up can be facilitated by seeing both the business and the financial statements in the same terms. This leads to improvement in understanding how the conventional (current) limited company audit should be approached.

However, improving the match up between the conventional audit and financial statements is not the purpose of our book. We want to transform both audit and business in a mutually connected fashion, with the transformation of business informing and being inspired by the transformation of audit (and vice versa). The spirit of such intent is captured nicely in the following comment by Tufan Erginbilgic in the Rolls-Royce 2025 Annual Report (p. 7) when explaining what business transformation means for Rolls-Royce:

> I have frequently been asked to describe the transformation we have undertaken at Rolls-Royce. My first point is to reiterate that we are not pursuing a turnaround or restructuring, rather a fundamental transformation of the business. When people think of a turnaround, the outcome is a return to the point in the past and past performance. Our transformation is about taking the business from point A to point B, where at point B the business is capable of things it could not even conceive at point A . Because of our differentiated mindset, capability and financial strength, we are well on the way to point B. What we are learning is that as we get closer, we see more opportunity, expand further and point B evolves.

In conclusion, the conventional limited company audit, focused upon the financial statements only gives a partial view of the business, its performance and prospects. How the financial statements match up with business activity and vice versa is essentially a correspondence audit rather than a progression audit. Moreover, it is an audit that falls a long way short of understanding the business in terms of society's values and the societal audit network (as set out in Chapter 1) of which it is a part. Developing a more 'transformative' audit to fully understand and progress the business is the principal focus of Chapters 7 and 8, whilst Chapter 9 outlines how traditional financial statements can themselves, as a consequence of our recommended new approach to auditing, also be reconfigured and developed to support this audit transformation.

Notes

1 As shown in Chapter 5 and its thought experiments, the audit 'eye' not only covers the sense of sight but also other senses such as the awareness of the snakebite through the sense of pain, the sense of logic (making sense through logic), and the emotional senses of anxiety and relief. The audit eye and its lens as used by us might therefore be considered the 'sensibility of audit', a combining of other more familiar senses that make sense of the audit pathways and capture the feelings (sense of emotion) associated with disruptions and potential disruptions.
2 Chapter 8 discusses the implications of innovation and creativity for an existing business.
3 Koch's book on the 'Power Laws of Business' introduces the similarities and differences between the physical and commercial worlds.
4 See Hawking (1988, p. 25) for a discussion of cones in the context of (light) cones in physics and Hawking (1988, p. 60) for Feynman's idea of a 'sum over histories'.
5 It takes many years to develop an engine through to its certification. See https://en.wikipedia.org/wiki/Rolls-Royce_Trent_1000#:~:text=The20%Trent%201000%20is%20a,powered%20by%20six%20axial%20turbines. This gives an idea of what a development pathway at Rolls-Royce looks like.
6 It should be noted that the choice of a year for the reporting period is essentially pragmatic. Logically it might be a period of time corresponding to the company's 'present'. If the 'present' is taken to be a period of stability (an extended 'now'), then the logical reporting period would vary from company to company with the shortest reporting periods being attributed to the most dynamic companies. However, the use of shorter reporting periods is constrained by accounting's allocation problem. A shorter reporting period may well better match the dynamic conditions facing the company, but it is also likely to make any allocation of revenues and expenses to specific time periods more problematic and potentially less reliable. In essence, this is an accounting version of Heisenberg's 'uncertainty principle', which states that the more we focus on knowing the speed of a particle the less we can know about its current position (and vice versa).
7 Investors immediately viewed the appointment as a positive disruption with the share price rising substantially in the new CE's first year of office, although other factors, especially the post pandemic revival of the airline industry, were also relevant.
8 A pandemic had been conceived by management as a threat to Rolls-Royce and was therefore not strictly a radical uncertainty which, at the time of the annual report, would need to have been a non-conceivable future event.
9 The notion of 'fields' is borrowed from the physical world where the 'force fields' of gravity, electromagnetism, the weak and the strong nuclear force pervade the physical universe. They too interact in complex ways that are not fully understood.

10 It should also be noted that the engine sale is a contract with the aircraft (airframe) manufacturer whilst the maintenance contract is with the airline that operates the plane, supporting the idea that engine sales and maintenance are separate pathways.

References

Big Innovation Centre, 2017, *The Purposeful Company*, https://thepurposefulcompany.org/wp-content/uploads/2021/01/feb-24_tpc_policy-report_final_printed-2.pdf

Hawking, S.W., 1988, *A Brief History of Time: From the Big Bang to Black Holes*, (Bantam Press, London).

Kay, J., and M., King, 2020, *Radical Uncertainty: Decision Making for an Unknowable Future*, (Bridge Street Press, London).

King, M., 2016, *The End of Alchemy: Money, Banking and the Future of the Global Economy* (Little Brown, London).

Koch, R., 2001, *The Power Laws of Business*, (Nicholas Brealey, London).

Mayer, C. 2021, 'The future of the corporation and the economics of purpose', *Journal of Management Studies*, 58(3), pp. 887–901, https://doi.org/10.1111/joms.12660.

Rolls-Royce Holdings plc, *Annual Reports 2019, 2022 and 2025*, https://rolls-royce.com/investors/results-reports-and-presentations/ar-annual-report-archive/ar-annual-reports.aspx.

Rovelli, C., 2019, *The Order of Time*, (Penguin, London).

7

AUDIT AS DESERVED CONFIDENCE

According to Sir Donald Brydon, "The purpose of an audit is to help establish and maintain deserved confidence in a company and in the information for which they have responsibility to report including the financial statements" (The Brydon Report, 2019, p. 22, paragraph 5.1.4). Central to Brydon's independent review into the quality and effectiveness of audit, this statement is a clear recommendation that the audit needs to do more than provide assurance on financial statements. It talks in terms of confidence not just in the information for which management is responsible but confidence in the company itself. Moreover, it represents the role of audit as being to help establish and maintain such confidence and ensure that it is deserved. Brydon did not elaborate on the notion of deserved confidence but we believe it is of critical significance in the process of reconceptualising the role and future purpose of audit. Indeed, we would extend Brydon's conceptualisation by emphasising that our central emphasis on 'thinking differently' should mean that audits do not just provide declarations of confidence in the company's current standing and position but can also enable the company to advance confidence in itself, in its ability to survive and thrive.

This chapter, therefore, examines the notion of 'deserved confidence' and how its formal incorporation in the purpose of audit extends the audit lens beyond the financial statements to the values of the company itself, and the societies or society in which it operates. Gaining and building deserved confidence goes to the very heart or overall purpose of the company and is something that positions the role of audit as also being deeply connected with societal values and expectations – through consideration of the company's actions and values, and those of its stakeholders/society. We consider deserved confidence in a company to have four central focal elements that we call 'pillars';

DOI: 10.4324/9781032721293-7

namely creativity, sustainability, resilience and fair treatment of stakeholders.[1] The chapter discusses each of these pillars, the connections between them and their interactions with a range of external forces (environmental, societal, economic and technological). Deserved confidence flows from confidence in the way a company situates itself on and across such pillars - including the way it shapes its strategic intent and its associated operational activities as it engages with external forces.

Ideally, a company or other organisation within society, and the society of which it is a part/member should share the same (societal) values. However, in practice, a company's values and those of society may not be identical at any point in time and can be in tension rather than in agreement or equilibrium – with the company wanting to influence society and vice versa. A company that does not have identical values or place the same weight as society across the four pillars is not necessarily undeserving of confidence. This is for the auditor to decide given the circumstances and intentions of both the company and society. It is a dynamic relationship between the company and society, with the auditor seeking to make it a positive dynamic. It is also important to recognise that these values are qualities (and not just financial quantities) and that values in the sense of financial or other numbers can only ever be evidence of, or in part represent, the strength of the underlying qualities possessed by the company. It is the underlying qualities (the realities) that matter whilst the assessment and representation of those qualities is made by the auditor based upon the available relevant evidence, including financial information. Accordingly, instead of the audit supporting the status of the financial statements, it is the financial statements that provide supporting evidence for the audit of the status of the company in terms of deserved confidence.

Figure 7.1 is our diagrammatic representation of how a limited company could be seen by the auditor, incorporating, at its head, the four pillars of deserved confidence. At the base of Figure 7.1 is the reality faced by the company in terms of the external, interrelated, pressures or forces enabling or constraining its development: namely, environmental, societal, economic and technological forces. They operate upon the business but, at the same time, the business impacts on them.

In Figure 7.1 the business provides two channels between reality and its representation; channels that provide two sources of evidence to support assessments of deserved confidence. The first (left-hand) channel is through the business activity itself – the purposeful pathways and disruptions. Evidence of this underlying business activity primarily takes the form of qualitative descriptions or indications of what the business does (its pathways), why (the purpose of the business pathway), and how that purpose is influenced by disruptions flowing from the external forces. Evidence is based, for instance, upon discussion and upon direct observation and experience of the company's

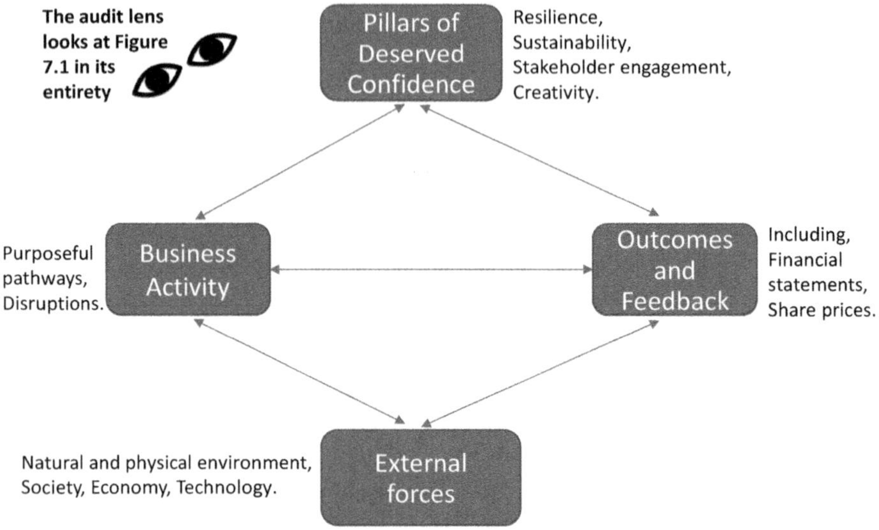

FIGURE 7.1 **The auditor's representation of a limited company and the pursuit of deserved confidence.**

operations, but is also supported by understanding the relations with external forces, with the pillars, and with outcomes and accompanying feedback.

The second (right-hand) channel between the external forces and the pillars is concerned with outcomes of/feedback on the business activity. The feedback is not only the company's financial statements, together with the underlying production numbers and market prices, but also takes other forms. These other forms can flow from the pillars and include, for example, customer surveys, credit ratings and analyst reports that relate to stakeholder engagement. The two-headed arrow between the pillars and outcomes/feedback treats the assessment of the four pillars as a form of feedback, with the outcomes themselves feeding forward to inform that assessment. Feedback can also relate to the external forces such as the impact of the business on the environment and vice versa. For quoted companies the share price is another form of feedback.

Whilst the right-hand channel comprises primarily numerical (quantitative) evidence, the left-hand (qualitative) channel comprises purposeful pathways implemented by the company to respond to disruption from external forces (their threats and opportunities) with the ultimate purpose being deserved confidence. The financial numbers (a key part of the right-hand channel) should relate to and inform the purposeful pathways and disruptions but the financials' role and relevance differ depending upon the purpose of the pathway and the nature of disruption. Together, the two channels result in the auditor considering connections with and between the purposeful pathways and disruptions and their impact/outcomes (the feedback, both financial and non-financial).

The core intent of the audit is to see the company (1) interacting with the (various) external forces that impinge on/enable its operations and (2) addressing the component pillars of what constitutes deserved confidence, so as to assess whether the company is suitably resilient in the present context, sustainable in terms of the future context, responsibly engaged with its stakeholders and sufficiently creative. This requires the auditor to have in view and engage with the entirety of the network - a holistic requirement shown graphically by the inclusion of the audit lens or 'eye' in Figure 7.1.

Whilst management run the business, the auditor sees the running of the business, through the audit lens provided by Figure 7.1, as a mediation between the external forces and the four pillars. If the auditor's thinking follows Figure 7.1, then it is plausible that management, if wanting to earn the auditor's deserved confidence, might be persuaded to think in the same terms. However, in the company's annual report, management make their own claims regarding resilience, sustainability, stakeholder engagement and creativity. These claims and accompanying discussion with management will provide evidence for the auditor; but if thinking differently is the key to audit independence, this may well require the auditor to report separately on such matters.

In this chapter we give an assessment of each of the four pillars in turn, although, as the discussion will reveal, the pillars are deeply inter-connected and, consequently, no particular significance can be given to the order in which they are presented. Indeed, there is a lot of inter-connection going on throughout Figure 7.1. This can be illustrated by comparing the lower half of Figure 7.1 to the FEB network (financials, environment, business) introduced in Chapter 2. 'Financials' have become 'outcomes and feedback', the environment has extended to include all of the external forces and business (activity) now incorporates purposeful pathways and disruption. In Chapter 2 it was shown that the financials, the environment and business can each serve not just as an entity (which is potentially subject to audit), but also as a channel/intermediary or as a (force) field. In assessing the FEB network, it was emphasised that it was not possible to do an audit of one entity or element in such a network without an accompanying assessment of the other elements. F, E and B are a conjugate threesome.

Figure 7.1's version of the FEB network is expanded by the incorporation of the 'pillars of deserved confidence'. To audit these pillars (and, through the pillars, to assess deserved confidence) requires an assessment of the other elements in the network. Under present arrangements, there is an audit of the company's financial statements but consideration should be extended to other forms of feedback including an assessment of the company's share price as might currently be conducted by an investor or investment analyst. In terms of the external forces, it is primarily the company's relations with the physical and natural environment that receives the greatest (formal) attention from the auditor but this should also be extended to the other forces. The audit of business pathways and their relations with disruption and the financials will typically be considered as a focus of internal audit, but the external auditor will also perform some of this work. What is typically missing and what we are advocating here is the audit of deserved confidence and the company's standing in relation to the four central pillars through which any consideration of deserved confidence is framed.

Setting the purpose of the audit in terms of an assessment of deserved confidence gives the audit an essentially integrative and holistic quality. It requires the auditor to consider the purposefulness of the company's chosen pathways and their contribution and capabilities in terms of providing the requisite levels of creativity, sustainability, resilience and engaged stakeholders (the four pillars) that lead to or drive deserved confidence. The 'two headed' arrows in Figure 7.1 are there to emphasise that all the connections in Figure 7.1 are reciprocal.

Accordingly, in assessing the company's standing across the four pillars, Figure 7.1 could be turned on its head – such that it is the company's relations with the 'environment' that are capable of being considered as a primary driver of the confidence in which it is held/ seen to be deserving. We take the term 'environment' to include not just the natural and physical environment but society, the economy and technology – such that it is also possible, in this different framing, to deem that a company that is improving its impact upon the physical and natural environment, promoting society's goals, improving the economy and advancing/adopting technology is deserving of our confidence. The respective emphasis here will likely vary across audited companies depending on the context in which they operate, with pillars and forces combining and interacting in differing ways. This will not just influence the way in which stakeholder interests are framed but also impact on the capacities and propensities that companies have for self-determination and being proactive rather than just responsive to the circumstances they encounter. For example, a chosen strategic direction can gain or lose its sense of purposefulness as notions and values of what is 'enlightened' corporate behaviour transform, or as disruptions are encountered and cause a re-assessment of the company's overall standing and position.

As such, the assessment of deserved confidence by the auditor can be classified as the outcome of the auditor's consideration and contemplation of the nature of interactions between the pillars and external forces, and how those interactions have been shaped by the business through its purposeful pathways, in response to disruptions and resulting outcomes, both financial and non-financial.

In the analysis that follows, the chapter considers each pillar in turn and discusses its key relations with the other pillars and with the external forces.

Resilience

The Brydon Report (2019, pp. 80–82) supported the idea of a resilience statement. Recommendation 18.1.2 (p. 81) is "That the Board make a Resilience Statement that incorporates, enhances and builds on the [current] Going Concern and Viability Statements". Brydon saw the resilience statement as coming from the Board and being commented upon by auditors, but it could come directly from the auditors, perhaps as part of the audit report.[2] There are strong connections between resilience and the strength of the other pillars, particularly sustainability; the purpose of resilience being in some sense to make the business sustainable.

An assessment of resilience should consider both the likely need for resilience, and the resilience available. Likely need derives from the risk of various disruptions and the possible impact of these upon sustainability. An assessment of likely need requires a good knowledge of the outside forces. The resilience available can be addressed through a series of probing questions. Does the company have the creativity that might be needed in the event of disruption? Is the stakeholder engagement strong enough that key stakeholders, including management, will stick with the company? In particular, does the management have the necessary tenacity and ability to deal with disruption? These are all questions that address the relations between resilience and the other pillars. Further questions relate more directly to potential disruption and to the financial numbers. Does the company have pathways (including policies and practices) to deal with possible disruption and does the company have the financial strength to deal with, or take advantage of, disruption? Thus resilience, both financial and non-financial, is built up and judged by reference to future possible disruptions and their likely impact.

Without creativity and stakeholder engagement, financial strength alone may not provide resilience and yet there is a clear financial dimension to resilience. The 'traditional' balance sheet items of fixed assets plus working capital minus long-term debt might taken together be regarded as a 'fund' available in the event of disruption. In particular having a store of liquid net assets, especially cash, to fall back on helps. So when (reversionary) disruption occurs and resilience is called upon to return the business to its pre-disruption levels of activity and profit, the necessary finance is there. The cash flow issues created by the disruption can be tackled by applying the existing cash or other liquid assets of the fund, by the company eliminating or reducing dividends which would otherwise be paid from the fund, or by redirecting the resources of the business including the net assets to alternative activities that are less impacted by the disruption. Any or all of these might impact stakeholders; notably any reduction of dividends might affect the share price.

Shareholders play an important role with regard to resilience. A business does not fund the totality of its activities through debt as this does not give sufficient resilience when there is disruption to the continuity of the business. A business copes with disruption better when it is funded, at least in significant part, by shares on which a return (dividend) does not always have to be paid. Moreover, share capital, unlike debt, does not have a set time for repayment. Thus, the more that a business is funded by shares rather than debt (the lower the leverage), the better the business is able to cope with disruption because of its greater capacity to retain cash.

All of the issues in this section can be covered in a 'statement of resilience' connecting resilience to the risk of disruption, evaluating whether the size/strength and nature of the existing resilience is appropriate and highlighting the pathways in place to make resilience more appropriate to the company's circumstances. A key purpose of shareholder financial capital is to provide financial resilience and this gives the resilience pillar a financial dimension. Of course, resilience is not just a question of funding but also of whether the stakeholders, and particularly the management, have the necessary loyalty, tenacity and ability to deal with disruption. To a significant extent therefore, the statement of resilience should assess the strength of the stakeholder network, including the motives of the shareholders and the company's ability and willingness to respond to the emerging stakeholder landscape consequent to environmental, societal, economic and technological forces. This assessment cannot be made purely by considering financial matters.

For the assessment of resilience there is a strong connection with sustainability. The function of resilience is primarily to act as a buffer between disruption on the one hand and sustainability on the other. However, resilience can be associated with not just the pillar of sustainability but also with that of 'creativity', especially whenever innovation is the key to dealing with/avoiding negative disruption, or creating positive disruption.

The resurgence of Rolls-Royce since the Covid-19 pandemic is a case of resilience that goes beyond a return to pre-Covid levels; a resilience brought about by new, determined, management with different ideas and improved financial structures. Resilience relies upon a coming together of personal and financial strength. Resilience could be treated as if it was a form of insurance designed to give comfort that, should a disruption occur, it can be managed and dealt with. In this sense, all companies are in the insurance business. However, to reiterate, financial resilience by itself is seldom enough, especially when faced with 'game-changing' disruptions.

Resilience in the form of both strong finances and a determined management, capable of creative thinking and of taking a well-considered business risk, is key to survival. By way of contrast, potentially reversible disruption can become game-changing given inadequate resilience in terms of management attention and funding; witness the banking sector and the financial crash of 2007/2008 that was driven by excessive risk taking and a failure to give sufficient consideration to the sustainability of profits being earned and the resilience, especially financial, of banking business models.

Sustainability

Understanding the pillars and their relationship with the forces is a key function of audit. This is particularly the case for sustainability. A business is considered unsustainable if continuing its current activities or level of activity is incompatible with the future needs of society, and it is unlikely to be able to switch to other activities that are compatible. An assessment of sustainability requires consideration of future changes, and the company's response to such changes, in the environment, the economy, the rate of technological development and what society sees as the fair treatment of stakeholders and their interests.

Business activities differ in that they have different environmental issues and are exposed to different social concerns, different macro-economic variables and different technologies. These are the four external forces to which companies are subject. Companies differentiate themselves by creating their own stakeholder networks that have different susceptibilities to these forces. The forces are pervasive across the four pillars and impact through their potential to generate both positive disruptions (opportunities) and negative disruptions (threats). To predict disruption and its impact requires understanding of the pillars and their relationships with such forces. Disruptions caused by the forces can impact all of the four pillars but are illustratively discussed in the following paragraphs by focusing on the forces' potential impacts on business sustainability.

Understanding the physical and natural environment

The connection between business and the natural environment is very high-profile at the time of writing and any company failing to meet societal expectations is clearly exposed in terms of the sustainability of its business. However, the auditor must also consider the continuity of current trends in societal attitudes and the possibility of future disruptions accelerating, decelerating or even reversing the trend. Disruption follows from a new understanding of connections and the most striking example in recent times of a disruption is the realisation of the connection between climate change and certain human activities facilitated or carried out by business.

It is also evident that there can be a significant interval between recognition by the science community and recognition by the wider community, including investors. Appropriate foresight and highlighting by the auditor might help to reduce this interval. Relations between business and the environment is an excellent example of reciprocity. Business activity shapes the natural environment. In turn, the environment, along with society's sentiments regarding the environment, shapes business. In a similar fashion, the securing of deserved confidence rests upon how well the business anticipates, assesses and controls any adverse impact it has on the environment and any adverse impact that a changing environment may come to have on the business.

Understanding society

Societal sustainability risk is the risk that the company's activity is not sustainable due to changing societal attitudes. To understand this risk, the auditor needs to understand society, giving an explicit connection between the audit of the company and the audit of society. We cannot complete the audit of the company without an assessment of society, at least to a level at which societal issues relevant to the company audit are understood. If we take society to exhibit both similarities and differences between individuals and between groupings within society, then the audit of society is to understand how similarities and differences can come together to generate both economic and social progress (and potential disruptions).

In one sense, the construction of society is similar to the construction of an audit. Audit evidence has to exhibit both similarities and differences; the similarities allow evidence to come together to give a more complete picture whilst reconciliation of the differences gives us new understanding. In a societal context, similarity can be expressed as uniformity or equality, and differences as variation or diversity.

At the extreme, equality and diversity are apparent opposites. If everyone is the same there is no diversity and if everyone is different there is no equality. Too much emphasis on equality can come at the expense of economic progress and the economic growth that may be necessary to tackle many social problems. Too much emphasis on diversity can come at the expense of social cohesion, creating potential social problems and a sense of unfairness as different groups may need to be treated differently for differences to sustain. The company auditor needs to make a judgement as to how the (apparent) opposites of equality and diversity are being managed at both the company and societal level.

It is not enough for either society or the company to state that they are in favour of equality and diversity and to produce a list of measures promoting each. They must explain how the measures connect the two opposites to best effect (e.g., so that neither disadvantages the other); and how, therefore, together they contribute to both economic progress and a fairer society.

Where the company and society are diverging on this issue there is a direct sustainability risk for the company since the company may face legislation or regulation forcing change, or a backlash from stakeholders unwilling to deal with the company. However, if society does not find the right balance, then there is sustainability risk for (either or both) a harmonious society and for the economy; and hence an indirect sustainability risk for the company. The auditor needs to assess the impact of future societal attitudes on the sustainability of the company. By explaining this assessment, the audit can also be performative and influential in enabling both the company and society to find the right balance.[3]

An excellent example of opposites working together rather than against each other is discussed by Ridley in his book assessing 'nature via nurture' (Ridley, 2003). He explains how the apparent opposites of 'nature' (our natural talents in the form of our genes), and 'nurture' (in the form of our experiences) come together to shape the human beings that we are.[4] His discussion extends to the issue of fairness. He states

> There is heavy irony in the fact that the more egalitarian a society is, the more innate factors will matter......in a world where everybody gets the same education, the best jobs will go to those with the most native talent......Is the world more fair when every bright kid, even the one from the slums, gets a place at the best university, and so gets the best job? Is it fair on the stupid ones left behind?......a meritocracy is not a fair place...... Society stratified by wealth is unfair, because the rich can buy comforts and privileges. But a society stratified by intelligence is also unfair because the clever can buy comforts and privileges.
>
> (p. 263)

And, yet, if the most talented do not get the jobs that require their talent, the economy will suffer and this might affect everyone. If wealth does not buy comforts and privileges, how much incentive is there for the talented to succeed? If the pattern of ability and talent in society does not match the needs of the economy or of society, what is the incentive for the talented to adapt?

There may be a connection (possibly a creative tension) between a 'fair' society and a 'successful' economy that requires understanding, imagination and management at both the corporate and societal levels. It is important to search for the balance point where fairness promotes economic success and economic success promotes fairness. This may involve challenging ideas on what constitutes fairness and what constitutes economic success. The auditor's understanding of the issue can play a role here.

It is in the area of social sustainability that the auditor most clearly becomes an actor or influencer rather than an observer. For example, Humphrey (2020) highlights the use by payday lenders of exorbitant interest rates (reaching 1460 percent) and questions the passive role of auditors whereby financial statements disclosing profits made from charging such rates of interest were deemed 'true and fair' without any accompanying consideration of, or comment on, the underlying fairness of such loan charges and the extent to which such a business model was sustainable. Additionally, large numbers of borrowers who do not or cannot repay their loans are hugely subsidised by those who do and both groups experience substantial emotional and financial stress. The auditor of the lender might recognise that such a situation is unlikely to be considered appropriate by society and choose to highlight the substantial sustainability risk in their assessment of the extent to which the lender was deserving of confidence.

Understanding the economy

Understanding and influencing the economy, its interaction with society and the implications of those interactions for the company and its sustainability are some of the biggest challenges for the company audit. A sense of unfairness around inequality of wealth and income weakens social cohesion that, in turn, can feed through to weaker economic performance – highlighting the connectivity between the economy and society and consequently between the social and economic 'dynamics' of audit. A stronger society and a stronger economy need stronger companies whilst stronger companies need a stronger society and economy. The auditor of a company must be aware of these connections and the opportunities and risks they present.

As a general rule, social problems are a drag on economic performance (and vice versa) and so it is logical to divert some of the country's economic performance to 'invest in' tackling social problems. However, 'moral hazard' can be an issue here. The idea of moral hazard is that trying to 'invest' in the reduction of social problems can serve to accentuate those problems. For example, if support is increased for those out of work, more workers might choose to give up work. The extent of moral hazard depends upon the 'values' of members of society and in particular their 'work ethic'.

Hence, assessing and securing deserved confidence in a company and its sustainability requires understanding of both the economy and society (or economies and societies) in which the company operates and/or to which it is exposed. The question addressed in this section is 'how is the sustainability of the company affected if there are changes in the macro-economic environment(s)'?

The auditor of the company considers the economy in trying to understand the connections between various rates and levels of economic performance, including the future trajectory of the economy and its implications for society and the company. In essence, the auditor is assessing the economy's scale of creativity, sustainability, resilience and stakeholder engagement. For a global company, these matters should be considered for each country in which the company or its stakeholders operate. For example, if the current exchange rate of the Chinese currency (informally fixed against the US dollar) cannot be sustained then this would have consequences for all companies that depend upon Chinese suppliers.

Disruption to both the economy and a company operating in an economy can come from inflation, interest, taxation and foreign exchange rate changes. These changes, in turn, connect with other economic indicators such as GDP, employment, trade and fiscal deficits. Some may question whether an assessment of economic impact upon a global company such as Rolls-Royce is feasible but it is assessment that has to be routinely made, for example, by investors. To an extent, therefore, the auditor is putting themselves in the position of, and providing assistance to, the investor.

In *The End of Alchemy* (King, 2016), Mervyn King, a former Governor of the Bank of England, distinguishes stability and sustainability. He argues that stability of politically sensitive economic rates (including interest, inflation, tax and foreign exchange) is government's priority but that such stability, if achieved, might not be sustainable in the longer term when there is a persistent imbalance in the economy. If so, this presents a direct challenge to an auditor trying to assess the sustainability of a company's economic environment.

In the case of the UK, for instance, there is a long-standing trading imbalance. It follows that any company with a strong export performance is making a strong contribution to the economy. If sterling is supported by the sale of UK assets and bonds to overseas buyers then the current exchange rate is unlikely to be sustainable in the long run since the country will most likely run out of assets to sell and the market for its bonds would be weaker. This, in turn, has implications for other rates. In such circumstances, the challenge is one of judging sustainability risk, with this risk being lower for a UK company that is a net exporter compared to one that is heavily dependent on imports. But challenges can also bring rewards. For instance, by highlighting sustainability risk and encouraging corporate behaviour that has a more positive economic impact, the overall business and societal significance of audit would be enhanced.

It is a complication for any low interest or low tax rate policy if the policy results in further increased demand for imports rather than a surge in UK investment in the domestic economy. If a weakening currency leads to price rises for imported goods, then the inflation rate would rise, possibly prompting the central bank to raise nominal interest rates (but not necessarily real interest rates), and any low tax or low interest policy would not be sustainable. The auditor needs to assess the extent to which the company is exposed to changes in exchange, interest or tax rates. In respect of interest rates, a company is more exposed if it is highly leveraged and also if it does not score well on environmental criteria in so far as banks are bringing such criteria into their interest rate charging policy.

The short-lived, 2022, UK government of Liz Truss focused upon tax rates (cuts) rather than interest or inflation rates on the basis that this would encourage entrepreneurship and economic growth. The money markets were not convinced and increased the government's cost of borrowing substantially. Her policy would have created a substantial fiscal deficit, at least in the short term, since her administration did not specify cuts in governmental expenditure. Modern Monetary Theory (MMT) suggests that government deficits do not matter because any government that has its own currency can 'print' money to pay the bills. Nevertheless, Stephanie Kelton, an MMT economist, concedes that "once an economy reaches its full employment potential, any additional spending – whether it comes from the government, the domestic private sector (US households and businesses), or the rest of the world (foreign demand for our exports) – carries inflation risk" (Kelton, 2021, pp. 256–7). This implies that fiscal deficits are not sustainable unless the supply side of the economy can cope. The problem is, at least in the UK, the tendency for easy money (whether for the government, individuals or businesses) to stimulate demand rather than supply (investment); an undermining of financial discipline leading to additional monies not being used wisely.

It seems that to central bankers, stability for some rates is more important than for others and low stable inflation (sound money) is a priority, whilst interest rates are merely a tool to enable the target inflation rate to be attained. But the impact of interest rates upon investment also needs to be considered, especially as expanding the supply potential of the economy is so important. In the UK, the interest rate and inflation have gone up and down together but the real interest rate has been low and on occasion ultra-low or negative. It must be doubtful whether an economy in need of many forms of investment in order to sustain itself, let alone grow, can do so on the basis of such low real returns for its domestic investors (savers).

A reasonable assumption might be that low interest rates would make more projects attractive and increase investment. However, it appears that lowering interest rates, like tax cuts, may have more impact upon consumption and upon asset prices than upon investment. For instance, notably since the financial crash of 2007/2008, exceptionally low (real) interest rates have been associated with exceptionally low (real) investment for the future. If creativity is key to the revival of the economy, then the number one audit priority becomes to promote creativity.

Companies need to be creative to create new investment opportunities capable of providing and encouraging new investment and investors with high real rates of return. This is a crucial contribution that companies can make to the economy. A successful, productive economy is not singularly characterised by ultra-low real interest rates, nor just by high levels of investment. It is characterised by high levels of investment in high returning projects that give an appropriate incentive for delayed consumption. Pinpointing what a successful economy looks like carries over to assessments of what a successful company looks like and the degree of confidence that should be placed in it. Like an economy, a business that does not engage with risk taking is unlikely to be sustainable in a dynamic business environment and, hence, becomes a high risk. Business success requires a willingness to run a well-considered risk.[5]

A related argument is that in so far as the interest rate is the price of time (Chancellor, 2023), then it is a signal to the economy (by society or its central bank) as to how society values the future relative to the present. A lower interest rate signals that society is valuing the future less than before. The question is why would an economy respond to such a signal by increasing its growth rate so as to benefit a less valued future? To expect both low interest rates and high growth rates might be unrealistic.

It seems that stability, recovery or improvement in one part of the economy can simply disguise the fact that an economic problem has been moved elsewhere, and this 'elsewhere' is typically to the future. Economic management easily becomes a form of burden shifting. For instance, the UK government has taken on overseas borrowing with the effect that a significant proportion of future GDP will go overseas, shifting the burden of debt to future generations. It also leaves the UK with a less resilient economy.

The UK economy might have benefited from conserving more of its GDP to deal with disruptions. Instead, the UK has dealt with disruptions through borrowing and this reduces still further the UK's resilience. If the UK economy not only lacks resilience, but is also deemed to be high in terms of sustainability risk, over-promises its stakeholders and, due to low investment, is low on future growth prospects (that is, it does not have high creativity value), then any UK company that is resilient, low on sustainability risk, does not over-promise and invests on the basis of creativity will contribute to a strengthening of the UK economy. If a company invests in its people, making them more talented and creative, then it is making a contribution not just to the economy but to society. Companies that make a strong contribution to the economy and to society are, in principle, going to be more deserving of our confidence.

While the economy and society are deeply intertwined, the nature of their connection can be controversial. For example, the impact of an ultra-low (sometimes negative in real terms) interest rate policy on 'well-offness' is not entirely straightforward. Piketty (2014) held that the rate of return on capital (r) exceeding the economic growth rate (g) was a primary cause of wealth inequality. According to Piketty, falling returns and interest rates reduce inequality. However, this might not hold if growth is also reduced as a consequence of falling returns. Chancellor (2023, pp. 216–7) challenged Piketty by arguing that when interest rates are lowered, capital values of assets increase – benefiting those who are already asset rich. The wealthy are also likely to be able to borrow, or have savings, to invest in more assets so as to benefit further from any prolonged period of declining interest rates. The likely effect, he argues, is to increase rather than decrease inequality.

Since the introduction of low interest rates consequent to the 2007/2008 financial crisis, the value of assets relative to GDP has risen substantially – implying that the wealth holders have done well relative to income earners. But the value of assets is a capital sum whilst GDP (income) is a flow. Not all wealth holders are in the same position. For those reliant upon income from assets, such as those holding a pension pot, the key question is whether asset values have increased sufficiently to maintain the (interest) income that the assets provide. If they haven't, then, from an income perspective, such people are not better off. However, for those who do not need assets to provide income it is a different story and they may be able to spend any capital gains without threatening the sustainability of their current standard of living.

The problem for the economy and for society is any performance measurement that sees performance in terms of capital gain (and in so far as such gains have been readily achievable) can promote the diversion of the country's brightest and best into the search for such gains, regardless of whether they are matched by the development and underpinning of income-generating companies.

Learning from the 2007/2008 financial crash, at the company (financial institution) level, any such mis-specification of performance and diversion of talent are likely to lead to a financial crisis for the company and this is a risk that must be recognised by the auditor in the assessment of sustainability and deserved confidence. In respect of the 2007/2008 crash, the mis-specification of performance together with the lack of recognition or warning by the auditors ultimately led to a widespread economic crisis from which we are still suffering. It was a crisis in which society as a whole, rather than those responsible, bore the consequences.

In a critical commentary on the management of the (UK) economy, Chancellor (2023, p. 187) states that "we have come to live in a controlled environment, with its fake money, fake interest rates, fake economy, fake jobs and fake politicians". This controlled environment of 'fake' might promote fake companies with fake (financial) reporting in the sense that the reports make the company look good but, in reality, do not justify confidence in the company.

Audit should serve both society and the economy by being the 'promoter of the genuine' and of action to remove the 'fake'. If everything is fake then a fake society becomes the reality! To protect reality from this fate, it is necessary for some things, protected and supported by audit, not to be fake. The audit can seek to detect fakeness through identifying inconsistencies between the fake and the genuine, with the overall justification of purpose resting in the notion that what is fake is ultimately not sustainable. The audit needs to reverse any trend towards Chancellor's 'controlled environment of fake' from becoming a reality.

Understanding technology

A further consideration in terms of sustainability and sustainability risk is the potential impact of changing technology. Problems can come from backing or developing the wrong new technology (as once happened to Rolls-Royce in respect of carbon blades for the RB211 engine – materials matter to engine performance and the carbon blades disintegrated in a bird strike), or it can come from failure to spot and back a winning new technology or its adoption.

Research and development pathways relative to those of competitors are relevant, as is the possible development of products by those not yet considered as competitors. Technology is a key factor in the competitive landscape. Creativity as a driver of research and development pathways is going to shape the future of the company and of society and the economy. Technology connects to both sustainability and growth and to the likely need for resilience and adaptability in the face of change. Technology can bring benefits that support sustainability and growth but also risks. For example, the more we dismantle the off-line in favour of the on-line, the more susceptible we become to computer viruses. A computer viral pandemic could indeed be game-changing, with society, post-Covid-19, having become more dependent upon the internet and more exposed to computer viruses. The one issue is a platform for the next and the issues are not independent. Another connection between technology and increased risk is the spread of social media and the consequent risk of deterioration in mental health. In recent times this possible connection has attracted much attention.

There is also much contemporary interest in the future impact of artificial intelligence (AI), with the possibility that AI might one day provide everything we need, leaving humans to pursue hobbies that give pleasure rather than the work demanded by the economic and political systems. However, there will likely always be scarcities such as land, human (emotional) intelligence and probably expertise in AI. Economic and political systems need to continue to allocate scarcity. AI might help us to allocate scarcity better but it is unlikely to remove all scarcity. Moreover, given that AI is dynamic, there will be a continuing need for talented individuals to develop improved AI, to find new uses for it and to find ways of auditing and controlling it, without relying on people's interest in AI as a hobby. It can be dangerous to assume that AI or any computer system works as intended; witness the 700 or so wrongful convictions of postmasters by the UK Post Office on the basis of information given by its now notorious computer system, Horizon.

Nevertheless, it is important that the future impact of AI on a company is considered along with whether this is an opportunity or a threat. Either way it is likely to impact the assessment of sustainability. AI, by recognising patterns and connections in data much more quickly than humans, can be highly efficient. In the sense of recognising new patterns in data, it can be creative but much depends upon the quality of the data and the quality of the algorithm. If the data and algorithms were to be largely generated by the results of past AI application, then the AI might be performative (in the sense of inducing conformity) rather than creative (in the sense of stimulating innovation).[6] Whilst most human actions are done from memory the human brain also deals with critical or creative functions. It becomes important to recognise when actions can be based upon memory of (conformity with) past actions and when they require new and different thinking. The concern is that if, in circumstances where new thinking is required or would be beneficial, we rely upon AI that is trained on the basis of past actions then we will not progress. Moreover, our ability to think differently will not progress and might decline through lack of use.

Awareness and understanding of how the positive and negative disruptive forces of technology are being understood and managed, at both a company and a societal level, are important considerations in assessing the scale to which the audited company is deserving of our confidence. It also serves to reinforce the significance of the connections between the four identified pillars of deserved confidence, namely, sustainability, creativity, resilience and stakeholder engagement. Sustainability requires investment in creativity if there is to be a pipeline of new products to maintain the business when the existing products become tired. At the same time, the company needs a resilience fund of cash and liquid assets to see it through unexpected disruptions and perhaps to take advantage of unexpected opportunities. Sustainability also needs to maintain the engagement of creative and resilient stakeholders, an engagement that will have both direct and connected financial implications.

If the audit, and in particular the auditor's understanding of the external forces, is influential upon management then such understanding can lower the sustainability risk. If so, the audit, in judging sustainability risk, is, in part, shaping the foundations of the audit's future performance and influence. One argument of our book is that audit should promote understanding and that, in this regard, audit is pervasive – in effect, becoming a further external force established to understand, control and manage the other forces that impact on, and are impacted by, the company being audited.

Stakeholder engagement

The four external forces (environmental, societal, economic, technological) influence a company through its stakeholder network and so to deal with these forces, the company needs a strong and engaged stakeholder network. A company deserves confidence if it has engaged supportive stakeholders relevant to its purpose and treats them fairly. The auditor needs to search for evidence of the continuing engagement, support, relevant expertise and financial health of each stakeholder group.

The stakeholder network is formed of propositions to stakeholder groups including customers, employees and suppliers. It is the stakeholders who execute the company's pathways so that the business activity and the stakeholder network are deeply connected. Propositions cover not just the pathways in which the stakeholder is invited to participate but also the financial consequences of such participation. Stakeholder propositions need to be attractive for each of the stakeholder groups and it is crucial that the auditor considers the strength of the propositions in the light of changing and prospective market and competitive conditions. There is competition for customers, suppliers, employees, management etc. and, thus, competition manifests itself through the stakeholder net – which changes in response. We can call this the changing stakeholder landscape within which stakeholder propositions have to remain attractive and competitive.

The stakeholder net can be thought of as connecting stakeholders together through a series of propositions in order to give the company substance. Thus, the pathways that are presented for stakeholders to perform or participate in should not just be attractive to specific stakeholder groups but should bring stakeholders together and help to manage or resolve any tensions between them.

Returning to Figure 7.1, it is possible to see the pathways and disruptions as having varying financial consequences for stakeholders, and those consequences will in turn impact the participation of stakeholders in the pathways. There is scope here for thinking differently about stakeholder propositions. For instance, in their paper 'Reimagining profits and stakeholder capital to address tensions among stakeholders', Hatherly et al. (2020) suggest that any reported profits coming from wealth transfer between stakeholders (rather than wealth creation for all stakeholders) should be 'switched off' for purposes of performance measurement and distribution and retained in a stakeholder capital fund. The idea is that stakeholders adversely affected by wealth transfer are given a stake in this fund, helping to reduce tension and encouraging stakeholders to come together in building a stronger, more sustainable company in the long-term interests of all. In so far as the four forces (i.e., the environment, society, the economy and technology) operate on and through stakeholders, then, at a different level, the stakeholder net can be thought of as bringing together these four forces.

With regard to the present, an assessment of the stakeholder network might be based upon current stakeholder propositions compared to opportunities elsewhere, but also upon experience of management's behaviour towards stakeholders. This would be indicated, for example, by customer reviews and reviews by employees. With regard to the future, a developing stakeholder net is essential to capture value from creativity and growth – and not only formal promises but also the less formal prospects the company provides play a part in this. The stakeholder net needs to adapt, innovate and develop.

Prospects, which are in effect informal promises to share the company's future with its stakeholders, can provide an important element of the relationship with customers, employees, suppliers and other stakeholders.

In addition to prospects, there are formal contractual or legislated promises which can include, for example, a defined benefit pension scheme, deferred tax,[7] derivatives and warranties. The outstanding balances on such contracts give a financial dimension (recognised on a company's balance sheet) to the pillar of stakeholder engagement. For the most part, such formal promises are legacy items relating to business conducted in the past but which have acquired a higher or lower value than was originally anticipated and consequently represent a change in the sharing of the future between shareholders and other stakeholders (or, alternatively, a change in the value of the protection (insurance) provided for non-shareholders against future downside risks).

Promises could also include formal agreements relating to future business such as agreements to share future profits. A company's portfolio of such promises is, in effect, a portfolio of financial contracts, each of which is managed by the company or its appointed manager through a purposeful pathway (with potential disruptions) crafted for the promise in question; but the overall management of the portfolio of promises is through the company's Board. The different promises – pensions, warranties, deferred tax, derivatives – form a portfolio of uncertainties and, consequently, may be looked at in that light; that is, any negative correlation between such risks might reduce the overall risk of the portfolio.

The defined benefit pension scheme is perhaps the clearest example of a relevant financial contract. Pensions and other promises often have susceptibility to future disruptions. The audit engages or draws on expertise in each of the different promises to enhance understanding of the relationship between their valuation and their unpredictability.[8] Formal legacy promises are agreements made with stakeholders in the past to be fulfilled in the future. Their value changes over time as circumstances change and they are valued at the best estimate of their current value. The volatility of such values increases if there is high leverage (for instance, the pension fund balance responds disproportionately to a change in the value of the pension fund assets). In this case the company's resilience may be impacted by the pension fund. Another connection is with sustainability risk. Where there are volatile macro-economic factors (whether they be rates of interest, tax, inflation or foreign exchange), it is possible through derivatives to smooth (manage/normalise) earnings but whilst this reduces the (apparent) sustainability risk, the risk (and measurement difficulty) is passed to valuing those derivatives. Because the uncertainty may be less visible doesn't mean it matters less. The implication might be that the auditor should be sceptical of any extensive use of derivatives.

Towards an overall evaluation of the stakeholder net

Promises form one part of an overall assessment of the strength of the stakeholder network (its influence, strength and foresight). In recent times activities such as the end of defined benefit pensions, outsourcing and the growth of the 'gig' economy, the exploitation of long-term customers and changes in corporation tax rates have altered the stakeholder landscape. In one sense, they have helped company resilience by providing the company with more funds and greater flexibility. However, there is a trade-off here in that such activities can transfer wealth and security from other stakeholders to shareholders and to those directors whose interests are (supposedly) aligned with shareholders through long-term incentive plans. Hence these activities are potentially damaging to the strength of the stakeholder net and any profits that flow from these actions may not be sustainable or might need to be reversed before opportunities for growth can be taken.[9]

Such activities may serve not only to transfer wealth to shareholders but to transfer wealth between different non-shareholder stakeholder groups or between different sub-groups within a stakeholder class. For example, off-shoring benefits customers and offshore workers at the expense of 'on-shore' employees. Adoption of robots and the development of AI will help employees with AI skills but replace the jobs of others. Thus, there is a complex pattern of winners and losers across national and skills boundaries.

In the longer term, this can create political difficulties and national government interference on behalf of the losers; losers that can of course include government itself. Government and the society that it represents are salient stakeholders in the corporate sector in a broad sense and the company should anticipate society's response to its treatment of stakeholders. It should try and do the right thing by society both as a matter of ethics and as 'enlightened' self-interest in building long-term reciprocal relations.[10]

Companies that treat their stakeholders well can suffer short-term pressure from less scrupulous competitors, including foreign competition from firms that do not subscribe to the same societal environment. There is an issue of resilience here that stakeholders may have to help with. As with the company itself, stakeholders have to be creative and adaptive – accepting, even embracing, change that might be essential for the longer-term 'progress' of the company and also the economy and society as a whole. Auditors may have a role here in highlighting this issue and how stakeholder relationships are impacting/will impact the sustainability of the company.

In this regard, it is important to recognise that stakeholder engagement is closely related to the other pillars of deserved confidence. A company's resilience, sustainability and creativity come in large measure from the ability to engage stakeholders possessing those qualities. Stakeholder propositions that are engaging can have both financial and non-financial elements or dimensions. For example, a company that overcharges its customers and underpays its employees and suppliers may, at least for now, show higher profits than its competitors but carries a higher risk of losing stakeholder engagement and hence a higher sustainability risk. Stakeholders can also be attracted by things beyond the financial such as a belief in what the company is trying to do (its purpose) or how it goes about it (the pathways), including its treatment of other stakeholders.

The basis of any assessment of the stakeholder net by the auditor needs to be explained. The evaluation is again challenging but is an opportunity to develop auditing and its value proposition to society as a whole, servicing the social foundations of the market and the company's 'licence' from society to operate.

Creativity: Leading to growth

Du Sautoy (2019, pp. 9–13) follows Boden (2003) in identifying three types of creativity. The first is *exploratory* creativity which according to Du Sautoy (pp. 9–10) "involves taking what is already there and exploiting its outer edges, extending the limits of what is possible while remaining bound by the rules". Thus, it is exploring from a base or platform of established rules. The second form of creativity involves *combination*, taking two completely different constructs and seeking to combine them. "Often the rules governing one world will suggest an interesting new framework for the other" (p, 10). The third form of creativity is *transformational.* "This describes those rare moments that are complete game changers......transformational moments hinge on changing the rules of the game or dropping an assumption that previous generations have been working under" (pp. 11–12).

To a significant extent, creativity drives growth and the company's future progress. A company deserves confidence if it is finding and taking opportunities to be creative and turning that creativity into growth. The ability to be creative and to grow the business on the basis of that creativity will be reflected in its openness to ideas, its commitment to research, the nature and success of its research and the development of the business on the basis of that success. Given that the outside forces are changing, some creative success may be required just to sustain the existing level of business. It is the potential (expected) future growth from the existing level of business that underpins the value of creativity. Creativity generated the company's products, existing and new, and it is the anticipated growth in these products, together with the potential for future products, that drives the value of creativity. Moreover, future growth should, in order to be sustainable, respond to expected future external forces so as, following Mayer (2021), to do no harm.

As with the other pillars, creativity has both a financial and non-financial dimension. Non-financial evidence is provided by an assessment of the future external forces and how existing products will respond, by a technical assessment of research and subsequent development of new and future products and by an assessment of how new products and existing products will interact with each other and with the external forces that are shaping the future. These non-financial assessments can be crucial and require the auditor to have access to abilities that are not financial. The financial dimension stems, for a quoted company, from the share price which indirectly gives the stock market's assessment of the value of creativity. Just as the auditor should challenge management on their reported profits, we argue that the auditor should apply an inquisitive mind to the market's (implied) assessment of the value of such creativity. Creativity and consequent growth prospects are highly material to investors since they often account for a major portion of the share price and market capitalisation. Creativity and growth also put a company in a good position to reward and obtain commitment from other stakeholders.

Concluding thoughts

This chapter has introduced audit as the provision of deserved confidence; an audit judgement based upon assessment of resilience, sustainability, stakeholder engagement and creativity – what we have classified as the four pillars of deserved confidence. A major consequence is that the 'matching up' of business activity and the financial statements as discussed in Chapter 6 is no longer the primary purpose and focus of the audit. Instead, the audit becomes an important source of feedback on business (activity) in terms of its impact on and relationship with the four pillars and external forces. This is the core analytical framing of the chapter captured in Figure 7.1, to which it is worth returning in summarising the chapter's contribution. The four pillars are shown at the top of the diagram, representing the core parameters for an assessment of deserved confidence. We have discussed each pillar in turn, recognising and emphasising their interconnectedness. At the base of Figure 7.1 are the four external forces (society, environment, economy, technology) that can be deemed capable of impacting on the pillars. The forces similarly have a vivid sense of connectivity, notably the mutual reliance of the economy and society, and we have provided illustrations of the level and nature of such connectivity through consideration of the impact of such forces on the pillar of sustainability.

Figure 7.1 represents the business and its activities as a process of navigation, constructing and pursuing purposeful pathways and responding to disruptions and their resulting consequences in ways that it believes are best. The role of the auditor is to determine the degree or scale to which such purposeful activities (i.e., the way the business is navigating between core pillars and forces) are collectively deserving of confidence.

Considering business activity in terms of purposeful pathways and disruption and their consequences provides one, largely qualitative, source of evidence of the connections between the pillars and the forces. Consideration of financial consequences and requirements provides predominantly quantitative evidence of the connections between pillars and forces, and in accordance with the analytical framing in Chapter 6, the auditor should be assessing and examining whether the quantitative and qualitative evidence of the business 'match up'; but matching up is not enough, the ultimate question being whether the evidence taken as a whole demonstrates the company's progression, both present and future. Figure 7.1 also reminds the reader of the overall importance of feedback on business activity and its capacity not only to reflect but also to shape the connections between the pillars and the forces. Audit is an important source of feedback.

In many respects, Figure 7.1 can be treated as audit's (the auditor's) mental model; a graphic representation of how the audit process is centred on understanding the nature and significance of the connections between the purposeful pathways and disruptions and the pillars and forces driving and shaping the activities of the business being audited. Just as business is a navigation process, so too is the audit as its investigations and assessments develop understanding of the achievements and standing of the business. Mental models in relation to cognition are discussed and explored in *The Oxford Handbook of 4E Cognition* (Newen, A., De Bruin, L. and Gallagher, S., (eds.), 2018). On the inside cover of the *Handbook*, it states: "4E cognition (Embodied, Embedded, Enactive, and Extended) is a relatively young and thriving field of interdisciplinary research. It assumes that cognition is shaped and structured by dynamic interactions between the brain, body, and both the physical and social environments".

In this regard, it is important to recognise that confidence (especially assessments of 'deserved confidence'), judgement, resilience, sustainability, engagement and creativity are all ultimately feelings or senses associated with the right hemisphere of the brain, and so Figure 7.1 is in large measure sensory and perceptive. Some of the senses involve parts of the body outside of the brain such as observation (eyes) and discussion (ears). Smell, in the sense of a smell test, and touch, especially in the context of creativity, are also used to invoke understanding of audit experience. The mental model of Figure 7.1 can, therefore, be classified as being 'embodied' in that it involves parts of the body other than the brain. Observation and discussion may involve other people whose interpretation of events becomes shared with the auditor, invoking the notion of shared or joint cognition. This is very much the case when the auditor employs a specialist, and so audit cognition might be considered as being 'extended' to include reciprocity and relations with other people and their brains. Further, the introduction of disruption from external forces in Figure 7.1 emphasises that the mental model is a dynamic system. The inclusion of purposeful pathways into Figure 7.1 suggests that the model is 'activist' since it relates to and learns from action. The mental model of the auditor is 'embedded' within society's framing of the purpose of audit.

The model also engages the left hemisphere of the brain in that it is representational and computes on the basis of those representations. For instance, the financial evidence is a representation and computation of the financial consequences of business activity. Ultimately, as explained further in Chapter 9, deserved confidence is itself a representation based upon all the elements and connections of the model.

We believe that the future of audit will include greater understanding of cognition as a mental model representing the dynamic interactions between deserved confidence, business activity, financial expression and the environment. In this respect, audit (and its delineation in Figure 7.1) is a creative mental process. Audit develops through its modelling of the company being audited, and, at the same time, frames (or even reframes) the company's existence. Accordingly, audit, through this mental model, can be seen as both shaping existence and simultaneously auditing that existence by, in the terms laid out in this chapter, assigning it an attributed level of deserved confidence. In this sense, audit can be regarded as creating what it audits and auditing what it creates and, as such, has to be treated as fundamentally dynamic in its construction.

If we combine this with the longstanding claims in the auditing literature of audit being "wholly utilitarian" (e.g., see Flint, 1988), then the innate dynamism in audit has to be driven by what makes or enables audit to be most socially purposeful. Framing audit around an assessment of deserved confidence is not just an extension in the current, standardised practical representation of audit. More significantly, it conceptually roots or integrates the practice of audit with considerations of the interactions between business and society and it is in this conceptual space that the essential professional spirit of a public-interested audit function should be situated and in which it can thrive. The implication of a public-interested audit function is that you cannot answer the question of what type of audit it is that society wants without addressing the question as to what type of society is wanted in terms of conformity, creativity and thinking differently.

For too long, and particularly in the literature on the notion of an audit expectations gap, there has been a structural resistance, despite references to its utilitarianism and social construction, to moving beyond standard representations of what is audit and what comprises 'legitimate' audit practice. Responding to societal expectations by merely stating what is not audit and what is not proper audit practice is not sufficient, nor legitimate.

Contemplating what audit can become and pinpointing the conceptual roots that can substantiate the development of its practice need to be seen as the way forward.

In this regard, resetting the purpose of audit around the assessment of deserved confidence is just the starting point, or base camp, from which subsequent development of the nature and scope of audit practice can develop. Such development paths will be considered in the next two chapters of the book and, notably, will assess the capacity for audit (a) to extend beyond notions of correspondence to matters of progression and (b) to set the grounds for what needs to be accounted for rather than the latter determining what has to be audited. In Chapter 8 we look at the implications of our concept of audit for the development of corporate governance as progression and in Chapter 9 at the implications for the future of corporate reporting.

Notes

1 Carney (2022, p. 442) utilised a a similar categorisation when when describing corporate values as (being) "inclusive, fair, sustainable, resilient and dynamic".

2 What the risks mean for shareholder value is a question that auditors could help to answer, pointing to potential business opportunities. Auditors could, for example, provide not only the resilience statement but resilience ratings for shareholders akin to credit ratings for debt investors – building upon the Statement of Principal Risks prepared by the company.

3 The idea of balance resonates with Aristotle's idea of virtue as the middle way between two extremes. Aristotle's middle way or mean is not always a compromise but rather a matter of using reason and 'practical wisdom' to find what works in the circumstances of the case (see Grayling, 2020, pp. 93–4).

4 Nurture works through or via nature and vice versa. It is presumably unwise for society to set up nurture in competition to nature but rather society should help nurture and nature to come together.

5 A point made back in February 1942 in a letter to *The Accountant* by N.C. Dibben.

6 This issue has been discussed recently on BBC Sounds, on *The Inquiry* programme.. See 'The Inquiry: Is AI eroding our critical thinking', www.bbc.co.uk/sounds/play/w3ct722s.

7 Governments have used the deferral of corporation tax payments to encourage companies to engage in investment. The value of this deferral can be disrupted by changes in tax rates or by changes in expected future profits.

8 To learn more about how auditors currently use specialists to deal with fair value, see Barr-Pulliam et al. (2019). The valuation of promises by specialists can involve mathematical models. These are based upon distributional assumptions which need careful consideration. The models may be 'self-fulfilling' in the sense that if everyone accepts them then they do determine value in the market place (this is classic performativity). The auditor needs to examine distributional assumptions. Auditors should not shelter behind general acceptance but should be prepared to challenge it.

9 A reduction in corporation tax rates reduces society's 'equity like' stake in the company. 'Equity like' in the sense that the corporation tax take, like the shareholders' share of profits, goes up and down with company profits. A reduction of corporation tax rates is a reduction of society's stake in the corporate sector.
10 In spite of doubts expressed in some quarters as to its effectiveness, such as by Jonathan Ford (2020), it is likely that some form of stakeholder capitalism will remain on the political agenda.

References

Barr-Pulliam, D., Joe, J.R., Mason, S.A. and K-A. Sanderson, 2019, *Unlocking the Black Box in Fair Value Measurement (FVM): Examining How Valuation Specialists Prepare and Evaluate FVMs*, Research Publication, (Institute of Chartered Accountants of Scotland, Edinburgh).

Boden, M., 2003, *The Creative Mind: Myths and Mechanisms*, (Routledge, London), https://archive.org/details/margareta.bodenthecreativemindmythsandmechanismsroutledge2003.

Brydon, D., 2019, *Assess, Assure and Inform: Improving Audit Quality and Effectiveness, Report of the Independent Review into the Quality and Effectiveness of Audit*, https://assets.publishing.service.gov.uk/media/5df8edfced915d0938597e1f/brydon-review-final-report.pdf

Carney, M., 2022, *Values: An Economist's Guide to Everything That Matters*, (William Collins, London).

Chancellor, E., 2023, *The Price of Time: The Real Story of Interest*, (Penguin, London).

Dibben, N.C., 1942 (February), *Letter to The Accountant.*

Du Sautoy, M., 2019, *The Creativity Code: How AI Is Learning to Write, Paint and Think*, (Fourth Estate, London).

Flint, D., 1988, *Philosophy and Principles of Auditing: An Introduction*, (Macmillan Education, New York, NY).

Ford, J., 2020, 'We should beware the rise of stakeholderism', *Financial Times*, 8th March, www.ft.com/content/c082635c-5fd4-11ea-8033-fa40a0d65a98.

Grayling, A.C., 2020, *The History of Philosophy: Three Millenia of Thought from the West and Beyond*, (Penguin, Random House, London).

Hatherly, D., Mitchell, R.K., Mitchell, J.R. and J.H. Lee, 2020, 'Reimagining profits and stakeholder capital to address tensions among stakeholders', *Business & Society*, 59:2, pp. 322–350, https://doi.org/10.1177/0007650317745637.

Humphrey, C., 2020, *Thinking Differently Is 'Audit'*, (Audit Futures, ICAEW, London), https://icaew.access.preservica.com/portal/asset/sdb%3AIO%7C3c14db66-e5bb-4aa0-b043-90c3a0b3f472.

Kelton, S., 2021, *The Deficit Myth: How to Build a Better Economy* (John Murray, London).

King, M., 2016, *The End of Alchemy: Money, Banking and the Future of the Global Economy*, (Little Brown, London).

Mayer, C., 2021, 'The future of the corporation and the economics of purpose', *Journal of Management Studies*, 58:3, pp. 887–901, https://doi.org/10.1111/joms.12660.

Newen, A., De Bruin, L. and S. Gallagher (eds.), 2018, *The Oxford Handbook of 4E Cognition*, (Oxford University Press, Oxford).

Piketty, T., 2014, *Capital in the Twenty-First Century*, (Belknap Press of Harvard University, Cambridge, MA).

Ridley, M., 2003, *Nature via Nuture: Genes, Experience and What Makes Us Human*, (Harper Perennial, London).

8

AUDIT AS GOVERNANCE

Tackling the governance deficit

This chapter starts by explaining how modern investment theory and practice has deprioritised effective corporate governance but goes on to explain how an audit based upon deserved confidence can improve, reinstate and promote good governance not in terms of rules and regulations but by leading the way to improved corporate performance on behalf of all stakeholders. Good governance extends not just to corporate management but to corporate investors. Indeed, good governance comes from the auditor, management, investors and committed stakeholders working together to develop a common understanding of the business, the challenges it faces and the transitional pathways it needs. Audit should be fundamental to the development of this common understanding and mutual responsibility. An audit centred on the assessment of deserved confidence is one that can inspire a governance regime focused on progression and not just correspondence.

Investment theory and practice: A brief overview

Lo and Foerster (2023) give an informative review of the ideas that dominate modern-day investing. Most notably, Markowitz introduced the idea of a portfolio to diversify and consequently lower the risk for any required return. What matters for a portfolio of stocks is how the individual stocks vary in price relative to one another. Diversification does not stop with investing in stocks but can be applied to a portfolio of different asset classes including bonds (loans), real estate and other types of investment. William Sharpe showed that with diversification the optimum portfolio should be the portfolio of all assets, with each asset weighted according to its size or market capitalisation. In this case the risk for the investor becomes the risk of the market or volatility of the

DOI: 10.4324/9781032721293-8

market as a whole. This is the systematic risk that cannot be diversified away. In fact, much of the unsystematic risk can be diversified away through a portfolio of just 30–40 randomly selected stocks.[1]

Eugene Fama introduced the efficient market hypothesis; the hypothesis being that markets reflect investors' collective best guess as to the underlying intrinsic value of stocks. Thus, the market quickly and efficiently absorbs any new information into stock prices. If stocks are appropriately priced by the market then investors shouldn't spend time trying to outperform the market. Consequently, Jack Bogle pioneered indexed funds that concentrated on low management cost rather than outperformance. There is periodic rebalancing of the portfolio to keep in line with share price changes but in essence shares are held for the long term since long-term time horizons help to reduce risk.[2] Index funds, including the Vanguard funds that Bogle started, have become a major component of the fund management business. In respect of personal savings and pension pots, much is invested in mutual funds which are professionally managed. There are a variety of investment styles on offer but with index funds being very popular. Black, Scholes and Merton developed a formula for valuing options that enabled markets in options and option-like contracts to develop, allowing market participants to 'inexpensively' amplify or dampen their risk/reward exposures.[3] Options and option-like contracts are themselves marketable securities but are called derivatives because their value is derived from the value of the underlying securities to which the contracts relate.

What this very brief outline of ideas in investment pinpoints is the growth in investment practices that, though reliant upon the intrinsic value of the underlying businesses in which they invest, pay little attention to the underlying businesses themselves on an individual basis. This results not only from the increased use of derivatives but from the growing use of passive investment. Passive investment is derivative in the sense of paying little attention to the underlying businesses. This causes the investment industry to distance itself from its governance role in terms of improving the performance of those businesses upon which it depends.

Another area of fund management is liability-driven investment (LDI). Here the role is one of meeting the various risk and return requirements of pension funds, insurers and others who have future liabilities to meet. The objective of LDI is not so much a high return coming from improving businesses but rather a return from assets (many of which are not equity investments) that matches the financial obligations or liabilities. It is particularly popular with defined benefit pension scheme trustees and advisors. Once again it tends to be distant from any governance role with respect to individual companies.[4]

The word 'active' as the opposite of 'passive' investing can cover those funds who trade because their analysis shows the share is fundamentally under- or over-priced, or those whose 'technical' analysis leads them to believe the momentum of a share is about to change.[5] Technical analysis of past share price movements and patterns can lead to automated trading when certain price thresholds are met. Such trading has little or nothing to do with the intrinsic value or quality of the underlying businesses.

In fundamental analysis, however, the investor (fund manager) trades, at least in principle, after analysing and getting to understand the company. These are so-called 'active investors' in the sense that they are active in the stock market but they may not be active in terms of their governance role in pressing companies and company managers to perform better. It remains difficult for an investment fund with just a small percentage holding of a company to exert influence on company management. Jeff Ubben co-founded the hedge fund ValueAct Capital with the intention of taking a substantial position in a concentrated (small) number of companies after considerable study of each company and whether their share price was understated.[6] Ubben did not like the term 'activist investor' and preferred to describe it as "a governance-based approach" to value investing, with a close engagement with management and other long-term investors.

We take the view that auditing should be very similar to what ValueAct does (or claims to do) in respect of understanding the company, but the auditor does not take a stake in the company and makes the results of the audit study of the company and its assessment of the company and its share price available to all. Audit's role is to support a governance-based approach to investing and to promote a set of values that good governance should require of investors, management and other stakeholders. ValueAct's values (https://valueact.com/ - accessed 1 October 2025) are as follows.[7] A similar set of values could well be promoted by the audit firm to its portfolio of clients.

Relationships & trust
We place great value on our relationships with current and former portfolio companies, as well as the institutional investor community: we always consider what is in the best interest of the company and all stakeholders.

Responsibility & long-term thinking
We believe in investing for the long term and managing companies for the long term. This requires the highest standard of integrity, a deep understanding of industry structure and business strategy, and a consideration of relevant social, ethical and environmental issues.

Transparency & respect
Our team culture promotes openness, shared learning and shared rewards. We succeed or fail together. We apply this same approach to working with our portfolio companies.

Ubben relates that before setting up ValueAct he might have held a much smaller holding in a company he had identified as under-priced but his analysis and understanding were private and, having invested, he might have had to wait a considerable time before the rest of the market came around to the same understanding and lifted the share price. Meanwhile the fund's performance would have been reported as low. Our conception of the audit changes this situation since the audit would search for different thinking, just as ValueAct did, but would give that thinking a clear voice in the market. There would be early pressure on management and the market to address the new thinking.

Thematic investing seeks to follow macro trends including geopolitics, society, the environment, technology and demographics. Recently, a most visible theme has been 'ESG' investing, prioritising companies that do well in terms of their environmental, social and governance performance. In 2020 Ubben left ValueAct to start Inclusive Capital Partners. This fund would invest not only in companies with green credentials, for example, one producing wood pellets and another involved in vertical farming, but also in major companies such as ExxonMobil and Bayer (a company entwined in litigation over its weedkiller, Roundup); huge, profitable companies that would be screened out by conventional ESG funds. The idea was for Inclusive Capital Partners to use its significant stake to pressure such companies to improve their ESG performance. Such companies need a pathway through which the profits from non-green activities can be invested in the development of greener alternatives. The expectation was that whilst the shares of these major companies were depressed through their exposure to green issues, the execution of such a pathway would revive the share price.

However, in November 2023, Inclusive Capital Partners was closed having raised only a fraction of the funds hoped for from institutional investors. The Financial Times reported that Inclusive blamed its closure on public markets, saying they had not rewarded its mission.[8] It seems that whatever insight Inclusive had was not convincing investors. The idea of investing in the likes of Exxon was not popular with ESG investors or with other investors who did not want to give up their dividends in order for Exxon to invest in green projects. Essentially, Inclusive had fallen between two investment buckets or silos, those silos being the very silos that Inclusive was trying to connect.

It could be argued, alternatively, that companies performing poorly on ESG criteria should continue to pay high dividends to institutional investors who would then allocate the cash to ESG funds. In effect the 'recycling' would be done by the investment institutions rather than by the companies generating the cash, although the investment industry would have to ensure that its fund mandates did not make investment too 'siloed', thereby preventing dividends being used to boost ESG impact investment. This highlights that governance takes place at two levels. The first is at the company level where the concern is that any loss, or decline, of the company adversely impacts non-diversified, dependent (committed) stakeholders. At a second level the concern is the governance of the investment funds (and companies that manage funds) and their performance both for the providers of their funds and for society at large.

At both governance levels, such concerns point to the importance of the evaluation of pathways to improvement of any poor ESG performance and of the impact of such improvement on assessments of deserved confidence in the company or portfolio. For such evaluations, step forward the auditors.

Future value from correspondence and progression

In essence, the stress between continuing or refining the existing business (and even creating a new business that might ultimately render the existing business redundant) is at the heart of every company. It is the tension between exploiting the existing business platform and creating a radically new one to replace it. Creativity value comes from both past creativity (the potential extension or expansion of existing business) and from new/future creativity underpinning radically new business platforms. The extent to which it is attributable to one rather than the other is vital to an understanding of the company and the tensions at its heart. A concern of audit is the temptation for management to focus on extension and expansion of the existing business at the expense of new platforms. In so far as extension relies on continuity of the existing business platform and new platforms constitute progression to something radically different, then the tension at the heart of a business is between correspondence and progression.[9]

Where the envisioned radically new business (platform) is entirely separate from and independent of the existing business, one business does not replace the other and both can grow simultaneously, but management does have to decide which is most deserving of any scarce resources. The existing business is likely to provide most of the growth in the near future but the envisioned business may have the greater potential. Where the envisioned business is a radical improvement of the existing business and will ultimately replace the existing business, the main issue is one of transition (i.e., its transition pathway).[10] Given time, the existing business moves to contraction, and growth depends upon the success of the incoming radical alternative. If the expected loss of value from future contraction exceeds the expected growth from the replacement, then the sustainability risk premium is high and the creativity value, from past, present and future creativity, may be negative. It follows that the auditor must assess not only future growth potential of the existing and radically different platforms but also the interaction between them. It is this interaction – the interaction between correspondence and progression – that can be an important driver of both creativity and sustainability.

To assess growth of the established business, the auditor starts with the existing business (continuity) and then looks for the future amendments and adjacencies that refine and advance the existing business. This search can involve a certain amount of innovative and creative thinking. Though continuity and correspondence are dominant, such amendments and adjacencies introduce an element of discontinuity/progression in the sense that they are a development of, rather than a repetition of, the existing business. However, for both management and the auditor, the direction of thought is (a) to understand the existing business and (b) to search for developments that matter. In other words, firstly understand continuity and then understand the potential expansion, contraction or refinement of existing products and markets.

Any assessment of growth to be generated from a radically new business starts with the vision and analyses the future pathway, including possible disruptions necessary to bring it about. Now, the direction of thought is to (a) understand the discontinuity consequent to the vision and (b) search for a pathway(s) to bring the vision about and generate visibility (the visionary pathway). A well-constructed visionary pathway reintroduces a sense of continuity by connecting the past to the future even though there will be surprises, both good and bad, on the way. In so far as this continuity is achieved the visionary pathway is also a transition pathway. Surprises might be of the nature of reversionary disruptions from which it is possible to re-join the visionary pathway. However, to the extent that the surprise suggests the envisioned pathway is not do-able or needs a substantial re-think, the value associated with progression is lost, although there may be some recovery in the value of the existing business. In this case, the surprise is dis-confirmatory evidence. In determining whether a company is deserving of confidence, the auditor will seek and consider both confirming and disconfirming evidence and assess management's response to both, judging whether the company's optimism and caution, taken together, are appropriate.

The relationship between visibility and materiality has already been discussed in Chapter 5. The audit is planned by thinking in both directions; from the end to the beginning in terms of materiality and from the beginning to the end in terms of what is visible. Materiality, leading to the identification of where to give attention, flows backwards from the future, whilst visibility, coming from the acquisition and evaluation of evidence, flows forwards from the beginning. To make an assessment of correspondence (continuity) value the auditor's thinking follows visibility, whilst the assessment of progression (discontinuity) value follows materiality. Thus, an overall assessment of the future impact of past and present/future creativity is thinking in both directions by thinking forwards to the future and backwards from the future. The audit exists at (is created by) the intersection of visibility and materiality.

Conceptually, the distinction between (a) the value of thinking that is substantially based upon correspondence with existing thought and (b) the value of progression to radically different thinking is illustrated in Table 8.1. Correspondence value comes from an analysis of the development potential of the existing (level of) business (i.e., thinking from the present about the future). Progression value comes from a different and more visionary future (i.e., thinking from the future about the present). In Table 8.1, radical uncertainty represents the future's future, which is difficult to think about because there is no 'conceived' connection to the present. In Table 8.1, the 'present' present is thinking about the existing business without thought being given to the future beyond the continuation or sustainability of the present (in the sense of repetition of current levels of residual income). The 'present' present provides the benchmark against which the future can be evaluated.

An auditor's assessment of correspondence and progression is helpful to the investor trying to decide whether the prospects in either are over or understated and whether the balance between the two corresponds to their own preferences between investing in the currently visible and investing in a future vision. Some funds and fund managers will offer visibility rather than vision, whilst others are prepared to invest in radically new products or situations. The latter type of investor has conviction attributable to belief, imagination, visualisation, intuition, vision etc. In this case, the pathway that supports the value is envisioned and can be associated with thinking differently. To quote Jonathan Swift, the author of *Gulliver's Travels*, "vision is the art of seeing what is invisible to others".[11]

Such investors are trying to be creative, paralleling the research creativity of their investees. Creativity involves joining the dots (i.e., making connections) which others do not see, possibly because their thinking is too linear and too dependent on giving primacy to the present or viewing the present as an extension of the past. Drawing on direct quotes on creativity from Asimov, Poincare and Steve Jobs, McGilchrist

TABLE 8.1 Correspondence and progression value

Thinking about the/ from the	*Present*	*Future*
Present	Thinking about the present business without contemplating the future	Developing pathways to build and expand upon the existing platform, *taking the present business to the future*
Future	Developing pathways to implement the vision of a new platform, *bringing the future to the present business*	Radical uncertainty being future disruptions that are not easily conceivable at present

(2021, p. 244) highlights a collective emphasis on the making of what (to the left hemisphere of the brain) seem to be distant connections. To begin with, a new idea or connection can seem outlandish. With the passing of time, it comes to be seen as obvious. Being innovative serves to reveal that something typically treated as self-evident is open to challenge and, ultimately, replaced by completely different thinking that itself, in time, becomes the newly obvious and open to challenge.

The assessment of risk

It is important that the auditor's assessment of deserved confidence is based upon an appropriate assessment of risk. A company might excel at creating many new and exciting ideas but not at turning those ideas into profitable products, perhaps because it is 'out of its depth' in respect of production. Difficulty in turning exciting ideas into successful products can, given an enthusiastic management and investor following, easily be underestimated and, as a consequence, the company's risk is not fully recognised and the assessment of creativity value is too high. Meanwhile, focusing on a highly successful product could be appropriate because the company realises that it is on to a 'good thing' and does not want to lose concentration by attempting to develop new ones. Maintaining concentration can reduce the risk of growth potential not being met. However, it could also indicate that management is insufficiently visionary or feels 'out of its depth' with regard to creative thinking. The auditor (and investors) will need to consider the company's long-term sustainable future and whether an absence of new ideas makes a sustainable future relatively risky. Risk appetite varies between different investors and there can be a tendency for those with low-risk appetite to invest in established companies where the risk is a lack of vision and this risk may be underestimated. Those with a high-risk appetite, however, might be attracted to visionary companies where the risk of failing to translate that vision is higher than realised. A contribution of audit should be to enable investors (and management) to recognise and consider risk appropriately whatever their risk appetite.

Using the terminology of the popular '2 by 2' Boston Matrix, a company (or corporate activity) with low correspondence and progression is a 'dog' with little chance of improvement. One with high correspondence but low progression is a 'cash cow' with a risk that the company will not have a long-term future. A company with high progression potential whilst low in correspondence with existing thought is a 'question mark' with valuation dependent upon belief and conviction in the company's ability to convert creativity into new successful products. A company with both (successful) correspondence and progressive activities is most likely to be a 'star'. Over time, some question marks will fall by the wayside and be re-classified as dogs but the natural lifetime (entropic) pathway of a single line of business is to go from a question mark to a star to a cash cow to a dog. A company might have several lines of business with each business being either a dog, star, cash cow or question mark. A low-risk company (or investment fund) will tend to have a well-balanced mix of question marks, stars and cash cows.

The auditor can discuss the balance and consequent risk with management and also look at the investment philosophies of participants in the market for the company's shares to see how the market views the company in terms of risk.

The idea of platforms

A platform is a representation of the core continuity of an activity: a common and lasting base from which related activities or new versions of the activity can be developed. These developments are, in essence, incremental in contrast to non-incremental development based upon thinking differently. In the classroom, it is popular to introduce the idea of a platform through a discussion of chess, a non-co-operative, competitive game.

Chess is a game with a clear purpose (to achieve checkmate) and rules that apply to all chess games. Thinking in one direction, it is the purpose and rules that represent a starting 'platform' for the execution of individual matches. However, thinking from an opposite direction, it is the vision or 'feel' for the game of chess and its creative possibilities which is the starting platform for the top player and the rules are simply there to enable, express and action that vision. If all you understand about chess is the rules of the game then you are not going to be a very good player. The key question is how do I develop the deep understanding of the game which will turn me into a top player? It is possible to develop the ability to think several moves ahead in terms of both attack and defence. This is essentially serial thinking of the 'if A then B' kind. Within the rules each player plans pathways (successive moves) to cover both attack and defence and each player plans to anticipate and disrupt the opponent's pathways. At this point one is still only an average player.

Neither of us, as chess players, ever got beyond this point and so the rest of this paragraph is somewhat speculative. The brain's ability to cover all the possible permutations of moves ahead is strictly limited. To get better you need to develop more holistic thinking in which to place your serial thinking skills. This means thinking in terms of recognising and developing positions that dominate the board. This is greatly helped by direct experience of playing high-level chess yourself but also indirect experience obtained by studying the games of top chess players. What is learnt is the shape or pattern of board positions that have proved dominant. It is seen from this brief discussion that chess is played through the application of two platforms, being the rules (used to think ahead on a serial move by move basis) and a platform of experience represented as patterns of pieces on the board and their associated outcomes (used to think ahead in terms of re-shaping the board). The overall aim is to build a platform of understanding superior to that of other players.

By studying a large number of games, a player can observe resemblances between winning positions to identify their pattern characteristics and, for the expert, this becomes 'instinctive' but it is instinct formed of experience and understanding as well as natural ability. The key to becoming an expert is to adapt your ability to recognise this 'global' knowledge so as to be able to draw upon it in the particulars of an individual game. The individual games produce the input for the global knowledge, which then feeds back into the individual matches. Each match is against a different opponent or against the same opponent whose own platform of understanding has developed. Each match, therefore, has its idiosyncratic element and the truly top player is able to recognise and respond to this.[12] This again highlights the two platforms, one formed of rules and serial thinking, the other of the 'feel' for a dominant position based upon experience; and a game is the interaction or connection between the two platforms in the context of the 'idiosyncrasies' of a particular match. In terms of evidence (understanding) we have the logic (rules) of the game, the big picture of pattern recognition in big 'data' and specific data relating to the particular game and the individual opponent.

There is a resemblance here to audit practice. Each audit employs auditing standards and although the profession does not regard them as rules, they are designed for universal application. However, each audit could be viewed as a particularity with its own 'idiosyncrasies'. A study of past audits reveals the commonalities (pattern) of both successful and problematic audits and provides a base of understanding employed in individual audits. That base of understanding may not be effective in an individual audit if the audit's 'idiosyncrasies' are not taken into account. The experienced, 'expert', auditor is able to do this; to recognise whether an anomaly or idiosyncrasy is immaterial to the big picture or whether it is a clue to a material issue to which existing expertise must adapt.

Returning to chess, through artificial intelligence (AI), a computer can build a knowledge platform from previous chess games to develop its own understanding based upon pattern recognition. The 'understanding' of the computer has advanced as its pattern recognition capability has improved and it can now beat human players including chess masters except perhaps when the chess master can come up with an innovative winning way which is outside the machine's learnt experience. As the machine learns more this becomes progressively difficult. Human creativity is captured and represented by the machine's AI which is, of itself, not creative in terms of chess but creative in terms of how creative chess played by others is identified and represented. This could in principle lead to AI that learns to be creative (Boden, 2004).

If the game becomes dominated by machines, chess becomes a competition between AI developers. However, while a computer can beat a chess master, a computer did not invent the game of chess. For now, at least, humans retain a visionary capability for the invention of games beyond that of the computer, and the relevant question for auditing is, do auditors as humans need to create new audit 'games'/purposes?

There is an important distinction here to make between high-validity and low-validity environments. In high-validity environments the rules of the game (no matter how complex they are, as for example, in chess) stay predominantly the same. In low-validity environments the rules of the game are either not well defined or keep changing – and games keep declining in popularity due to the invention of new games. Today's computer capabilities have provided a platform for a whole new games industry, where the computer serves as a platform for human creativity. Thus, we have a further platform (a technology platform) facilitating the invention of games by humans that would otherwise not be doable. Many of these games allow a player(s) to indulge their imagination and/or reflex skills. Technology has spawned a whole new genre of games, though it seems unlikely any of these games will survive as long as chess, since the technology behind the games will develop along with the possibility of more game creations. The technology platform is an 'affordance' that invites (or affords) human creativity, but it can also restrict human creativity if the development of new games is limited to those affordances provided by technology. This is a different relationship or connection between humans and machines to that where the machine completely captures people's creativity.[13]

Where we have a game such as chess played on the internet between humans there is no radical change to the game itself and the game corresponds to the rules of chess. At the other extreme where the machine affords new games (e.g., based on virtual reality), this is a radical (progressive) development. Where the machine captures human expertise through an assessment of 'big data' that is beyond an individual human's capability, it can be argued that, since there is no radical change to the game itself, this development is closer to correspondence than progression. Judgement is necessary to classify a development as correspondence or progression. In principle, if a comparison of the old and the new is dominated by similarity then there is correspondence; if the comparison is dominated by difference, the development is progression.

What matters in a business setting is the purpose of business pathways (actions) with the idea, introduced in Chapter 4, that the management of business activity should consider, as part of its purpose, the intended balance between 'correspondence' (i.e., moving towards or maintaining accepted norms) and 'progression' (i.e., moving away from, challenging and potentially changing accepted norms by developing fundamentally new perspectives). Correspondence constitutes 'exploratory creativity', described by Du Sautoy

(2019, p. 9) as taking what is already there and exploring its outer edges, extending the limits of what is possible while remaining bound by the rules (in our case, by the rules of the platform).

If, however, a company develops a platform that is completely different to the existing platform then that may be considered 'transformational creativity'. Transformational creativity results from removing one or more of the basic rules or constraints accepted as part of the fabric of the subject (the platform) (Du Sautoy, 2019, p. 11). Transformation is risky but it is also risky for a company in a dynamic environment not to take risks. Deserved confidence is not so much associated with low risk but with a company that puts itself in a position to take risks as required by, or given the opportunity by, that environment.

The auditor's consideration of platforms

In considering the sustainability, resilience and growth of the business, the auditor will need to consider the platforms upon which the business is based. Business platforms play much the same role as they do in chess, in the sense that one platform involves looking a relatively small number of moves ahead to exploit and develop the current situation. Exploiting the current situation is essentially short term and does not take the player to a new platform. A top manager will also have a feel for what a longer-term dominant position looks like and knows how to get there. This is progression to a new platform.

The key feature of a platform is that it endures for a significant period in time and space without there being a game-changing disruption. It is multi-purpose and endures for a significant time as a pathway or linked pathways, common to multiple products. When a product fails to perform, its replacement may well use the same platform and so reversionary disruption does not threaten the platform. The end of a platform's life comes from game-changing disruption. However, a certain amount of change to the role of the platform during its life is likely and adaptability will enhance its longevity and postpone/reduce the risk of game-changing disruption.

In business the feature of a platform is that it can be the base for increasing volumes of a number of different final products (say A--->B1, A--->B2, A--->B3, where A is the common platform for B1 etc., the different products) and this gives management various strategic options. One is to treat the platform as a product, with the purpose of the company being to build and rent the platform – thereby, enabling other companies to produce B1, B2 and B3. Another is for the company to both retain the platform and produce B1, B2 and B3 itself so that it can become multi-purpose with an element of risk spreading. Another option is a hybrid of the first two so that the company retains the platform and, say, one of the products. More radical is to sell the platform but continue to produce one or more of B1, B2 and B3 by renting space on the platform from the platform's purchaser. It is tempting for management to present its chosen option as something radical and significant. Nevertheless, in our terms none of the strategies are radical since there is no change to the underlying platform.

In looking to the future, the auditor might work through the options with management as the best way to gauge management's intentions. There is an element of serendipity in the development of platforms whenever they are initially constructed for one product or purpose and then found to be good for others. Looking to the future, the auditor must be alert to such possible developments. Whenever a platform is retained, it becomes the 'core competence' (Prahalad and Hamel, 1990) or 'core continuity' and the basis from which future options can be considered. If these options relate to the future role of the existing platform rather than the development of new platforms then it is considered correspondence activity and relatively minor in terms of (new) creativity.

Platforms and deserved confidence: A summary

A well-recognised platform can enhance resilience in so far as it offers the flexibility outlined in the previous section; flexibility that can help deal with reversionary disruption. However, a game-changing disruption is likely to require more radical thinking associated with progression. The balance between correspondence and progression is a major factor influencing sustainability risk. If a company is reliant upon continuation of an existing platform, then sustainability risk could be higher than for a company that is (also) developing new ideas; new ideas that can create or respond to game-changing disruption. In some of such cases (where increasing progression value does not compensate for reducing correspondence value) creativity value might be judged as negative. If a company is dependent upon progression, then it might be riskier than a company that (also) has an existing platform to fall back on (and help finance progression). It follows from this that confidence is going to be more deserved when the auditor is satisfied that the company (in light of its activities, finances and the outside forces it faces) has secured a good balance between correspondence and progression.

An additional, underlying, issue is whether the auditor (a) follows (and then subsequently comments upon) or (b) influences (and, in that sense, leads) the insights and judgements of management and of investors. We consider that if the core foundation of auditing is thinking differently, then this fits much better with notions of influence than followership. High-quality management and investment can be inspired by, but can also facilitate, high-quality auditing.

Big data as a platform: 'Smart' auditing leads to smarter investing

An important step in the audit process is identifying through analysis of big data (that is, data that covers many companies and time periods) unexpected differences (or similarities) between companies. Companies/time periods identified as being unexpected outliers (that is, different to their peers) are targeted for audit investigation as to why they are outliers. Are they outliers because they are (reflective of) thinking differently to, smarter than, or ahead of, the others? Or are they outliers because they are not performing their operations as well as others? Or, are they outliers because the information that made them appear as outliers is defective? The analysis to identify outliers is generally statistical and computerised, but the examination of why there are outliers requires further (this time, human) investigation.

However, what makes smart auditing 'smart' is not the use of statistical or computerised analysis *per se* but the choice of factor(s) on the basis of which a company can be considered an outlier. Here the smart auditor thinks differently to (ahead of) other auditors. Auditing is dynamic and the auditor (and auditing) gets smarter not by following standards ('standardised' behavioural patterns) but by thinking differently to other auditors. Our work in this book suggests a number of factors for testing. For instance, the auditor might search for unusual or unexpected relations or change in relations between correspondence and progression, or between creativity and other pillars of deserved confidence. Smart auditors will develop their own ideas and relations for testing, because audit is (and always needs to be) dynamic.

As explained earlier in this chapter, a relatively recent phenomenon has been the growth of investment ideas (such as passive investing) which disconnect increases in value from developments in underlying business structures, whether visible or envisioned. Investment strategies which cut the link between the dynamics of business and the dynamics of value take us towards a 'Ponzi'-like economy of value extraction rather than value creation. One form of (adjusted) passive investment is so-called smart beta. With smart beta, the investment is deemed to be a portfolio of factors. Smart beta starts as a passive investment that follows the market but then actively seeks to find, through a statistical analysis of big data, factors identified in individual businesses that mark the share as an outlier and enable the portfolio to be adjusted so as to 'outsmart' the market. However, factor investing is essentially passive since there is no direct study by the investor of the underlying fundamentals (platforms and pathways) of any of the businesses in the portfolio and hence no understanding of how value flows and business activity flows connect.[14]

A variety of factors can be created and backtested to see if a portfolio based upon them outperforms a relevant market index.[15] Two factors that are frequently used as a basis for portfolio construction are 'book to value' and 'momentum'. In the first (value investing), the portfolio is biased towards stocks (shares) with high book to market value and in the second (momentum investing), the bias is towards stocks with a recent record of increasing values. Volatility is another factor that is popular with smart beta investors. A smart beta portfolio can cover one or more of these factors and others found by statistical testing to be associated with share value movement.[16]

In future, the investor might learn more, through the work of smart auditors, about fundamental business factors that are of more causal force in shaping why particular companies are outliers. Accompanying explanations and reasons given by the auditor will help to refine both the case for inclusion and any portfolio weighting. For example, if the reason is that the company is strategically distinctive in its approach and thinking, the company may well be worthy of inclusion in the portfolio; but if it is an outlier due to defective information, then it should be excluded. Thus, smart auditing can act as a service to the fund manager by enabling the passive investor to become more 'active', connecting exceptional performance with the business actions (pathways) that have generated that performance through a deep understanding of underlying business fundamentals. As such, it can be said that smart auditing and investing place emphasis on those factors that are a part of the framing of deserved confidence.

Although smart auditing can enable smarter investing, it is not the role of the auditor to identify investment 'opportunities' per se. Rather, the smart auditor's work enhances the empirical basis on which investment decisions are made – with resulting share price patterns more directly reflecting the auditor's assessment of the level of confidence that can be deservedly placed in the audited company. Auditing, in this respect, can be viewed as the key to a wider confidence-building exercise in companies right across the corporate stakeholder network. In other words, the share prices are not just fair to buyers and sellers of shares but are fair to all stakeholders in the sense that the proportion of corporate-generated wealth and well-being assigned to shareholders is appropriate.

Assessing the performance of fund management

Through governance afforded by audits focused upon deserved confidence, the purpose of fund management can centre on improving the performance of invested companies whilst creating the variety of investment products that meet the various needs of investors. This should attract investors and promote investment that enhances the economy for all stakeholders. The purpose of fund management as a whole cannot just be to outperform a market index. That is not possible except by extracting value from those who do not invest via a fund.

A variety of funds allow subscribing investors to share in the success of quoted companies on their (the investors') terms. It is through smarter audits that fund managers can enhance their understanding of both companies and funds, allowing them to progress the companies and their fund products and to avoid the fund management industry being largely one of value transfer. At present, the performance of a fund is primarily represented by drawing together (a) its performance in financial share value terms against a benchmark index chosen by the fund managers and (b) an indication from the managers of the risk attaching to the fund on a scale from, say, 1 (low risk) to 7 (high risk).

The problem with the first of these is that the fund, wanting above all to avoid coming in behind its benchmark, will tend to invest in the benchmark. When supposedly active funds invest in their benchmark it is known as 'closet benchmarking' – a clear case of performativity. A problem with the second is when the risk rating for the fund is based upon the rate at which the fund has moved up and down in the past and is, therefore, not forward looking. There is much room for improvement in the understanding of fund performance by regulators and in the audit of the behaviour and performance of fund managers.[17] If portfolios based on smart auditing out-perform the market then this suggests that smart thinking based upon factors that frame deserved confidence arrives at the fair market price more quickly than the standard thinking of the time. It encourages the remainder of the market to adopt the same thinking shaped around the pillars of deserved confidence that we have taken to be creativity, sustainability, resilience and fair treatment of stakeholders. Consequently, the auditor can serve as the identifier and carrier of new thinking as well as the instigator of action.

It is important that the audit of an investment fund, the audit of an investment company that manages funds, and the audit of companies in which funds are invested follow the same underlying audit philosophy built on a commitment to deserved confidence. This allows investors, managers, other stakeholders and auditors to have deserved confidence in each other, and to develop governance as a mutual activity. It is the philosophy of audit that is shared in the sense that all share the commitment to thinking differently and bringing their different ideas together creatively in order to progress in terms of the four pillars - progress that can benefit all stakeholders.

Success of a portfolio comes when deserved confidence in the portfolio is increasing. In the case of fund management, it needs to take into account the fair treatment of stakeholders, including whether the needs of the subscribers (investors) to the fund are met; that is, does it fulfil the purpose specified to subscribers and follow the direction of necessary engagement with the investee companies? The proposition to subscribers should specify the extent to which the fund currently invests in (a) new creativity (potentially leading to progression), (b) exploiting past creativity and (c) sustainability and resilience. Engagement with investees should help drive down sustainability risk by ensuring, for example, that the companies take appropriate measures in relation to societal issues including those relating to the economy, the environment, climate change, advances in technology and the treatment of employees and other stakeholders. Other things being equal, improvement in the income of the portfolio and its sustainability indicates a contribution to the economy or economies in which the fund is invested. Sustainability risk attaching to the portfolio can be reduced through diversification but this should not reduce engagement with individual companies on their individual sustainability. Resilience risk needs to be assessed by reference to the probability of disruptions and the portfolio's ability to withstand them or to benefit from them. Diversification can be considered as giving less exposure of the portfolio to the specific risks (and opportunities) of disruption.

Smart thinking has to function as evidence of the future, evidence that brings the future into view more quickly. Fundamentally, smart thinking is not about outperformance but about progress based upon improved understanding and the opportunities that brings to all investors and stakeholders. The governance of fund management needs to bring this about, with the auditors of the funds helping to inspire such a shift through their assessments of deserved confidence.

Concluding summary

The opening sections of the chapter discussed investment priorities and highlighted the fact that many investment practices pay little attention to the underlying businesses in which investment is made. Consequently, governance by the investment community of individual businesses may be somewhat ineffective. Even when investors do analyse the companies in which they invest, they may not hold sufficient shares to have an effective 'voice' or hold company directors to account. This situation has opened the door to activist investors (hedge funds) including those who concentrate not on diversification but on building a substantial shareholding in a small number of companies that their analysis has shown to have value potential. Such hedge funds are private and the benefits of their work, if successful, are only enjoyed by a few.

The failure of Inclusive Capital Partners was used as a case to highlight the problems of governance in relation to the transition away from an established business (platform) that performs well in terms of profitability but badly in terms of its ESG impact. This is seen as illustrative of the general need for all companies to identify an appropriate pathway from the existing business ('correspondence value') to new business platforms ('progression value'). Correspondence value results from anticipating the future exploitation of the present business platform. It is thinking from the past and the present to the future and is often influenced by the expected continuation of trends. Progression value results from anticipating the development and exploitation of future platforms that may be radically different and can represent different thinking. How long the existing platforms can be used depends upon movements in the force fields of the commercial universe; that is, when and where are there likely to be game-changing disruptions. These fields form a threat but they also provide an opportunity to create radically new platforms.

Such analysis serves to build a framework for the judgement of overall creativity value based upon both correspondence and progression and the interaction between them; a framework which embraces both continuity and discontinuity. It is the successful handling of these opposite processes that is key to progress.

We cannot know the future but we can develop ways in which the mind can address the future and this, whilst a big challenge for auditing, can give it new strategic direction. The future of auditing in many respects rests on auditing the future! Auditing is currently rooted in an understanding of the past and present but our conception of audit based upon assessment of deserved confidence requires that auditors have a better understanding of and engagement with the future (and what it holds or could hold for the company being audited and for the society in which it operates).

A discussion of chess was employed in the chapter to introduce an understanding of platforms and how they exist at different levels. Two key platforms were distinguished – one formed around rules and serial thinking, the other centred on a sense of 'feel' and assessing the dominance of a particular position based upon experience. A game (such as chess) is the interaction or connection between the two platforms in the context of the idiosyncrasies of a particular match. In terms of evidence (understanding) we have the logic (rules) of the game, the big picture of pattern recognition in big data and specific data relating to the particular game and the individual opponent. Transferring these thoughts to auditing, we discussed how the smart auditor like the 'top' chess player has to be creative, bringing together the logics of auditing and the recognition of important patterns of evidence emerging from the idiosyncrasies of the particular client.

The final section discussed big data as a platform through which smart auditing can encourage smart investing. Smart auditing starts by looking at big data and then looks at individual companies shown on a statistical basis to be outliers. What makes smart auditing 'smart' is the choice of factor(s) on which to search for exception. It is argued that smart auditing should choose factors that frame the construct of deserved confidence, being factors that relate to creativity, sustainability, resilience and stakeholder engagement. The auditor explains the reasons for any exceptional performance on and across these factors. However, it is emphasised that the role of the auditor is not to identify investment opportunities but, through their assessment in terms of deserved confidence, to provide valuable insight that can help in the establishment of fair share prices.

In summary, this chapter has explored and sought to strengthen understanding of the connections between audit, management, investment and governance. Audit should seek a major role in aligning share prices with levels of deserved confidence in underlying business activities, helping investment and management (rewards) to move to those companies and activities with better prospects, whilst at the same time improving the prospects of all companies. The objective of investing in shares becomes not so much to gain at the expense of other investors or other stakeholders but to share in the increasing prosperity of the business sector. Good governance comes from the auditor, management, investors and committed stakeholders working together in delivering greater understanding of business.

The provided framing for audit demonstrates its fundamentality in terms of promoting and securing development of this common understanding; an understanding that enables governance to operate more as a lateral concept promoting connections and hence creativity across stakeholders, rather than a hierarchical concept in which the governors supervise the governed. Good governance does not come from over-reliance on rules, codes and committees that may indeed hinder the application of the principles, spirit and creativity that underlie the establishment of better companies. The future of audit is shaping the future of mutual governance, a governance based upon common understanding of, and confidence in, the future. The auditor is ideally placed to reshape governance and through this to tackle the governance deficit. Governance should be seen as an (implementation) arm of progression audit, with progress looking to the future and judging the need to move on from established ways of business in order to deal with outside forces. In this respect, it is important to appreciate that the best form of oversight is foresight.[18]

Notes

1 It is noted that the market as a whole can be invested in some risk exposures more than others and consequently investing across the whole market might not provide 'maximum' risk diversification.

2 Jeremy Siegel demonstrated that, in the long run, real returns on equity reverted to a mean, reducing their riskiness (Lo and Foerster, 2023, p. 295) and reducing their riskiness relative to bonds, although others such as Robert Shiller (e.g., Shiller, 2000) have long emphasised that markets could suffer from bouts of irrational exuberance leading to boom and bust.

3 It is inexpensive to buy a position (exposure to price movements) using a derivative instrument but that position is highly exposed to price movement and, hence, is highly leveraged. Scholes and Merton were among the founders of a hedge fund called Long Term Capital Management (LTCM) that used quantitative models related to option pricing to identify price discrepancies between similar assets as

the basis of a trading strategy that assumed the discrepancy would close over time. The subsequent failure of this strategy followed when Russia defaulted on its debt, the discrepancy widened rather than closed and LTCM collapsed spectacularly. The case serves to highlight the importance of auditing all potentially significant financial institutions with reference to sustainability and resilience in light of the volatility of their promises (derivative positions).

4 In 2022 there was an LDI crisis in the UK. This had some similarity with the LTCM case (see endnote 3) in that both cases were looking for a convergence that, because of a financial disruption, did not take place at the required point in time. LDI managers held substantial volumes of gilts but were forced to sell gilts to meet unexpected (disruptive) shortfalls, driving down the price of gilts, increasing the shortfall and creating a downward spiral. Ultimately the Bank of England had to intervene (see Arjalies et al., 2017, pp. 62–67).

5 For a discussion of technical and fundamental analysis, see Malkiel (2019, pp. 113–181).

6 ValueAct was not a hedge fund of the 'hit and run' variety.

7 It is not clear how well these values were adhered to in the case of Rolls-Royce. ValueAct bought a significant (10 percent) share of Rolls-Royce in 2015, pushed for the disposal of its poorly performing marine division which was consequently sold and then ValueAct disposed of its entire shareholding in 2020 during the Covid, pandemic, incurring an estimated 20 percent loss (*Financial Times*, 6 August 2020, 'ValueAct sells entire stake in Rolls-Royce', www.ft.com/content/e7dd1939-dadb-43d0-9444-4622bb0f1b88). Since the end of the pandemic the value of Rolls-Royce's shares has risen considerably.

8 The cited article in the *Financial Times* can be accessed at the following link www.ft.com/content/349bdf63-cd38-4328-890a-e94c9fe4849e?syn-25a6b1a6=1.

9 For example, in the case of Rolls-Royce, further development of new engines in the Trent family represents continuity and correspondence with existing technology predominating, whilst development of the electric plane represents a discontinuity and progression to a new technology. Management must judge the boundary between correspondence and progression – including how much resource to put into each of these developments.

10 If continuity is associated with purpose and discontinuity with disruption, then the transition pathway connects purpose and disruption.

11 For a theatrical illustration of the inspiring nature of Swift's observation and how it can help to bring an actor's character to life, see https://alwaysactingup.wordpress.com/2009/08/26/"vision-is-the-art-of-seeing-what-is-invisible-to-others-"/.

12 McGilchrist (2021, p. 695) also discusses chess playing as an illustration of expertise and its development.

13 The computer games industry is one of low validity and hence one where pattern recognition cannot be employed as effectively as it might in complex but relatively unchanging environments. We should be aware that the development of technology has been and continues to have a disruptive effect on the games industry, with the majority of contemporary growth being in computer games rather than in traditional 'board' games.

14 To take an example, in 2015, one unlisted mainland Chinese company had a subsidiary listed in Hong Kong (Hanergy Thin Film Power Group Ltd) with high

share price momentum. Funds heavily invested globally in momentum would have had the company in Hong Kong as a big contributor to the fund's outperformance. However, Hanergy's price collapsed in May 2015 and subsequently the company was de-listed due to fraud. Momentum up to May 2015 seems to have been driven by the listed subsidiary selling increasing numbers of solar panels to the unlisted Chinese parent which had simply been accumulating stocks. This highlights the problem of passive investors not knowing what is going on in a company. It also represents presumably an audit failure. In the Hanergy case, inquiry as to who the main customers were (it would turn out be the parent company), their financial status and their relationship to the auditee was key. Gathering evidence on the nature of relations with key stakeholders should be important for any audit. For a more general appraisal of management fraud and corporate collapse, see *The Unaccountable & Ungovernable Corporation* (Clarke, Dean and Egan, 2014).

15 Such backtesting work typically invokes a statistical 'arsenal' of (normal) distributions, measures of normalised returns, significance, skewness, risk and volatility, Sharpe ratios and factor correlation.

16 As an exercise in smart investing, Edinburgh MBA students Alasdair Cummings and Mikey Salvador, for their dissertations, separately backtested portfolios constructed upon their own 'smart choice' of factors based upon identifying unusual relations between the financial dimensions of the four pillars. The results were promising in terms of market outperformance, although it is wise to be cautious about making claims outside the periods tested. In one case, results were noticeably driven by the behaviour of the Indian stock market over the period and in another by a relatively small number of companies, of which Hanergy was one!

17 Observational research of the workings of fund management by Arjalies et al. (2017) utilised the notion of investment chains to reflect the complexity of relations between the various actors forming the investment industry: chains being something that can restrict but also secure. However, what chains don't do is encourage thinking differently. Arjalies et al. also discussed evidence of the inefficiency of financial intermediation, of which the investment industry is part, and also ineffectiveness implied by the increasing cost of financial intermediation relative to GDP (pp. 11–13). It may be that the finance industry is more successful at value transfer than value creation. Complexity allows for specialisation but not necessarily improvement in the performance of the financial industry, especially if the performance of the industry and the firms and governments into which it invests are mis-specified.

18 A similar claim was made by Humphrey and Moizer (2008, p. 277) in relation to the functionality of audit regulation.

References

Arjalies, D-L., Grant, P., Hardie, I., MacKenzie, D. and E. Svetlova, 2017, *Chains of Finance: How Investment Management Is Shaped*, (Oxford University Press, Oxford).

Boden, M., 2004, *The Creative Mind: Myths and Mechanisms*, 2nd edition (Routledge, London).

Clarke, F., Dean, G. and M. Egan, 2014, *The Unaccountable & Ungovernable Corporation*, (Routledge, London).

Du Sautoy, M., 2019, *The Creativity Code: How AI Is Learning to Write, Paint and Think*, (Fourth Estate, London).

Humphrey, C. and P. Moizer, 2008, 'Understanding regulation in its global context', in *Auditing, Trust and Governance: Regulation in Europe*, Quick, R., Turley, S. and M. Willekens (eds.), pp. 262–278, (Routledge, Abingdon).

Lo, A.W. and S.R. Foerster, 2023, *In Pursuit of the Perfect Portfolio*, (Princeton University Press, Princeton, NJ).

Malkiel, B.G., 2019, *A Random Walk Down Wall Street: The Time-Tested Strategy for Successful Investing*, (Norton Publishing, NY).

McGilchrist, I., 2021, *The Matter with Things: Our Brains, Our Delusions, and the Unmaking of the World*, (Perspectiva Press, London).

Prahalad, C.K. and G. Hamel, 1990, 'The core competence of the corporation', *Harvard Business Review*, 68:3, pp. 79–91, https://hbr.org/1990/05/the-core-competence-of-the-corporation.

Shiller, R.J., 2000, *Irrational Exuberance*, (Princeton University Press, Princeton, NJ).

9

AUDIT AS THE ENGAGEMENT OF THE FINANCIAL AND NON-FINANCIAL

This chapter examines in more detail the relationship between financial evidence, non-financial evidence and deserved confidence. It starts with consideration of some of the key intricacies associated with the auditor's assessment of deserved confidence. The chapter then contemplates the potential to reconfigure an audited company's financial statements so that they, in conjunction with pertinent non-financial evidence, are better able to facilitate the auditor's assessment of deserved confidence. The financial statements' reconfiguration put forward in the chapter is not absolute. Indeed, we want it to stimulate and encourage fresh ideas and perspectives on how to improve the functionality of financial statements. However, the provided illustrative reconfiguration serves three definitive purposes. First, it reinforces the more holistic nature of the reconceptualised audit function proposed in this book compared to the current, traditional, limited company audit. Secondly, it establishes that a company's financial statements do not have primacy over the audit but rather have to be seen in more subordinate terms - as 'servicing' the function of audit rather than being its essential focus. Thirdly, the proposed reconfiguration helps to illuminate and appreciate that the auditor's assessment of deserved confidence is not a fixed process – but is something capable of being stimulated, in a reverberative fashion, through the continual development of new ways of thinking about the relationship between a company's achievements, obligations and interactions with its business environment.

Thinking further about the assessment of deserved confidence

In the physical world, position can be described in terms of four co-ordinates, being the three space dimensions (height, width and depth) plus time. In

DOI: 10.4324/9781032721293-9

business, a company's position can also be described in terms of four co-ordinates (pillars), being creativity, sustainability, resilience and stakeholder engagement. The first three of these exhibit (represent) different relationships between the past, present and future. Creativity is concerned with growth in the future, sustainability is the continuance of the present into the future and resilience conserves and learns from the past to prepare for future disruption. Thus, these three pillars are all concerned with time. The pillar of stakeholder engagement is a 'spatial' dimension or co-ordinate connecting shareholders and other stakeholders. If performance is a measure of the movement of a company over time between an opening and a closing position determined by all four pillars (creativity, sustainability, resilience and stakeholder engagement), then any (re)presentation of deserved confidence must explain the changes in and across the four pillars and the impact of such changes on deserved confidence.

Deserved confidence is an idea that spans time, space, feeling and depth. For confidence as a feeling to have depth there must not only be confidence about what is known (the occupied space and the past) but confidence about what is left to find out (the unoccupied space and the future). Having confidence about the past but not the future is shallow. Deserved confidence is not only having confidence about what has been achieved, why and how. It is also having confidence about the ability both to shape the future and respond to the unexpected that it will bring.

To have depth, an assessment of deserved confidence must be based upon a creative flow or spirit: a creativity that senses the what, why and how of future achievement; a creativity that inspires – and inspires not just auditing professionals but also those who engage with, depend on and are assessed through the audit process. It is also a capacity not to be underestimated in terms of its quality and purposefulness. At its conceptual core, assessing deserved confidence (and for any such assessment to be both pertinent and respected) requires the ability to think creatively; in essence, to be able 'to create creativity'.

When we talk of a creative footballer, we mean a player who has a 'feel' for the game, who can through touch and unexpected movement make time and space; who can see the visionary pass or connection, bring others into the game, get them moving and 'make it happen'. A creative manager recognises the qualities of the players, works with them and positions them to 'create' a team that plays exciting football for the benefit of players and fans. Professional football is a business and needs an attractive product. In a similar fashion, a 'creative' auditor should have a 'feel' for the production of deserved confidence, an eye for the visionary connection and the instinct to react insightfully to any surprise positioning of the company across the four pillars.

Evidence can be viewed in both financial and non-financial terms – with non-financial evidence extending beyond financial outcomes, providing additional insight and delineation of what business activity is going on in respect of purposeful pathways, disruptions and potential disruptions, of the outside forces the business is subjected to and of the non-financial outcomes of the business activity, including those for society and the environment.

The deserved confidence audit requires that the connections between non-financial and financial evidence and each of the pillars are understood. Each pillar and the flows between them are brought to life, reflected and captured in the provision (incorporating both the contrasts between and the coming together) of non-financial and financial evidence.

The creativity of the auditor flows to the client company and vice versa, with varying analytical emphasis dependent on contextual circumstances. If the company being audited is placing too much emphasis on the financial numbers or over-relying on non-financial evidence, the auditor's creative responsibility will be to challenge and to change such emphasis for the better.

Emphasising the creativity inherent in the auditor's analytical focus reinforces that the audit should be seen as anything but routine and standardised – instead, the audit has to be treated and regarded as a unique and dynamic investigation of how confidence emanates from within and flows across the four pillars of deserved confidence and an assessment of the merits (or merited nature) of the company's current and potential future positioning on such pillars.

Such assessment considers the nature of the pillars together with evidential representations of business activities and the likelihood of, and capacity for, future development and progress. Deserved confidence in this regard is both an assessment of the way the business has engaged with the nature and demands of the different pillars and how well it is set to respond to future shifts in its own business environment (the outside forces) and in the constituency of the pillars themselves. This includes the capability of the business to progress commercially and to have a more desirable or meaningful societal impact.

The financial and the non-financial serve to challenge each other as evidential sources. Do the financial numbers make sense given the auditor's knowledge of the business and its environment? And does our knowledge of the business and its environment make sense given the financial numbers? The audit is continually asking both questions at the same time which, conceptually, emphasises the reverberative nature of audit as a process.

Audit establishes or pinpoints the appropriate scale of deserved confidence by drawing together and mediating between the senses – combining evidence that is both financial and non-financial (which, in turn, shapes – and reshapes – such evidence and its representation). It could even be said that audit, through deserved confidence, is the 'queen' of the senses. It draws together, and in that 'sense' is created by, the other senses whilst at the same time it frames and influences those other senses. The ultimate potential here for audit is not only to represent and assess achieved and prospective business outcomes but also to influence, in a progressive fashion, such outcomes, the company's future positioning on the pillars of deserved confidence and, even, what comes to be recognised as central to the make-up and identity of such pillars. This points directly to the fundamental dynamism of audit as a concept and a practice – and what follows in the remainder of this chapter is just one, but a very important, example of what can transpire (and serve to challenge) when recognising that 'thinking differently' is audit.

Connections and classifications

In nature, we know that the insect and the flower connect with and support each other. The insect fertilises the plant and the plant provides food for the insect. This connection is encouraged by the smell and colour of the plant and the receptors of the insect that respond to these senses. Classification into insects and flowers follows their (obvious) differences whilst their connection is organised around the common interest in survival, facilitated through the senses.

Money can be regarded as an 'artificial' sense in so far as monetary value enables the very different to connect. Buyers and sellers can connect via a price considered value for money by both. Recipients and providers of public funds connect at a level of funding considered fair by society. So, a sense of (fair) value for money is possessed by humans and society alongside the natural senses of seeing, smelling, hearing and touching (feeling). Value for money is an instinct and, as with other instincts, it is shaped by preference, experience and context – capable of being seen as having a strong connection with notions of fairness, for example, in not paying or being charged 'over the odds' for something. Value for money is a feeling that brings together a sense of the financial and of the non-financial.

In Chapter 5 it was argued that evidence comes from the senses – primarily combining visibility in the form of macro and micro data and a 'sense' of logic that connects the two. Logic itself arguably spans the two hemispheres of the brain, being not only processual (such as the orderly or 'if… then' thinking of chess or mathematics) but also instinctive or beautiful (such as the beauty of mathematics or chess). Evidence as a 'sense' extends to a sense of time and a sense of space. Chapter 5 also identified that evidence is itself a representation and 'to represent' is 'to evidence'.

Audit, in essence, is searching for a (new) representation of reality that can guide and influence societal and business action together with the individual and collective sense of value. Through its influence audit not only seeks to reflect but to change and improve reality. However, the reality is that 'reality' can never be fully understood and 'tamed' and the concept of 'progress' must be understood in that context. What we see and represent is not reality but a 'sense' of reality.

We have in this book represented the world through notions of classification and connection. It is possible to think of (re)classification as the progression from the micro to the macro, from the individual to the collective, from the quantum to the universal (and vice versa). Each (business) activity is placed in a box (that is, it is classified) and connected to other boxes to form a bigger box or network. Each network is connected to other networks and this continues until we have the network that represents the four pillars and their connectivity, and ultimately the 'single' or 'collective' box of deserved confidence.

It also has to be appreciated that this is not a static set of positions or perspectives. Deserved confidence and the connections and pillars on which it rests are fundamentally dynamic and open to transformation – with new forms of classification and fresh or different connections capable of shifting what deserved confidence comprises, how it is to be assessed and what can be provided and illuminated through analysis and reflection. In other words, we gain insight on deserved confidence by addressing it from different directions; that is, through contemplation of different networks of classification, connection and consequence.

Chapter 7 introduced deserved confidence in the business, with the three key layers or levels of Figure 7.1 being (1) the four pillars through which deserved confidence is assessed – resilience, sustainability, stakeholder engagement and creativity, (2) the external forces impacting on the audited business and (3) the business activities, informed by its outcomes (both financial and non-financial) and positioned as a reflective or responsive intermediating level between the pillars and the external forces. The narrative in Chapter 7 discussed what might need consideration and response during this intermediation. The discussion considered each pillar's connection to business activity, to the other three pillars and, directly or indirectly, to the external forces coming from the natural/physical environment, society, the economy and technology.

In Figure 9.1, in order to explore the nature of a company's 'financials' as a source of audit evidence, the elements first introduced in Chapter 7 are reorganised into (1) financial evidence (being the financial outcomes), (2) non-financial evidence (taken to include consideration of business activity, disruptions, non-financial outcomes and both the impact of and impact upon external forces) and (3) the four pillars, positioned as vehicles for bringing together or framing (i.e., making sense of) both the financial and non-financial evidence.

Whereas in Figure 7.1 the focus was on business activity as the intermediary between the four pillars and the external forces, our discussion of Figure 9.1 will focus on the four pillars as the intermediaries between financial and non-financial evidence. Figure 9.1 does not replace Figure 7.1 but, by reconfiguring all the elements introduced in Figure 7.1, it leads to discussion and analysis that provides insight on the contributions and limitations of financial evidence and consequently additional insight of the analytical priorities of the deserved confidence audit. Overall deserved confidence comes from confidence in the company and how it is run (Figure 7.1), combined with confidence in the audit's ability to bring together financial and non-financial evidence in an insightful manner (Figure 9.1). In essence, Figure 7.1 presents the auditor's cognitive model of the audited company, whilst Figure 9.1 depicts the

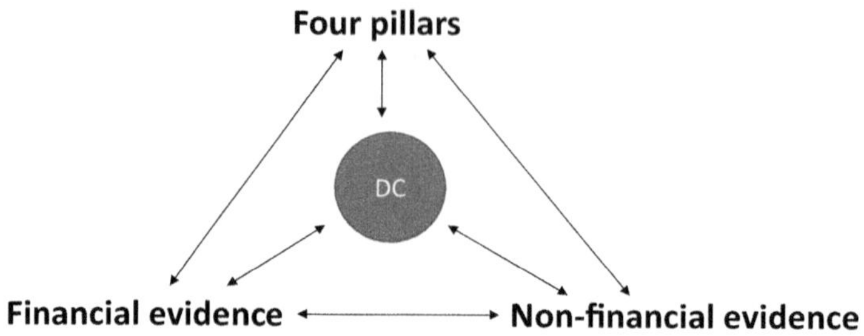

FIGURE 9.1 **Financial and non-financial evidence, the four pillars and deserved confidence (DC).**

auditor's cognitive model of the confidence that could flow from bringing the financial and non-financial together in a reconfigured manner around the four pillars.

The remainder of this chapter considers the processes by which an auditor could develop confidence through bringing the financial and the non-financial together. Since the auditor is seeking an assessment of the company's positioning on and across the four pillars, financial numbers along with business activity have to be understood in the context of each other and the outside business environment. In terms of interaction, better financial evidence or better understanding of such evidence can lead to better understanding of the non-financial and vice versa, leading to a better understanding of the four pillars and their connectedness. For example, introduction of Environmental, Social and Governance (ESG) assessment (a form of non-financial evidence) can lead to better understanding of the limitations of the financial evidence and of how the company's financial and ESG performance should come together to evidence (the pillars of) deserved confidence.

The importance of the pillars in assessing deserved confidence

It has to be remembered that in our reconceptualised audit, the financials (including financial funds and transfers) are only individual elements of evidence of the four pillars and do not by themselves fully delineate either the pillars or the flows between the pillars. Indeed, other evidence in the form of the purposeful pathways undertaken by the company to reposition itself with respect to the pillars and external forces is essential to any assessment of the degree to which the company is deserving of confidence.

Such assessment could include, for example, discussions with management about how and why they are repositioning and/or responding to the pillars, discussion with key employees and evidence of communication with stakeholders – coming together with an appreciation of relations between the company and pertinent outside forces, including impacts on society and the environment. In addition to a sense of where the company is, what it is doing and why, such assessment will also need to incorporate study of the financial outcomes relevant to an understanding of the company's position on and across the four pillars. The scale or strength of confidence that the company is 'deserving of' is centrally dependent on the auditor's assessment of such positioning and the need for any potential strategic repositioning regarding the pillars.

The auditor could be said to have in mind, ultimately, a set of relationships and representations as depicted in Figure 9.2. What connects the pillars in Figure 9.2 are not only flows of financial and non-financial evidence (or even resources) between them but the confidence that emanates from the knowledge that the auditor has built up and consolidated through the audit. It is a collective sense of belief in, and recognition of, the company's creative capacity, the sustainability and resilience of its business activities and the nature and strength of its stakeholder relationships that enables the auditor to declare that the company is deserving of confidence. Such considerations can incorporate assessment of the company's ability (a) to create new knowledge or understanding (**'creation'**), (b) to convert such knowledge into

FIGURE 9.2 **The audit ring of confidence.**

sustainable business propositions ('**conversion**'), (c) to cover commitments to stakeholders ('**coverage**') and (d) to conserve resources and stakeholder and shareholder connections in the business – and give it a sense of resilience and solidity ('**conservation**').

The collective framing embodied in Figure 9.2 represents the audit as a process of inquiry, reflection and engagement that assesses and engenders the holding of the most appropriate or deserving level of confidence in its operations and its destiny. It is the confidence flowing from and across the pillars and the appropriateness of such processes and acts of **creation, conversion, coverage and conservation** that enable or underpin the auditor's attribution of deserved confidence – such that Figure 9.2 can be categorised as a diagrammatic representation of the audit 'ring of confidence'.

Notions of creativity, sustainability, resilience or stakeholder engagement, and hence deserved confidence, are all open to the outside forces that impact and are impacted upon by the business. Thus, the cognitive system for understanding, assessing and developing deserved confidence depicted in Figure 9.2 is both internally interactive and open to the outside. According to the interactive hypothesis of systems theory (Lamb and Chemero, 2018, p. 151), "a state or behavior that is strongly dependent on some other set of states or behaviors cannot be adequately characterized without also saying something about the states and behaviors it is dependent upon". It is this openness that gives the network new information, energy and a persistent lack of equilibrium (Lamb and Chemero, 2018, p. 154) in which changes can occur both in terms of the company's position on and across the four pillars and also the nature of the pillars themselves in terms of what they comprise or how their particular dimensions are represented.

Accordingly, the four pillars should not be seen or classified in static, fixed terms. If the network as a whole is interactive and open to the outside, then what counts as being creative or sustainable, for instance, can shift over time and across contexts. In this regard, the auditor not only assesses the positioning or repositioning of the company in terms of its position on any given pillar but also retains a sensitivity to changes in the nature of each pillar. As such, it becomes possible to view creativity not only as the creativity behind the company's product but as an awareness of the potential for definitional shifts in the pillars themselves.

The function of the audit is to challenge management on the creativity of its products and (re)positioning and consequently to assess the level of confidence management, and hence the company itself, deserves. To make this challenge effectively, the auditor also needs to be creative, to be prepared to 'think differently' and to think differently from management. Confidence flows from seeing a 'creative' network of creativity, sustainability, resilience and stakeholder engagement, positioned to achieve an even stronger (more creative) network in future.[1] The auditor should 'push/pull' management towards a stronger network: a case of leadership rather than followership. It is audit as progression rather than correspondence.

In Figure 9.2 the external forces are pervasive and impact the pillars and deserved confidence through the company's purposeful pathways whilst, at the same time, the company's activities impact those forces. For instance, there is a need in assessing deserved confidence to recognise the impact of the company on the environment's resilience, sustainability, creativity and other stakeholders in the environment. In making a judgement of the impact on the environment, the auditor considers both the numerical (metrics) and non-numerical evidence in the context of relations between the environment, society, the economy and technology. There has been much exploration of different means of bringing environmental 'costs' into the financial statements. For example, most recently Barker and Mayer (2025) advocated a form of replacement cost accounting that recognises the replacement cost of business impact on the environment, whilst Friedrich and Kunkel (2025) argue that a new transnational body is required to respond to the global importance of maintaining the environment and to ensure that environmental liabilities are recorded on the balance sheet.[2] Rather than thinking in terms of disclosure or financial accounting, we are thinking (in this chapter) of the auditor and the company working together to build deserved confidence for all stakeholders in the company's commitment and success in dealing with its responsibilities to the environment and other external forces.

Treating the audit as the primary function – accounting implications and opportunities

A direct conceptual implication of what has been said so far in this chapter (and the book more generally) is that instead of audit accommodating a particular set of company accounts, it is the company accounts that should respond to the needs of the audit. Thus, it is the deserved confidence audit and its four pillars that drive the way the auditor looks at the accounts and the interpretation of the non-financial evidence, enabling both forms of evidence to come together and give insights on the achievements of the company. If the non-financial evidence is employed to explain or to challenge financials that are framed in terms of the four pillars, then the non-financial evidence is also, in effect, taking on the same form as the financials, with both following the shape of the audit ring of confidence. It is the audit ring of confidence that brings the financial and non-financial evidence together.

The remainder of this chapter uses a hypothetical company in the aero engine industry to explore what a conceptual reconfiguration of audit around deserved confidence and the four pillars (Figure 9.2) implies or could stimulate in terms of the reconfiguration of the company's financial statements. The company has been lacking growth for a number of years but a new range of engines has been launched at the beginning of the financial year and it has sold well. However, the new engines have run into a number of problems in service that required or will require 'fixes'. A key feature of the illustration is how an assessment of the four pillars requires an understanding of this issue (the non-financial evidence) and of its financial consequences. Another issue covered by our illustration is a substantial change in the value of derivatives, the value of which is included in 'promises'. The forces that drive the engine problems are technical whilst the changes in derivative values flow from macro-economic forces, and so both issues illustrate the coming together of non-financial evidence (technical and economic) and financial evidence in the judgement of deserved confidence. The illustration starts with a summarised conventional set of financial statements and proceeds to explain what a reconfigured set of financial statements could comprise.

Reconfiguring the financials

Table 9.1 (Financial Position) and Table 9.2 (Movement in Financial Position) summarise the hypothetical company's published balance sheet and profit statement in a manner that enables the auditor's reconfiguration of company accounts to align more closely with the four pillars of deserved confidence. An initial suggested reconfiguration is given in Table 9.3.

Table 9.3 details the financial dimensions (and changes in the funds) associated with each of the four pillars, with the sum of the four funds being the

TABLE 9.1 Financial position

Opening £m	*Balance Sheet/Financial Position*	*Closing £m*
5080	Goodwill and intangibles[3]	5430
2865	(Net) Fixed assets plus working capital minus debt	2775
(6081)	Promises – Deferred tax, warranties, pensions, derivatives	(3049)
1864	**Book equity**	**5156**

TABLE 9.2 Movement in financial position

Movement in Financial Position	*£m*
Underlying profit	1022
Dividend	(216)
Change in value of promises	2536
Impairment of intangibles	(50)
Change in book equity	**3292**

TABLE 9.3 The financial dimensions of the four pillars

Creativity	*Sustainability*	*Stakeholder Engagement*	*Resilience*	*Market Equity*	*Flow/Transfer of Funds*
£m	*£m*	*£m*	*£m*	*£m*	
11306	5646	(6081)	2865	13736	Opening balance
2793				2793	External inflow
(5510)	5510				Internal transfer
(2536)		2536			Internal transfer
	(456)	496	(40)		Internal transfer
			(50)	(50)	External outflow
6053	**10700**	**(3049)**	**2775**	**16479**	**Closing balance**

market equity (market capitalisation) of the company.[4] In respect of financial position, goodwill and intangibles are replaced by a creativity fund. Fixed assets plus working capital minus debt are replaced by a resilience fund. Promises are assigned to a stakeholder engagement fund, while a sustainability fund is calculated based upon the underlying profit and business risk. Book equity is replaced by market equity. The movement in financial position is represented as a series of flows interacting with the outside world (the external inflow and outflow) together with a series of internal transfers between the four funds.

The opening and closing resilience funds shown in Table 9.3 are taken directly from the balance sheet data in Table 9.1 (being in each case the total of net assets plus working capital minus debt). The opening and closing stakeholder engagement funds similarly come directly from the balance sheet (in this case being the provisions for deferred tax, pension liabilities, warranties and derivatives).

To calculate the sustainability fund closing balance, underlying profit of £1,022m taken from Table 9.2 is split between what the auditor judges as a fair return on the resilience fund of £166m and the resulting, underlying residual profit (earnings) of £856m. The closing sustainability fund of £10,700m represents the determined present value of sustainable residual earnings which represents a significant increase on the opening sustainability fund of £5,646m (the calculations here will be explained in a later section).

The opening and closing market capitalisations for our hypothetical company are £13,736m and £16,479m respectively, these amounts being the number of shares in issue multiplied by the share price at the opening and closing dates of the financial year. The value of the creativity fund has been taken to be the market capitalisation of the company minus the other three funds. Thus, the closing creativity fund is £6,053m (£16,479m – £10,700m – £2,775m + £3,049m). Similarly, the opening creativity fund was calculated as £11,306m.

Understanding the movement in financial position

The flow of funds in Table 9.3 (right-hand column) gives the financial value created (and lost) through interaction of business activity with the outside (this value is initially taken to be the increase in its market capitalisation) and the value flows between the four funds to change the positioning of the company. The flow of funds becomes clearer when Table 9.3 is displayed in a 'shape' that follows the audit ring of confidence (see Figure 9.3), with the fund flows being labelled as (value) creation, conversion, coverage and conservation.

The outer ring of Figure 9.3 shows the financial funds and the flow/transfer of funds. This financial evidence comes together with identified, pertinent non-financial evidence to create or provide the basis for the auditor's deserved confidence (DC) assessment (positioned at the centre of the figure).

In Figure 9.3, the value created through interaction with outside forces is £2,793m – which equates to the change in the company's market capitalisation of £2743m (£16,479m – £13,736m) plus the amount of funds that the company chose to distribute as dividends to shareholders in excess of the return on the resilience fund (being £216m – £166m = £50m).

The return on the resilience fund is the auditor's assessment of what would be a fair return in light of the risks faced by the company and can be used to determine whether shareholders are unduly increasing or reducing the resilience fund; in our case the shareholders' contribution to the fund has

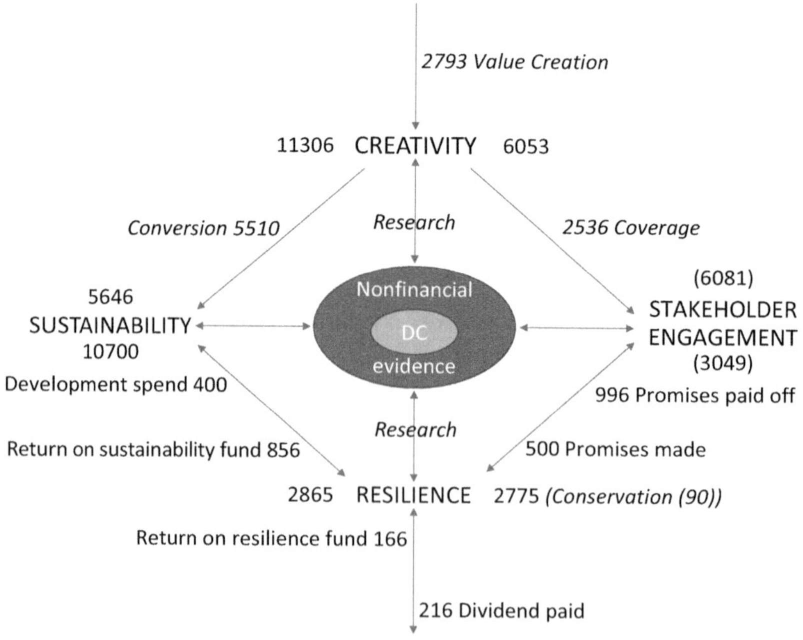

FIGURE 9.3 **Reconfiguring the financials to follow the 'audit ring of confidence'.**

been reduced by £50m, a reduction that may cause the auditors to question its appropriateness given the intended expansion of the business as a result of the launch of the new engines.

Creation (£2,793m) is the increase in the financial value implied by the change in market pricing of the company's prospects during the year, with prospects broadly defined to include the prospects for all four funds including stakeholder engagement. Market pricing is influenced by past, current and prospective creative activity and its expected impact upon future growth of new and existing products. The value of creativity initially reflects a judgement by the stock market. The auditor can start by taking the market's implied assessment of value created as shown in Figure 9.3 but this assessment is challenged by the auditor seeking to examine and explain the market's assessment through the collection of non-financial evidence, including evidence of prospects. Figure 9.3 uses the example of research as a form of expenditure capable of directly connecting resilience and creativity. As research has been written off in the accounts, research expenditure has been included as a deduction against income in calculating the sustainability fund and not incorporated as an asset in the financial resilience fund. However, the company's research efforts can still provide non-financial resilience in the form of creativity that can protect against future disruption and improve the company's prospects through its potential for value creation. The auditor will need to assess the scale of research progress and whether its potential to enhance the company's overall creativity has been under (or even over) valued by the market.

The creativity 'fund' of £11,306m at the start of the financial year becomes £6,053m at the end of the year due to the incoming flow of value creation and outgoing flows of conversion (£5,510m) and coverage (£2,536m). Coverage is the amount that the company's market value might be expected to increase during the year due to the company reducing its liabilities to stakeholders (other than shareholders). In Figure 9.3, the transfer of £2,536m from the creativity fund to the stakeholder engagement fund represents the reduction in the future stakeholder claims (in this case being a change in the fair value of financial instruments) that the company (and its prospective plans and actions) has to 'cover'.

Conversion, on the other hand, is the amount (£5,510m) of the creativity fund that has been realised during the year by turning prospects into the comparative 'reality' of sustainable, underlying residual profits. The sustainability fund moves from £5,646m to £10,700m as a consequence of the incoming flow of conversion (£5,510m) and the net outgoing flow of £456m (£856m – £400m) to the resilience fund. The £456m is the determined return on the sustainability fund of £856m, net of a £400m, one-off, cost incurred for the fixing of problems with the company's new engines – which will be discussed in more detail later in the chapter.

The opening resilience fund of £2,865m becomes £2,775m at the end of the year due to an overall conservation outflow of £90m. This outflow comprises a net inflow received from the sustainability fund of £456m, a net outflow to the stakeholder engagement fund of £496m (£996m – £500m) and a net outflow to shareholders of £50m (£216m – £166m).

The outflow to the stakeholder fund of £996m is a payment made to reduce the company's liability under past promises made to stakeholders (other than shareholders), whereas the £500m inflow is new promises made to such stakeholders (increasing the resilience fund because the company, for example, has chosen to reward employees with enhanced future pension entitlements rather than paying in cash the equivalent amount as an increase in current salaries). The outflow to shareholders is a dividend payment of £216m that exceeds the notional return on the resilience fund of £166m.

The liability (from a shareholder perspective) of the stakeholder engagement fund (promises made to non-shareholder stakeholders) is reduced from £6,081m to a closing £3,049m by the net £496m inflow from resilience and by the £2,536m inflow from the creativity fund.

Considering the collective significance of the financials and the non-financial

Understanding of the financial funds and flows comes from understanding of the activities of the company, and the relations of those activities with the four pillars and with external forces; whilst at the same time understanding of the company and its relations with the four pillars and with outside forces is informed by knowledge of the financial funds and flows, together with knowledge of other (non-financial) outcomes. Consequently, the greater holism of deserved confidence shown in Figure 9.2 extends beyond the (financial) holism of Figure 9.3 to embrace non-financial evidence.

The key point to take from Figure 9.3 is that all the funds are directly and indirectly connected to each other and a change in one fund, due to company activity and/or outside forces, impacts the other funds and hence the company's funding position as a whole. In this sense, understanding of the company's funding is holistic as is the understanding of the non-financial evidence and the assessment of deserved confidence in Figure 9.2. Or to put it another way, we can view the outer ring of Figure 9.3 as framing the funds and flows of financial evidence in the shape of the audit ring of confidence. When considered together with the non-financial evidence (shown in the inner ellipse) that flows to support or to contest the financial evidence, this collectively forms the basis for the auditor's overall assessment of deserved confidence (DC) as shown in Figure 9.2.

In the remaining sections of this chapter, we give some further insight into the significance of non-financial considerations in assessing the company's performance and standing, and in formulating the auditors' deserved confidence assessment. The analysis is moving from one predominantly driven by financials to consideration of non-financials and how they support and challenge each other and ultimately combine to form the audit ring of confidence that indicates whether there is consistency between the company's financials and its strategic intentions and prospects. In the UK the auditor of a company of a certain size/status is obliged to report whether the information given in the company's strategic report is consistent with the company's financial statements. However, such a correspondence orientation falls substantially short of the spirit of progression that is central to an auditor's assessment of deserved confidence.

The role of interest rates

In Figure 9.3, the flows of creation, conversion and coverage represent the changes between the opening and closing fund values for sustainability, stakeholder engagement and creativity, but only after the auditor has determined the annual returns on the resilience and sustainability funds. This requires consideration of what are fair and appropriate interest rates to apply to fund values, making such rates a key factor in connecting financial and non-financial evidence.

In our above illustrative example, the return on the resilience fund of £166m was calculated on the opening fund of £2,865m using an interest rate judged appropriate by the auditor, of 5.8%.[5] This left a residual underlying profit of £856m (£1,022m – £166m). The closing sustainability fund of £10,700m was arrived at by assuming the residual profit is sustainable (permanent) and calculating the present value of sustainable residual earnings of £856m using a sustainability rate of return, judged appropriate by the auditor, of 8% (8% of £10,700m = £856m). A similar calculation last year gave an opening sustainability fund of £5,646m.

The sustainability rate of return (8%) is at a premium (in this case 2.2%) to the resilience fund return (5.8%). The premium is a matter of the auditor's judgement but might be informed by that charged in similar situations across companies. The case for a premium is discussed in the next section. It should be noted that the return on the resilience fund is notionally paid before the return on the sustainability fund since it is the return on the sustainability fund that is the residual.

The returns shown in Figure 9.3 have been calculated by the auditor and as shown in Figure 9.3 both returns (£856m and £166m) flow into the resilience fund. This follows conventional accounting where the underlying profit of £1,022m, comprising both returns, flows into those book assets (net fixed assets plus working capital minus debt) that form the resilience fund. The dividend payments, promises made and paid and the development expenditure are already in the published financial statements and therefore do not present new audit challenges.

As previously stated, the flows of creation, conversion and coverage are the amounts necessary to be consistent with the movements in the funds of sustainability, stakeholder engagement and creativity during the year. In essence, the flow of financial value starts with creation since before creation there is nothing; this is then converted into sustainable business activity and such sustainability both supports and is supported by resilience and stakeholder engagement. Given the connectedness of the financial and the non-financial evidence, all business activity and changes in outside forces (i.e., all non-financial evidence) have the potential to change both the flow of financial value and our understanding of that flow of value and its consequences for deserved confidence.

The role of prospects

Prospects relate to future opportunities and threats and how the company intends to deal with them; opportunities and threats provided by pressures from and upon the natural environment, changing societal attitudes, economic trends and the technological developments available to the company. If prospects are good and risks are low then it is less likely that the resilience fund of assets will be called upon; and there are unlikely to be accounting losses that result in the resilience fund being diminished. Accordingly, the required rate of return on that fund might be low. If prospects are poor and the risk of losses is high, then the rate of return on the resilience fund should reflect this. In general, the sustainability risk might be expected to be higher than the resilience risk, even when prospects are good because the risk of not being able to maintain underlying profits (the sustainability risk) is higher than the risk of actual losses that would impact the resilience fund. In other words, the company might have lower profits rather than losses and this impacts sustainability before it impacts resilience. Of course, if prospects deteriorate then both the resilience and sustainability risks might increase with both funds requiring higher returns. Other factors such as financial leverage and non-financial resilience can, together with prospects, impact the risk relationship between the two funds and these other factors have been discussed in Chapter 7.

Prospects and the risks inherent in those prospects also impact relations between the sustainability and creativity funds. Whilst sustainability represents the ability to maintain current residual profits into the future, creativity represents the prospects for increasing current residual profit in the future. If prospects are good then there might be very little risk that the current level of residual underlying profit cannot be maintained, and a low rate of return for the sustainability fund would be appropriate. However, the creativity fund depends upon the residual profit achievable in future being above the current level of underlying residual profit. This is likely to be more unpredictable than achieving current profit and so the required rate of return implicit in the market's judgement as to the creativity fund value (of those future profit increases) is higher than the required rate for the sustainability fund. If prospects deteriorate, the impact on the creativity fund will depend on how the market reacts to the deterioration when valuing the company's shares and how the auditor reacts in terms of changing the required rates of return for the sustainability fund. The creativity fund is increased by the falling value of the sustainability fund but decreases as a consequence of declining market value. It is quite possible that the auditor and the market think and feel differently as to future prospects and their consequences, and any such differences, and changes to those differences, will impact the value assigned to the creativity fund.

The case of the engine fixes

In order to demonstrate how the circumstances of the business come together with the four funds to allow a judgement of deserved confidence, we consider the case of our hypothetical company and its engine fixes. The approach of the auditor is to construct the audit ring of confidence by bringing together both the financial evidence (Figure 9.3) and non-financial evidence (in this case, understanding of the engine fixes) and assessing how they challenge and support each other.

Table 9.3 shows that the market values the company more highly at the end of the year than at the beginning. It also shows that the resilience fund has remained at roughly the same level, that the company has achieved an increase in the sustainability fund and the claims upon the company by other stakeholders (promises made) have reduced. Nevertheless, the value attributed by the stock market to the creativity fund has declined substantially from £11,306m to £6,053m. This is mostly due to a transfer from creativity to sustainability shown in Figure 9.3 to be £5,510m. Whilst sustainability represents the ability to maintain current profit into the future, creativity represents the prospects for increasing current profit levels in the future. Since the new engines have boosted profit this year, much of last year's creativity value has materialised (it is no longer prospective), generating a value transfer from creativity to sustainability. However, problems with the new engines have put a break on the market's expectations of any further increase in profit, so that there is little new value arriving in the creativity fund to replace the transfer out.

In the published (conventional) accounts the cost and estimated future cost of the engine fixes (£400m) have been treated as one-off development expenditure reducing the company's current assets by £400m and increasing the intangible assets by the same amount. It has not impacted reported profit. However, what is important is not the accounting treatment *per se* but that the issue of the engine fixes has implications that go beyond direct financial consequences to confidence in the company as a whole.

In respect of the non-financial evidence the first stop for the auditor here would be with the Head of Development to get a handle on the success of the problem fixes, the costs and the timescales and to consider what impact on the four funds is to be expected. It is important to establish whether the problems are truly one-off and have been or can be dealt with from a technical point of view. If so, it would be reasonable to regard the cost of the fixes as a one-off hit to the resilience fund (book equity) rather than a charge to underlying profit. The engine fix costs become a continuation of the development cost of the new engines, albeit incurred after the launch and therefore expensive and unwelcome. In effect, one-off costs become a claim on the resilience fund in order to maintain sustainability but provided they are truly one-off then, although the size of the resilience fund is reduced by the charge, the risk and required return on the remaining resilience fund might be unaffected. The auditor needs to ensure that charges are appropriately claimed as one-off, or else increase the required return on the resilience fund to reflect any raised uncertainty in this regard. Assuming the total cost of the fixes (actual and expected) is £400m then this amount flows from the resilience fund to support the sustainability fund as shown in Figure 9.3.

If after investigation, for which the auditor probably needs specialist help, there remains doubt as to the competence or the cost of the fixes then there is likely to be a significant impact on the risk attaching to the continuation of the underlying residual profit and hence upon the value of the sustainability fund. In addition, there would need to be an increase in the resilience risk. These risks are compounded by the possible disengagement of disillusioned customers and the increasing value of warranties. However, on a more positive note the ability to make the fixes might speak well of the resilience of the company engineers in the face of disruption.

Identifying the origin of value

Figure 9.3 shows shareholder value entering the system at the top and flowing initially into the creativity fund. However, this value flow of £2,793m which originates with the changing valuation of the company by the stock market does not all remain in the creativity fund and £2,536m transfers to the stakeholder engagement fund. In effect the market's improved valuation of the company comes partly from creativity, for example, from any identified progress in research, but in this case mostly from a reduction in the valuation of stakeholder promises in response to outside forces. Thus, £2536m of the value entering the system is allocated to the revaluation of promises, leaving £257m as creation. This small increase suggests that the market did not come to see during the year a significant improvement in the company's prospects. The auditor needs to assess whether the market view is reasonable, particularly in the context of research progress.

In a sense, value enters the audit ring of confidence both through creativity and through the revaluation of stakeholder promises, but for simplicity Figure 9.3 shows only one entry point.[6] The auditor needs to consider whether the change in the value of the promises to non-shareholder stakeholders will, in fact, impact stakeholder engagement. However, in the case of our hypothetical company, the stakeholder mostly affected is the financial institution that is the counterparty to the foreign exchange derivatives that have changed in value. Our company's sales were made in dollars but the reporting currency was sterling. Consequently, the company purchased foreign exchange derivatives which changed substantially in value as a result of change in the exchange rate. This is unlikely to impact key stakeholder relations with customers, suppliers and employees.

In the case of the revaluation of promises, the non-financial evidence is provided by the changing economic environment and its influence on the (specialist) valuations of promises made to non-shareholder stakeholders. Confidence in these valuations becomes an important part of deserved confidence in the company.

Outside forces also play a key role in assessing the interest rates to be used in valuing the sustainability and resilience funds. The auditor needs to have confidence in the choice of these interest rates. Of course, there is much non-financial evidence left for the auditor to explore including the company's environmental commitment, its treatment of employees, the company's research efforts, prospects for the airline industry as a whole and the possible impact of the engine problems on future orders and sales. Having considered all of the non-financial evidence and its implications for the company, the auditor can assess the extent to which the company is deserving of confidence. Furthermore, if details of the auditor's thought process were to be revealed to management and investors then it might well highlight matters, including inconsistencies, not fully or properly recognised by management and/ or investors, pushing them towards delivering, and investing, in a better company.

Company directors' long-term incentive plans

To encourage management and investors to pursue such lines of thought, it is worth considering the implications that our conceptual reconfiguration of audit has for the design (or rather redesign) of company directors' long-term incentive plans (LTIPs).

Currently LTIPs reward management, often bountifully, according to a set of performance measures that are predominantly financial and hence significantly divorced from performance in terms of deserved confidence. LTIP's are often quite complex and bring together a mix of benchmarks and measures, arguably exhibiting little understanding of the connections between them. Financial measures can include earnings per share (EPS), return on investment (ROI) and total shareholder return (TSR), TSR being a combination of dividends and share price increase. Share repurchases (buybacks) give a short-term boost to share prices and to earnings per share. LTIPs that include rewards for higher share prices and/or higher earnings per share, therefore, encourage buybacks rather than the business creativity/pathways that associate with deserved confidence. Moreover, increasing share prices can be the result of falling central bank interest rates that have little to do with management.

Finally, performance assessment centred on ROI might lead to only the highest returning projects being undertaken, leaving many positive projects on the table and discouraging overall investment. Consequently, ROI might encourage companies and investors to accept projects that are capital asset light rather than heavy. If so, then across the economy assets are replaced by labour and the economy moves to a capital asset (investment) light service economy that can find it difficult to increase productivity (the productivity puzzle) and runs into balance of payment difficulties due to the import of manufactured goods; and if services growth is underpinned by immigration, there can be difficulty in maintaining GDP per head. Low levels of investment, albeit in high-returning projects, results in low overall demand for capital and, hence, a low cost of capital set against a high ROI. This is the situation reported by Mazzucato (2018, p. 176), based upon research by J.P. Morgan in 2014 of S&P 500 companies, that whilst the weighted average cost of capital was at 8.5% the hurdle rate needed for a new project was far higher, standing at 18%.

The problems with LTIPs illustrate the perils of constructing a business performance regime around metrics. While LTIPs typically include some non-financial metrics (such as customer satisfaction ratings), all metrics mask the wider and deeper judgemental issues associated with deserved confidence. However, if long-term incentive plans were to be designed around the auditor's assessment of the four pillars and deserved confidence, then these perils would be reduced and give the auditor's assessments a greater potential to impact on the determination of management rewards and related behaviour patterns.

Audit, interest rates and the resurrection of business risk auditing

The role and importance of interest rates to a holistic deserved confidence audit is considered in this section by reference to the determination of the rate of return required for the sustainability fund.

Consideration of the required rate of interest has three key elements: (1) the price of time, (2) the amount of risk and (3) the price of risk. The price of time is the interest that would be necessary even if there were no risk; a return required whenever consumption today is preferred to consumption tomorrow. It is the 'risk free' rate and often based upon a relevant central bank lending rate. Care must be taken in making the most appropriate choice since no central bank is entirely risk free. Central bank rates reflect the confidence that global capital markets have in a nation's economy and levels of confidence vary between countries and over time. Even if prospects and confidence were such that sustainability was guaranteed the rate of interest could not fall below the 'risk free' rate.

The second element is the amount of risk, taken to be a function of both the chances of an event and the (negative) consequences of the event. If chances are high and consequences high then the amount of risk is high. As the chances and/or consequences reduce the amount of risk reduces. The amount of risk depends upon the company's prospects in relation to exposure to outside forces, taken together with the company's ability to respond through resilience.[7] The company's prospects impact resilience and sustainability risk. In respect of sustainability the amount of sustainability risk determines the risk premium to be included in the interest rate over and above the risk-free rate. It is this risk premium that is the third element, the price of risk. It is that part of the interest rate that has to be paid to compensate for risk. The price of risk is the risk premium paid to compensate for risk aversion.

To be relevant to the valuation of the sustainability fund, the interest rate used must itself be sustainable. If any of the three elements of the required interest rate are not considered sustainable in the future then that adds to the overall sustainability risk and increases the required interest rate further. Preferring consumption today and risk aversion are common features of many societies that, if taken too far, can result in too little investment to sustain the economy. If this is the case then current interest rates and risk premiums may not be a good guide to what is a sustainable rate, and it might be necessary to study the historical pattern over time of relations between (1) interest rates, (2) societal attitudes to consumption, borrowing and risk and (3) economic performance, in order to find an interest rate consistent with a sustainable economy, and this might be significantly different to the rate society is currently experiencing. As a general point regarding the importance of interest rates, much of our inability to get the economy moving could be a misjudgement/misunderstanding of the role of interest rates – whereby they are set too low to reward the risks associated with creativity and appear more consistent with a society that avoids risks through the promotion of conformity, potentially to the detriment of growth.

Developing our understanding of interest rates, how they should be constructed and the role they play in bringing together the financial and non-financial dimensions of sustainability is a challenge but also an opportunity for audit to contribute to economic well-being, to the natural and physical environment and to society. This is because the interest rate used for valuing the sustainability fund can be adjusted by the auditor to ensure it reflects the company's impact, relative to its size, on the economy, on the environment and on social goals. The adjustment reflects, for example, sustainability risk coming through the exposure of the company to and upon economic, environmental and social decline and/or to government intervention designed to prevent such decline. Similarly, whenever the interest rate on the company's debt does not appropriately reflect the company's contribution to economic, environmental or social change, an adjustment can be made to interest charged by the auditor in the reconfigured financials on the debt finance and this will change residual income. The auditor can thus facilitate governance and provide incentives on sustainability at the company level (micro governance) in anticipation of, and in a sense on behalf of, governance of sustainability by the government (macro governance).[8]

In summary, the financial and non-financial expressions of sustainability are brought together through the medium of risk assessment and its relations with interest rates, and the auditor can lead on this because the collection of audit evidence also gives the auditor a handle on risk. Indeed, with so-called 'Business Risk Auditing' (BRA),[9] the assessment of business risk was taken to be the primary source of audit evidence. The above discussion has focused upon risk in the context of sustainability. It is also a major issue in the context of creativity where there may be a novel risk (Hardy and Maguire, 2020). A novel risk is more difficult to get a handle upon, since reliable evidence may not be readily available. If big data is missing then novel risk, initially at least, has a fuzzy visibility-time profile; however, the risk profile changes as more experience/data is obtained. At the beginning, creativity has as much to do with instinct and belief as it does with conventional forms of evidence.

Concluding thoughts

This chapter has introduced the audit ring of confidence as a thought process that shapes and brings together financial and non-financial evidence in the development of an assessment of deserved confidence. Company financial statements are no longer the subject of the audit but, instead, they provide a source of evidence for the auditor's assessment of deserved confidence in the company. Consequently, the chapter has explored how financial statements and the share price can be used to provide evidence which interacts with, and is supported/challenged by, non-financial evidence to allow an assessment of the four pillars and how they interact with each other, and drive deserved confidence.

The perils of relying on financials alone, or failing to challenge the financials and other metrics, are highlighted by the problems with management's LTIPs and their potentially negative impact on confidence. The market and the auditor should not have confidence in a company where the management incentives are not on a basis compatible with how the auditor assesses deserved confidence. The process of reconciling the financial and non-financial evidence can raise questions about the financial numbers and, in particular, the company share price and its suitability as evidence of creativity and creativity's value in terms of future growth. The audit report covering the assessment of deserved confidence might draw attention to this. As indicated in the discussion of LTIPs, the share price can be manipulated by management, notably through share buybacks. Share prices prior to the audit report can be over or undervalued due to a market that is underinformed. Prices can also be influenced by investor speculation rather than intrinsic value. According to the market mind hypothesis (Schotanus, 2023), the market has a mind of its own. Different stakeholders think differently. Whilst the auditor is attempting to influence stakeholders such as the market and management, so that they come closer to thinking the same as the auditor, the auditor is at the same time seeking to think differently to others and maintain the dynamic of improvement.

A function of audit is to encourage the market (mind) to focus upon intrinsic value rather than speculation, and to think of intrinsic value in terms of deserved confidence. Since deserved confidence responds to the external forces coming from society in terms, for example, of the fair treatment of stakeholders and respect for the environment then, if the audit is influential, such issues become embedded in the share price. Attempts to predict the future of share prices, as such, then become or equate to an exercise in predicting deserved confidence.

The chapter has used a form of four fund accounting (Hatherly, 2013) to help understand the connectivity implied by Figures 7.1 and 9.1. Underlying four fund accounting is the dual nature of the present; it is a coming together (coincidence) of opposites. What constitutes the present can be considered in two different ways, and four fund accounting shows how they may be drawn together.

Firstly, it can be said that the present does not exist or, at least, it does not exist for more than an instant. It is the interface or boundary between the past and the future and this interface is constantly changing due to the passage of time. As soon as the present arrives it expires and is replaced by a new present. Following this line of thinking, a present might exist but only when successive 'instants' are unchanging. Sustainability is the ability to 'expand' the present in the sense of continuing the present into the future (the future as a continuation of the present) and this is the approach taken in assigning a financial dimension (the sustainability 'fund') to the sustainability pillar. The financial value of the present comes from the present residual profit and the risk associated with its continuity.

Opposite to the idea that the present does not exist (or only exists if there is continuity) is the idea that the present is all that exists. The argument is that the past does not exist because it has gone and the future does not exist because it has not yet arrived. The past exists as recall and the future as anticipation and both recall and anticipation exist in the present. Following this line of thinking, market capitalisation at a point in time represents the present.

The approach taken by four fund accounting embraces both views of what comprises the present. It has a separate fund for the present – the sustainability fund – or the present can be taken as the combined financial dimensions of all four pillars (the sum of all four funds), the sum being represented by market capitalisation. Thus, four fund accounting connects two 'funded' representations of the present – in the shape of the sustainability fund and all four funds added together. However, the chapter shows that for this connection to have meaning it cannot be purely a financial reconciliation as it also requires consideration of the non-financial dimensions of all four pillars. Audit operates at the boundary between the financial and the non-financial, bringing the two dimensions together to provide a purposeful representation as to where the company stands with respect to the four pillars of deserved confidence. The audit ring of confidence, expressed as a combination of narrative explanation and (financial) numbers, is such a representation. It can be seen as the creative outcome of a coincidence of opposites – the financial and the non-financial.

At a deeper level audit flows from the coincidental existence and non-existence of the present, another coincidence of opposites that can, following McGilchrist (2021, p. 841), be profoundly creative. Audit operates at the boundary between existence and non-existence, with creativity, flowing from the creativity of the audit, providing a channel from non-existence to existence. In essence, audit operates as a research function but, most critically, its focal point is rooted centrally in an assessment of business strategy and risks that draws on, yet extends beyond, the company's financials. It should be the audit that drives the construction of the company's financial statements and not the other way around. Rather than traditionally viewing audit as reconciling back to the financial statements, we should see audit as a driving force that takes us well beyond traditional financial statements. It is audit that continually inspires the construction of new ways of not only representing but also enhancing the performance of the company. In this way, audit directly changes the relationship between the present and the future. It is the scale of creative reconfiguration and connectivity applied by the auditor that gives substantive meaning, weight and impact to the assessment of deserved confidence.

Notes

1 If everything exists courtesy of its relations with other things then creativity takes the form of a creative network and higher levels of creativity take the form of a network of creative networks.

2 Although we have cited two recent papers, environmental and social accounting and audit have a long history of academic debate. See Gray and Laughlin (2012).

3 Movement on this account has been: opening balance £5,080m, add development spend £400m, subtract impairment charge £50m, giving the closing balance of £5,430m. It does not provide any meaningful valuation of intangibles nor any

understanding of how they are managed, what they represent or how they interact with sustainability, resilience and stakeholder engagement.

4 This 'four fund' accounting is an adaptation of accounting for four slices of equity (Hatherly, 2013). This gives further illustration of the reconfiguration of accounts from published financial data.

5 Ultimately both required rates of interest (for the resilience and the sustainability funds) are judged in the context of the prospects for the company and the risks inherent in those prospects, including the risk of future inflation.

6 The company's shareholders are invested in the non-financial dimensions of the company's resilience, sustainability and stakeholder engagement. These, along with creativity, are the intangible assets of the company. What we, for reasons of simplification, take as the financial value of creativity is, in fact, the financial value of all these intangibles. Also, whilst Figure 9.3 shows/treats value created by the business from interaction with outside forces as entering through the one entry point – to the creativity fund – there are in reality three other entry points, being to stakeholder engagement (as discussed in the text), and sustainability and resilience primarily captured by changes in the required rates of return on those funds.

7 Leverage might be a factor here. For example, if there is high sustainability risk, then there is a need for a high resilience fund but this need could be moderated by low leverage.

8 The terms micro and macro governance are taken from Walker (2006). The study of physics is a study of the very small (quantum physics) and of the very large (the physics of the universe) and a search for the connection between the two. Similarly, the study of governance can be divided into a study of the small (the individual company), the large (the economy) and the connection between the company and its external environment.

9 Business risk auditing (BRA) was popular in the late 1990s with its advocates arguing that an in-depth understanding of business and business risk was the best way for an auditor to recognise management fraud and business failure risk (the two most common causes of litigation against auditors). However, audit practitioners were uncomfortable with the lack of linkage between the work they were doing on business risks and the expression of, and support for, their opinion on the financial statements (see Curtis and Turley, 2007; Curtis et al., 2016). The linkage between business risk and deserved confidence is stronger and more direct since the assessment of deserved confidence and the risk premium used to value the sustainability fund must be consistent.

References

Barker, R. and C. Mayer, 2025, 'Seeing double corporate reporting through the materiality lenses of both investors and nature', *Accounting Forum*, 49:2, pp. 259–289, https://doi.org/10.1080/01559982.2023.2277982.

Curtis, E., Humphrey, C. and S. Turley, 2016, 'Standards of innovation in auditing', *Auditing: A Journal of Practice and Theory*, 35:3, pp. 75–98.

Curtis, E. and S. Turley, 2007, 'The business risk audit – A longitudinal case study of an audit engagement', *Accounting, Organizations and Society*, 32:4–5, pp. 439–461, https://doi.org/10.1016/j.aos.2006.09.004.

Friedrich, J. and T. Kunkel, 2025, 'Reimagining the foundation of financial reporting: A rights-based approach to account for environmental externalities', *Critical Perspectives in Accounting*, 102, https://doi.org/10.1016/j.cpa.2025.102796.

Gray, R. and Laughlin, R. 2012, 'It was 20 years ago today: Sgt. Pepper, Accounting, Auditing & Accountability Journal, green accounting and the blue meanies', *Accounting, Auditing & Accountability Journal*, 25(2), pp. 228–255. https://doi.org/10.1108/09513571211198755.

Hardy, C. and S. Maguire, 2020, 'Organizations, risk translation, and the ecology of risks: The discursive construction of novel risk', *Academy of Management Journal*, 63:3, pp. 685–761, https://doi.org/10.546/amj2017.0987.

Hatherly, D., 2013, *The Failure and the Future of Accounting; Strategy, Stakeholders and Business Value*, (Routledge, London).

Lamb, M. and A. Chemero, 2018, 'Interacting in the open: Where dynamical systems become extended and embodied', in *The Oxford Handbook of 4E Cognition*, Newen, A., De Bruin, L. and S. Gallagher (eds.), pp. 147–162, (Oxford University Press, Oxford).

Mazzucato, M., 2018, *The Value of Everything: Making and Taking in the Global Economy*, (Allen Lane, London).

McGilchrist, I., 2021, *The Matter with Things: Our Brains, Our Delusions, and the Unmaking of the World*, (Perspectiva Press, London).

Schotanus, P., 2023, *The Market Mind Hypothesis: Understanding Markets and Minds Through Cognitive Economics*, (De Gruyter, Berlin).

Walker, M., 2006, 'How can business reporting be improved? A research perspective', *Accounting and Business Research*, 36:Supl, pp. 95–105, https://doi.org/10.1080/00014788.2006.9730050.

10

AUDIT IS THINKING DIFFERENTLY

Breaking free of Groundhog Day

Attempts at audit reform have frequently reminded us of *Groundhog Day*, the 1993 classic film where a weatherman played by Bill Murray, having been sent on an assignment, is shocked to find he is living the same day over and over.[1] In the UK, we have been in a repeat cycle of dissatisfaction with audit, followed by pressure for reform, followed by suggested reforms, followed by inaction, later followed by the same cycle all over again. In the following paragraphs, we reflect on two official studies of the future of auditing with which we were personally involved, being the McFarlane Report and the more recent Brydon Report.

In 1992, one year earlier than the release of *Groundhog Day*, the McFarlane Report (published by the Auditing Practices Board in 1992) proposed that the audit be redefined to include, inter alia, a report on the conduct of a company's affairs by its management including comment on the adequacy of internal financial controls and on corporate ethical standards; a longer ('non-stereotype') audit report that comments on a broad range of information contained in the Annual Report; and a comment on any substantial future risks attaching to the company. It was also proposed that there should be a debate on the extent to which auditors might report to a broader constituency of stakeholders than just shareholders. Such recommendations are entirely compatible with the ideas that had been proposed in 1942 in *The Accountant* (see Chapter 1).

The Auditing Practices Board (APB) was established not by government but by the audit profession but, nevertheless, the response of the professional bodies to the McFarlane report was underwhelming. Puxty, Sikka and

DOI: 10.4324/9781032721293-10

Willmott (1997) analysed their responses and concluded that they represented the interests of their members and that the public interest, though prominent in their mission statements, did not feature explicitly in their thinking.

McFarlane talked (para 2.5) of building public confidence in auditors and of providing a more solid foundation for the future development of the audit profession. This is a conversation that has run and run but subsequently we see neither an increase in public confidence nor the creation of a platform for development. Even though we have had several decades of independent audit regulation and inspection, the predominant emphasis is still on 'restoring trust' in audit. To us the logical conclusion is that to restore trust in audit we don't need yet more regulation and inspection, but rather we need to think differently about audit, its purpose and what audit can achieve. It is the need for such different conceptual thinking that has been the main motivation for writing this book.

We have been thinking both separately and together about audit for a considerable time. Whilst David Hatherly was a member of John McFarlane's working party and of the APB that published the report, Chris Humphrey was a member of the advisory board to Sir Donald Brydon's (2019) review. Brydon emphasised how little of McFarlane's report and recommendations had been implemented in the intervening 37 years. Paragraph 5.1.1 of the Report states:

> *There is no shortage of debate and discussion of the future of audit but I found, in the words of Professor Chris Humphrey, a member of the Review's Advisory Board, that the debate so far "encourages a form of analysis where incremental change is probably the most likely recommendation and outcome, where old 'hobby horses' (such as the expectation gaps or the value of IFRS and the case for prudence) frequently get resurrected, where people seek to dominate a collective discussion with their singular perspectives, and quite quickly we end up in a discussion that we seem to have had many times over; a debate that is notable only for its familiarity and circularity, and if any radicalism does emerge, it tends to come in the form of speculative proposals that antagonise rather than resolve, and which, ironically, reinforce or ground analysis in what we have come to accept and understand as audit with a frequent refrain to proposed extensions in the audit being dismissed as 'not audit'.*

The Brydon Report (2019) was a very philosophical report on audit and audit professionalism. Brydon determined (para 5.1.2) that the concept of audit needed to be rethought and given a more ambitious delineation of purpose. His recommendation (para 5.1.4) that "The purpose of an audit is to help establish and maintain deserved confidence in a company, in its directors and in the information for which they have responsibility to report, including the financial statements" is entirely compatible with the articles published in *The Accountant* in 1942.

Taking direct inspiration from the Brydon report, Chapters 1–5 of our book centred directly on constructing the philosophical basis for rethinking the nature and purpose of audit, while subsequent chapters focused more on exploring the highly significant implications of viewing audit in more conceptually dynamic and creative terms. Collectively, we have sought not only to stimulate new thinking about audit but also to represent audit itself as stimulating something new. This book is the product of a long but ultimately fascinating journey that has opened up our minds to new vistas, and to the realisation that opening new vistas should itself be the mission of audit.

New ideas on audit, however, do not easily take root in the minds of government or the profession. Not surprisingly, in true Groundhog Day terms, the UK government did not accept Brydon's proposals for a more evaluative, holistic, expansive audit (BEIS, 2022). The UK government formally seemed to prefer that Brydon's overall purpose of audit was treated as the overall objective of its programme of (corporate governance) reforms and for the regulator to regard it as a non-binding purpose statement for its own activities (BEIS, 2022, para 6.1.19). In para 6.1.8 the government response stated that Brydon could lead to a perception that audit is forward-looking, and provides confidence in an entity's continued viability. There was also some accompanying resistance from the profession, with claims that it was too ambitious, expansive and not suitably specified.

What our book stresses is the logical and emotional conclusion that for audit to be of fundamental value, it must be forward-looking and provide confidence; that audit is the mainstay of, and cannot be subordinate to, governance; that regulation, at least in its present form, is not a solution; and that the profession must be ambitious and expansive to succeed in its declared intent to serve the public interest (or, otherwise, the profession will continue to wither in influence, impact and relevance). We are not looking for a continuation of what is currently seen as audit but for a transformation of audit to promote better business, a better society and a better economy; and it is being 'better' that is in the public interest. We focus on what audit can become rather than what audit is or what it is not.

The potential for constructing a transformative philosophy of audit is well illustrated by the fact that it is over 60 years since the publication of Mautz and Sharaf's (1961) classic text 'The Philosophy of Auditing'. It is also embodied internationally in recent academic responses to the Brydon Report. For example, US auditing researcher Robert Knechel took the view that

> Sir Donald Brydon has done the audit profession a tremendous service by highlighting a broad path forward for reforms to the audit profession (and, by implication audit education). An historical obsession with rules and regulations has not allowed the profession to avoid audit scandals and failures. Whatever is done in the wake of the Brydon Report is unlikely to be perfect on its own. **However, a significant rethinking of the nature, structure and practices of auditing may help the profession improve where stringent rules making has lagged**.
>
> (Knechel, 2022, p. 30, emphasis added)

Whilst our book has examined and developed concepts in the context of the UK and the Brydon Report, we submit that those concepts are relevant internationally. In the UK there is a consensus that a better economy and a better society are deeply connected. The current UK government has set out its agenda for growth but transformation of audit does not figure in it. However, it needs to be a priority and until it is, Groundhog Day will continue both in the profession and in politics. We particularly need governments to think differently and recognise the profound potential of audit's role in the economy and in society.

It is also important that thinking differently about audit is continual and not a one-off event that merely resets Groundhog Day as reliving something different. The underlying premises and foundation of audit must continue to be challenged in line with the philosophy of audit itself as something dynamic that continues to open up new vistas. The case is for a dynamic repair and improvement of audit (Humphrey et al., 2021). The commitment is to 'holistic' reform that goes beyond 'hole-fixing' and is oriented to changing audit rather than adopting a position that defaults to arguing that everything must change except audit. Indeed, the very straplines of the auditing firms such as 'building a better working world', 'formulating a new equation' or promoting 'Omnia' (being ready for everything) invite a major and continuing reformulation of audit practice but this is unlikely to happen without a deeper commitment and willingness to explore and develop the core conceptualisation of audit.

In this regard, there is a vital comparison to draw between context and concept. Audit reforms for many years have been dominated by a concern with context and have largely treated the concept of audit as a given. Reform typically centres on the context within which a particular form of audit is practised and regulated – considering, for example, what services auditors can provide and what they should be prevented from providing, what length of audit tenure is acceptable, whether a single auditor is sufficient or whether having joint auditors is the better way forward, the timeliness of audit reports and what auditors need to reveal about their work and conclusions. However, in so much of this, the conceptual form of audit is not up for debate, reflecting a dominant sense that we all know what an audit is and what it isn't – phrases such as 'an audit is an audit' or the assumption that the expectations gap is largely an educational or ignorance gap are premised on the assumption that there is one particular, dominant, accepted conception of audit that requires little justification or critical reference. Even when it is suggested that the expectations gap is more driven by considerations of performance than education, performance improvement in terms of audit tends to be framed around auditors doing their existing function better rather than pursuing a different conceptual formulation of audit.

Independence and non-independence in the public interest

To reconceptualise audit, we have drawn on the philosophy of physics and, in particular, those ideas in physics that stress the importance of seeing the reality of existence as one of connection. Every 'thing' (entity, element, idea, feeling, classification) exists courtesy of its connection with other things. Like physics, audit is concerned with whether things exist and with representing the nature or reality of that existence to others (other things) in the system or network. Audit itself exists simultaneously both inside and outside the network. 'Inside' in order to have influence that changes society and the economy for the better, and 'outside' in the sense of thinking differently to others and, therefore, having the ability to make a contribution to change and improvement. And so, our first (re)conceptualisation is of audit independence. Audit independence is thinking differently in order to enhance the public interest. We should not have rules on independence that are solely driven by fear of audit and consultancy converging.

Our first chapter says a lot about the public interest and progress to a better society and that 'better' includes 'better' societal values that lie at the intersection of truth and fairness, two concepts that we see as pragmatic/relative rather than absolute. Audit challenges societal values and pushes society to understand itself and its complex connections better. A better society and economy based upon better shared values is where the public interest lies; audit and society are interactive and the public interest lies in there being such a connection.

Audit is a way of thinking

We stress that audit is a way of thinking, of thinking differently. Crucially, thinking differently requires an independence of thought that has the potential to be creative, to take both business and society to a better place, and to do this audit should be flexible and dynamic. The potential of audit is unrealised/held back under the current institutional arrangements. Just what has happened to audit professionalism? In the mind of government has the regulator become the profession and the auditor merely an extension of the regulator? Can an auditor think differently if the ethos of regulation is one of conformity through rules, codes and compliance testing? Our reconfiguration of audit can drive a renewed sense and significance of audit professionalism; connecting audit more directly to serving the public interest and enhancing understanding of what that requires.

Integrative thinking, the opposable mind and creativity

If audit is required to think differently and lead to progress then it is necessary to understand creativity. Creativity can be seen in terms of the coming together of opposites. This is the basis of 'integrative thinking' as advocated by authors such as Martin (2007) and Riel and Martin (2017). The sense of revelation is indicated by the title of Martin's book (2007) – *The Opposable Mind*. Instead of downplaying differences of perspective or interest, of largely assuming an integrated pursuit of a common set of goals to create value, Martin's notion of 'integrative thinking' embraces the existence of difference and tensions between differing views and ideas, and uses such tensions to think a way through to new and superior ideas. The auditor needs an opposable mind because in our conception of audit there are no enduring standards, only enduring tensions (Hatherly, 2009), and it is through the recognition and synthesis of these tensions that audit (and through audit), society and the economy make progress.

McGilchrist (2021) also sees creativity in terms of a coming together of opposites, especially with respect to the left and right hemispheres of the brain. Whilst the left hemisphere promotes order, control, rationality, agency and bureaucracy, the right hemisphere promotes experience, change, empathy, freedom and openness. It is the coming together of these two hemispheres through the brain's corpus callosum that gives the opportunity for creativity. Audit may be thought of in terms of the corpus callosum, that part of the brain that connects and brings the two hemispheres together. We follow McGilchrist in his idea that western society has become too dominated by the left hemisphere of the brain, is out of balance and is consequently running out of creativity, different thinking and hence progress. With regard to audit, both society and audit itself have become ever more formalised through laws, rules, standards, codes of practice. If society is to progress and audit to deliver on its mission of progress in the public interest, then this formalisation must be moderated in favour of audit's creative power. In this respect, audit can be regarded as a countervailing power that seeks a better balance between the left and right hemispheres of the brain and, in the process, generates a creative tension.

Performativity and evaluation

The essence of our book is to promote audit's creative capacities to serve as an engine of social and economic progress (hence the notion of a progression audit). This requires the release of audit from ever more formalised codes/rules/standards/best practice stipulations by recognising that audit creates and shapes through performativity.

Performativity is crucial to our conception of audit because it gives audit much of its creative power. Performativity is an example of how the (perceived) future shapes or creates the present. It recognises the fact that how you are going to be judged, assessed or evaluated shapes what you do. The more expansive and holistic the evaluation, the more holistic and better balanced the shaping of current activity and the lower the risk of disruption from unanticipated consequences. Understanding audit's creativity is essential if we are to move from audit's standard association with conformity (and, as we have seen in the literature, notions of negativity and regress) to audit being more vividly connected with corporate and social progress/improvement. In respect of the limited company audit, Brydon's desired transformation of audit from an opinion on the financial statements to an evaluation of the company as a whole (in terms of deserved confidence) is key to enhancing audit's performativity in a positive fashion.

Well-considered risk, deserved confidence and the four pillars

There cannot be deserved confidence in a company (or society) that does not take well-considered risks and, hence, audit can be seen as an evaluation of how well considered the business is in its risk taking. A large risk may be well considered if it offers a chance of large returns. The only thing that is certain in business is the risk and opportunity of change. Risks stem from outside forces and responsibilities that include, for a company, the natural and physical environment, society, the economy and technology. The company responds through activities that promote an appropriate balance of resilience, sustainability, creativity and stakeholder commitment. We call these the four pillars of deserved confidence. Deserved confidence depends upon an evaluation of both the response to, and the impact of the response on those outside forces.

Reversing the expectations gap

An audit must be about progression as well as correspondence. In this sense audit leads and challenges society and, in terms of the 'expectations gap', it is the audit profession that should be ahead of society and expecting more from audit than society does. Presumably this is what Deloitte[2] have in mind when they state:

> Meeting your expectations is where our Audit & Assurance services begin. By bringing bright minds, effective processes and world-class technologies from across our global organisation while drawing on our years of experience, we push ourselves to deliver an impact beyond your expectations.

Unfortunately, we have a long-standing expectations gap where the public persistently has expected more from audit than the profession does. This emphasises the need not just to restore or bolster confidence in the current form of audit, nor to 'educate' the public as to what an audit is not, but the need to transform audit – and to do so in ways that enable it to deliver something that even the public did not think it capable of doing.

It is thinking differently about audit that transforms audit and thinking differently during the audit that, taken together, transforms society and the economy. We submit that thinking differently is inspiring, not burdensome, and makes audit a profession to transfer into rather than away from.

A cognitive model: Audit and the 'dance of three'

We believe audit can advance through its development as a mental or cognitive model. As implied by Martin's integrative thinking and by McGilchrist's characterisation of western decline, the simplest cognitive model is a network of three entities or elements (three nodes), two in opposition (or tension) and one that emerges from, or is created by, that opposition, and is itself in tension or interaction with the other two. Rovelli (2021), a leading philosophical physicist, calls this network a 'dance of three'. In a dynamic environment, such a simple network, however, is unlikely to be in perfect balance and now consists of three interactions or tensions (a triangle of connections), from each of which a further entity or element can emerge. Thus, technically, the dance of three is capable of becoming a dance of four, five, six and so on, potentially ad infinitum. It is the concept of materiality that operates as a constraint on such potentially explosive growth.

Making and crossing boundaries

In auditing, materiality is the important professional judgement that brings together the desire to gather/wait for more evidence and the need to provide assurance in a timely fashion and normally within a cost constraint. Materiality sets the boundaries for the audit investigation and determines how extensive the investigation is to be. Inevitably there is uncertainty as to what lies on the other side of the boundary and hence materiality introduces risk. A quality audit might be considered as one where that risk is well considered and this, in turn, depends upon context and an understanding of the network of which both the audit and the subject of the audit are a part. In terms of the 'dance', it is materiality that determines the scope of the network and how many 'dancers' are to be included.

Thus, materiality restricts the audit and prevents it from becoming an endless regress. Nevertheless, it must be remembered that as well as creating boundaries, audit, in making connections, crosses boundaries, so that audit itself is the coming together of opposites – of making and crossing boundaries – and this is its creative potential. Materiality is a judgement as to whether crossing the boundary set by materiality is likely to have a material impact on the audit, and inevitably this requires some consideration of high-level evidence of what lies on the 'other side'. Materiality can be seen as the process through which connections are included in, or excluded from, the audit; a judgement as to which connections are switched on or switched off, and it is a judgement that changes as circumstances change.

Materiality classifies into that which 'matters' to the purpose of the audit and that which doesn't. In general, the act of classification is an introduction of boundaries. The categories have similarities and differences, and creativity becomes a process of classification followed by boundary crossing in the form of co-ordinating, connecting or combining the classifications in new ways. Boundary making is facilitated by differences and boundary crossing by similarities. Creativity comes by thinking differently either so as to identify new connections and entities, or to identify existing entities and connections for removal from the network. This is a process which emulates the process of materiality judgement in that it too involves both the addition and subtraction of connections. In this sense materiality is creative and, as shown in Chapter 5, is the process through which we understand audit evidence and its cumulative impact. Creativity can be associated with thinking differently about what matters.

Audit and business: Dancing to the same tune

It was also in Chapter 5 that audit was represented as a dance of three between purpose, pathways to achieve the purpose and external disruption(s). Two thought experiments involving snake bites were used to demonstrate that the concept of audit is not limited to businesses or organisations or anything financial or numerical, but is core to life experience and its emotions. It shows how the concepts of evidence (visibility) and materiality (what matters) come together to shape the overall audit pathway and how that pathway, visibility and materiality are dynamic, change and change each other as the pathway to collect evidence proceeds, time passes and circumstances evolve. Thus, there is a dance of three involving visibility, materiality and time. Time itself is another dance of three; between the past, the present and the future, and to understand audit we need to understand the connection(s) between audit and time.

Whilst time, or rather the passage of time, is 'the auditor of last resort', a key purpose of 'audit' in chapter 5 was to deliver assurance that the snake bite will be survived (or not suffered) and to deliver that assurance in timely fashion. Through the thought experiments and the subsequent chapter (Chapter 6) we demonstrated that audit and business can be seen in the same format (or 'dance steps') of purpose, pathways and disruption. Furthermore, an audit and the subject of the audit can be viewed not only as separate networks but as part of the same larger network. That is, the audit, in shaping the business, is part of the story of the business, which is another way of saying that the audit is performative and creative.

The implication of the audit and business performing the same dance is that when the audit is creative and changes its thinking about the business then the company will follow suit and change its thinking. The creativity of the auditor transmits to the company and its management, who in anticipation of a good audit evaluation might seek to be more creative themselves.

Illustrating our reconceptualisation of audit

We believe that conceptualisation of audit begins with the audit of life; that is, we start thinking about audit from the assumption that everything is audit rather than a narrow view of audit as being that with which we are most familiar. Nevertheless, we have illustrated the application of our conception of audit through the audit of a limited company.

Business activity can be seen in terms of purpose and pathways; the business environment is a source of disruption requiring a flexibility of purpose and pathways, and the financial statements represent the financial outcome of bringing the other elements together. The business audit is thus described as an 'FEB' (financials, environment, business) network, and for audit to promote progress it should be conceived as an audit of the network, its tensions and interactions, rather than an audit of one element or entity within the network. Accordingly, we cannot have an audit of business without considering and evaluating the environment in which the business exists. In most circumstances the future – the future of the natural and physical world, society, the economy, technology and their relations with the business – will be a highly material constituent of this environment.

Audit as part of the network of time

The past and the present cannot be audited without also evaluating the future. The future is a key (material) part of the environment in which the company operates and exists. In so far as you cannot go directly from the past to the future or vice versa without passing through the present then the past, present and future do not form a fully connected, reverberative network. The restriction is one of order, being that the present must sit between the past and the future. Thinking goes from evaluating the past, to evaluating the present and to evaluating the future – or vice versa – and the most creative thinking goes in both (opposite) directions at once.

First, in the network that consists of the past, present and future, the present is a channel of communication from the past to the future and vice versa. Secondly, the present serves as a point of convergence for the past and the future and is created by this convergence; that is, the past and the future come together to create the present. Thirdly, the experience of the present is a force that influences the past (our interpretation of the past) and the future (our expectation of the future). An audit does not seek to evaluate the past, the present or the future but is an evaluation of the network as a whole. At the same time, in so far as the audit has an influence on the evaluation of the past, the present and the future, it is connected to the network and becomes part of the 'past-present-future' network of time in relation to the company or other audit subject.

Introducing deserved confidence to the FEB network

Chapter 7 added Brydon's idea of audit as deserved confidence to the FEB network to give a cognitive model or 'network of networks' that comprises (1) the external forces, (2) the pillars of deserved confidence, (3) business activity comprising a network of purposeful pathways and disruption and (4) financial and non-financial outcomes and feedback. Figure 7.1 brought these four together to create the auditor's cognitive model of the audited business. It focuses on the impact of the business as a mediator between the external forces and the four pillars, and how the model shapes the assessment of deserved confidence.

The audit evaluates the impact of the business – past, present and future. The role of business and its outcomes is similar to the role of the present in the past-present-future network in so far as the business (and its outcomes) sits between the pillars and the forces. Does (has, will) business activity lead to more resilience, sustainability, stakeholder engagement and creativity? At the same time does it (has it, will it) contribute to an improved natural and physical environment, a better society, stronger economy and better (use of) technology?

The cognitive model is a framework for thinking differently about the connections in the model; and whether different thinking could lead to improvement, and for answering the question: how much confidence does this company deserve? The FEB network becomes the deserved confidence network as shown in Figure 7.1. The auditor should deal with how the business activity has impacted the strength and relative strength (repositioning) of the four pillars and how it has impacted the environment that gives rise to the external forces. Whilst the business impacts the four pillars and external forces, those pillars and forces also impact the activity of the business. Successful auditors are able to synthesise both impacts in forming their judgement of deserved confidence.

Following Brydon, the role of the auditor is not to evaluate a set of financial statements but to evaluate the business as a whole in terms of whether, why and to what extent it is deserving of confidence. The overall aim of the audit is to explain how deserved confidence relates to, and emerges from, the 'deserved confidence network' as a whole including the network of pillars and the network of external forces.

Deserved confidence is a judgement in the context of the business and cannot be reduced to compliance with a set of 'standards'. Auditors who add value by thinking differently to management, investors and other stakeholders have to communicate in ways that delineate and explain their insights and how they contributed to their assessment of deserved confidence. The Brydon report (2019) recommended (para. 2.1.3) that (decision useful) information provided by auditors should, on occasion, include original information not produced by the audited company for disclosure. Our view is that every audit, as a consequence of auditors thinking differently, is destined to produce original information.

A role for reconfigured financial statements?

Conventionally the financial statement auditor gives an opinion as to whether the financial statements 'match' the company's business activity. Chapter 6 addressed this conventional audit and its difficulties. The conventional financial statements, and hence the conventional audit, have a difficult relationship with the future and neither the financial statements nor the audit have a clear relationship with society's values (the four pillars). Furthermore, these difficulties were highlighted by the attempted application of Business Risk Auditing (BRA) in the late 1990s – with auditors struggling to connect (both conceptually and productively in terms of the use of audit resources) the assessment of the overall business (risk) subject to audit with their obligation to provide a specific opinion on the business' financial statements (see Curtis and Turley, 2007).

Chapter 9, however, recommended that this tension between the business and its financial statements should be addressed by treating the four pillars as a channel or bridge between the two – with financial statements providing details on four financial 'funds', one for each of the four pillars of deserved confidence. This illustrative reconfiguration of the financial statements is driven directly by our reconceptualisation of audit and its delineation of the holistic nature of the auditor's assessment of deserved confidence. In short, it means contemplating 'audit first, accounting second' and demands that the financial statements are more reflective of, and better connected to, the business' four pillars and associated risk.

However, because the four financial funds, and the flows between them, only indicate the financial dimension of each of the pillars, the auditor's assessment of deserved confidence has to extend to a consideration of non-financial matters. Each pillar has to be assessed in terms of its overall strength across both financial and non-financial considerations. The notion of the audit ring of confidence was introduced to capture this assessment process that shapes and brings together financial and non-financial dimensions of the audited company's functionality. It is possible that the non-financial dimension will frequently be a greater contributor than the financial. Nevertheless, the financial flows between the funds do provide important insight into the connections between the pillars, primarily the important role of interest rates in connecting and valuing the resilience and sustainability funds and hence in valuing the business. This raises a potentially important role for auditors in assessing and influencing interest rates and how they relate to the risks facing the business.

The connection between the creativity fund and the other funds was also highlighted, with the value assigned by the market to the creativity fund being recognised in the reconfigured financial statements. This assigned value is open to challenge by the auditors based in part upon their understanding of the connections between creativity and the strength, both financial and non-financial, of the other funds. In particular, the creativity fund should reflect the creativity of its engaged stakeholders, including its researchers and product developers. Creativity also plays a role in resilience and sustainability and might be considered the activity that holds the network together. Consequently, the work of the auditor has a potential role in questioning, even challenging, the company's share price, in so far as the auditor's analysis of the company and its business networks embodies and encourages thinking that is different to that in the share market.

At the time of its introduction, BRA was heralded as a new exciting era for audit (Perrin, 1998). Our reframing of audit and the directional ordering of the relationship between audit and the company's financial statements, at one level, has reset the case for business risk auditing. At a more profound level, however, it has pinpointed the centrality of audit to business and society – and provided the opportunity for reigniting audit professionalism.

You cannot, as was attempted previously, apply the BRA approach whilst assuming that the business' financial statements are a given and that whatever is included in them has primacy and forms the subject of the auditor's opinion. The logical implication of undertaking a BRA-based audit is that the auditor, through intuition, insight and assessment, determines what is important or vital to account for. It is the audit that should drive the accounting, not the other way round. Audit has to be a function that is direct and creative – assessing in what key areas insight (and information) is vital rather than assuming that audit is a verification/assurance process related to a given or predetermined information set. This also frees the auditor up in ways that enable the audit process to generate its own, original insights into the company being audited – rather than just having to verify a ready-made statement prepared by the company. In so far as audit is about assurance, it is assurance given by creativity and positioning for the future rather than conformity with the past.

Such a perspective reinforces the capacity for auditing to limit a never-ending regress in terms of the production of data that needs verifying, especially when so much generated data is increasingly difficult to verify or even defies verification. Rather than pushing auditors down the route of providing 'limited' assurance-type statements (that provide little more than a façade of verification), it instead forces us to recognise that there are certain forms of data where insight and evaluation matter more than, and are more feasible than, verification.

There is a clear implication here that no audit can be regarded or treated as standard, providing a direct reminder of the idiosyncratic nature of audit (Knechel et al., 2020). The auditor's assessment of deserved confidence is auditee specific – and has to be tailored to the particular position and context faced by the entity being audited. The skill and public interest commitments on the part of the auditor are what help them to determine the precise scope, depth and style of their audit investigation. It puts notions of professionalism central to any determination of the audit task – and places audit dialogue not in terms of what is 'standard' but rather what is 'special' and 'distinctive' about each audit investigation. Indeed, if audit is thinking differently, then we cannot be representing audit in standard or standardised terms. Thinking differently means audits will all be different – and we have to be much more sensitive to, and aware of, the limiting impact that standardisation tendencies have had on the development of audit insight.

A reinvigoration of audit professionalism can go hand in hand with a switch in the tone of conversations concerned with the determination and justification of the scope of audit inquiry. It no longer needs to be the case that audit scope is spoken of in negative terms (i.e., 'what you are requiring or expecting, while interesting, is **not** audit or **not** what an audit is about'). Instead, discussions on audit scope can be more positively framed in terms of what is needed to facilitate a determination of deserved confidence. It is about determining the possibilities of what can be done rather than asserting what is not possible or cannot possibly be considered.

There is a related consequence here too that shifts the audit profession's references to serving the public interest from ones of assertion ('this is what we have always done and we can assure you that it is the best we do in serving the public interest') to a more action-oriented framing of public interest commitments ('we are varying our approach this year because circumstances have changed and demand a different form of analysis/investigation').

Collectively, the central priority is taking auditors out of a certain routinised comfort zone and opening up the opportunities to think and behave differently. It is moving auditors away from standard accounting-based reporting templates (i.e., accountants determining conceptual accounting frameworks on the basis of what they have typically felt comfortable with) and determining what audit activity and what accounts will best help stakeholders to know whether the company being audited is deserving of the confidence they are placing in it. It is about determining what accounts matter to stakeholders rather than justifying why certain accounts have traditionally mattered to accountants.

The driver of governance

Those responsible for governance need to be confident that the management are positioning the company for a better future and for this an assessment of resilience, sustainability, stakeholder engagement (including its treatment of stakeholders) and creativity is required. At the same time, governance should consider the company's impact on the natural and physical environment, upon society and upon the company's involvement with technology. In effect audit, under our re-conceptualisation, could be regarded as the mainstay or driver of governance and the audit report should be a primary basis of whatever action those responsible for governance seek to implement.

As such, governance should be seen as an (implementation) arm or extension of the audit rather than the other way around. Governance and accountability should operate in a similar fashion to audit – thinking differently in a manner that connects the tensions existing in the company in such a way that serves to promote progress. Arguably there should be no such thing as a governance code that takes governance down a road of codes/rules/best practice plus compliance and away from a focus on the progress the company is making. Those responsible for governance understand, or should understand, that a well-run company takes well-considered risks and that even well-considered risk taking can result in things going wrong.

The same applies to the audit and the choice of materiality. A well-managed audit takes well-considered risks and, with any risk, things can be missed. There is little to be gained either for the company or for the audit by setting up a system where everyone shelters from risk by having a regime of codes and compliance. This is not the road to progress.

The same also applies to litigation. Damages and fines cannot be awarded on an assumption that if things go wrong then the risks taken were not well considered, or that if the auditor did not follow 'best practice' then the auditor is at fault. Litigation is a societal construct and if society has a risk tolerance that is too low then there is unlikely to be improvement in the economy or in societal values. What happens is an extension to the codes of best practice to build a bigger shelter! Unfortunately, this just doesn't work as it results in audits that tick boxes but do not think outside the box (Hayward, 2003). This brings us back to the connection between audit and society. A progressive society requires a progressive audit and legal arrangements and judgments that are enabling of a progressive audit, whilst ensuring that a progressive audit is not an excuse for the auditor being too casual.

Lenz and Jeppesen (2022) (also see Lenz and Enslin, 2025) labelled the auditor as the 'gardener of governance' to draw attention to the close relationship between audit and governance and the former's nurturing influence. Such work has been focused on the less statutory world of internal audit, but its claims regarding the significance of audit's role in terms of governance apply across all forms of audit. Humphrey et al. (2024) described the auditor as an 'ecosystem engineer', framing the 'audit ecosystem' as a dynamic, socially interactive phenomenon, with a community of auditors responding to shifting organisational and societal demands, contexts and circumstances.

> Thinking of auditors as 'ecosystem engineers' both reinforces this sense of dynamism and the socially connected qualities and attributes of audit. It invites consideration of the capacity and propensity of audit and auditors to act in ways that prove to be both protective (in mitigating against certain – societal – threats or risk exposures) and nurturing or enabling (helping to establish the circumstances and means that give or bolster – social – life). It gives a clear representation of audit as an agent of sustainable change and development – the very things that we should be directly contemplating when we talk of a 'public interested' audit function.
>
> (Humphrey et al., 2024, p. 684)

It is worth recalling that in Chapter 1 we noted how the philosopher Julian Baggini (2017) talks of truth as being like a garden; not fixed or absolute but something that needs nurturing and tendering. In response to the question 'What is an ecosystem in short answer?', Google (on 5 March 2025) gave the answer "a geographic area where plants, animals and other organisms, as well as weather and landscape, work together to form a bubble of life". From here, it becomes possible to view the auditor as a gardener working to maintain and promote a 'bubble' of truth, concerned with the delivery of a better and fairer world. Or as Humphrey et al. (2024) concluded, there are

> a myriad of possibilities as to what audit could entail and achieve, what auditors work with, what skills they have and how different forms of audit (in the audit ecosystem) could be used to best societal effect. It is an

> image and a form of thinking that is better attuned to, and offers a more attractive route for, engaging with developing debates on the future of the corporation and of capitalism more generally – especially when scholars and policy makers in these arenas are making such limited reference to the role of audit. Instead of talking about all parts of the financial reporting ecosystem 'being essential to help(ing) effectively narrow the audit expectations gap' (IAASB, 2020, p. 14), it offers an opportunity for the auditing profession to pursue a much more dynamic and productive agenda that is not haunted by what an audit is or is not supposed to be, but about what auditing could become and what the audit ecosystem can do for others.
>
> (Humphrey et al., 2024, p. 684)

The future is artificial intelligence?

We have presented an illustration of our reconceptualised audit using the format of a network to mimic how the human brain works as a neural network. Our reconceptualised audit might therefore promote itself as a candidate for artificial intelligence (AI) that mimics the human brain. AI sees the world through the data it is presented with and data can be bad data (Sturge, 2023). We could regard the current auditing standards and details of current audits as bad data and, based upon such data, AI would come up with a very different understanding of the audit than if it were to read our book! Its conduct of an audit or recommendations as to how to conduct an audit would be very different to ours.

Or could AI be creative and produce or improve upon our book, by itself thinking differently? Again, this is likely to depend upon the data it is presented with. If AI is presented with current thinking and our book, it might learn how we have been creative and use this to take auditing to a further level. If AI's creativity is rooted in the creativity residing in the data through which it sees the world, then it might be able to identify creativity over a far wider range of subject matter than auditing and apply that broader understanding of creativity to the development of auditing.

It is probably fair to say that our own creativity comes from, but might also be limited by, the subjects and data to which we have been exposed. The power of AI is that through its appetite for data, it can potentially see much more of the world than a human. The disadvantage, at least given the current state of AI development, is that the machine might be able to identify a case of emotion but cannot experience or feel emotion. It did not distinguish between ugly and beautiful chess (Kasparov, 2018). It can see patterns in data more quickly than the human can, but not necessarily the beauty of those patterns and whether one pattern is 'better' or more beautiful than another. If this is correct then the auditor might have a 'feel' for a (new) situation or an opportunity to create a new situation that the machine does not.

AI could well play a role in helping the auditor to think differently but it is a more open question as to the extent to which AI can be creative about creativity; that is, can it come up with new forms or patterns of creativity that are not to be found elsewhere? This is a critical issue because if audit is represented as a dynamic form of cognition/intelligence, there is an inherent obligation to keep thinking and reimagining audit's essential purpose. As Kasparov (2018, p. 259) reminds us in concluding his book entitled *Deep Thinking: Where Machine Intelligence Ends and Human Creativity Begins:*

> I have argued that our technology can make us more human by freeing us to be more creative, but there is more to being human than creativity. We have other qualities the machines cannot match. They have instructions while we have purpose. Machines cannot dream, not even in sleep mode. Humans can, and we will need our intelligent machines in order to turn our grandest dreams into reality. If we stop dreaming big dreams, if we stop looking for a greater purpose, then we may as well be machines ourselves.

The constituents of audit

We have to come to understand audit through its relations with multiple 'dance partners'. For instance, we have shown that audit is in a dance with conformity and creativity, reality and representation, pathways and purpose, the individual and the collective, purposeful pathways and disruption, progression and correspondence, visibility and time, the transparent and the opaque, the completed and the not yet started, the open and the closed, the convergent and the divergent, force and countervailing force, continuity and discontinuity, the past and the future, space and time, order and disorder, confidence and doubt. Likewise, with considerations of the material and the immaterial, the materiality of making things and materiality as thinking through what matters, detection and prevention, existence and non-existence, complexity and clarification, the macro and the micro, the emotional and the logical, values as feelings and values as financials, the instinctive and the thoughtful, the auditor as insider and the auditor as outsider, classification and combination, the incremental and the fundamental, as well as the linkages we have just seen with machine and human intelligence.

Potentially, through thinking differently, every audit represents a distinctive reality (with a particular set of dance partners) and generates a unique representation, the purpose of which is to facilitate and promote the individual progress of the represented in terms of the collective values of society. Thus, audit is ultimately concerned with the relations between the micro (the individual company or organisation within society) and the macro (society as a whole); connecting what matters to the micro-world and what matters to the macro-world, a function in this regard that is characterised by a connected, 'dual' materiality.

The pattern of audit is generated by dualities, tensions and opposites, and not by rigid standards. Each component of the pattern can be seen in terms of a dance for three (following Rovelli) in which the audit component completes the threesome; it is a coincidence of opposites (following McGilchrist, 2021) that creates or drives the audit component; as the product of an opposable mind (following Martin, 2007); or as a mediating, boundary-forming/crossing instrument (following Miller and O'Leary, 2007). Each component is a superposition of differences and similarities, of the potential for competition and the potential for co-ordination.

In this respect, it becomes possible to represent a correspondence audit as one that ascertains to what extent established thought is being followed. A progression audit, however, identifies different thinking to challenge, and be challenged by, established thought, with the purpose of generating progress. Audit, overall, is a creative coincidence of opposites. Correspondence resonates with continuity, convergence, similarity etc. and progression with discontinuity, divergence, difference etc. The audit domain can be the individual, society, societal organisation, society's environment and all these domains and, hence, all audits are connected. To exist, an audit must relate to all material connections and ignore the immaterial, with materiality deriving from a pattern of thought. From this, audit itself might be thought of as (identifying) the materiality inherent in (competing) patterns of thought.

Speaking to those responsible for (and those keen to change) the future of audit

This section summarises in point form how we see the purpose and functionality of audit and its professional and intellectual obligations. The points indicate how we have gone about the proposal for transforming audit throughout the book and our principal points of departure from much of the conventional thinking within the audit profession and government. It shows the direction of travel we regard as necessary for audit to deliver its potential to improve society and the economy. The points are set out as follows:

1 The spirit of the book is that audit really does matter – it is at the centre and not the periphery of society. As such, we can start from the premise that audit could be everything (ready for everything) rather than stressing that audit isn't something or is a burden that needs reducing. But remember we are not auditing everything, just that which matters and so there is no infinite regress of audit. The fundamental problem that audit has faced is not

one of trust and confidence in auditing but one of relevance and significance of purpose. It is the compelling and informative nature of what an auditor finds/feels/says and the impact this has that matters most.

2 Sustaining such a line of thinking has required a deeper and more holistic representation of audit's conceptual underpinnings. It also requires the profession and government to commit to a broader and deeper conceptual development of audit rather than trying to restore confidence through regulatory fixes to a very static conceptualisation of the role and nature of audit.
3 Such conceptual invigoration, by necessity, encompasses a reconsideration of audit's social significance, especially given the claims by both the profession and government that audit serves the public interest and common good. In particular, it can no longer be taken for granted that the current conception of audit is the way to serve the public interest to best effect. Do not presume purpose and do recognise the arbitrariness of existing boundaries. Do not assume that there is one best way of organising, structuring and regulating professional organisations/bodies that provide public-interested auditing services.
4 Audit cannot connect with the public interest by continually saying that the public's expectations are misplaced. A persistent one-sided audit expectations gap is an evident sign of failure; it signifies a public interest function failing to meet or satisfy the interests of the public. Instead, audit must connect with the values of society and recognise that the audit/auditor will be an important influence upon those values. Audit and audit judgements cannot and should not be value-free but function and are made in the context of society's values, including truth and fairness as society sees them.
5 An ambitious conceptual journey does not seek to fit concepts to audit but, rather, to develop audit through conceptual advancement. We can start by treating audit as primary and not as an activity secondary to another (for example, accounting) upon which audit's usefulness then depends. Once audit is classified as primary, accounting becomes secondary, not the other way around. Audit tells us what needs to be accounted for.
6 Audit can be seen as both a search for uniformity and correspondence (*a process of convergence*) and a search for novelty and thinking differently (*a process of divergence*). Managing opposites such as convergence and divergence is a key skill of the auditor and potentially highly creative – far removed from standard representations of audit as 'routine' and 'boring'. It is thinking differently that is required to bring about such creativity.
7 Reframing the philosophical foundations of audit not only invites but embraces and justifies alternative forms of audit and audit practice. Contemplating audit in terms of various needs and interests, and through different lenses, standpoints or situations (i.e., considering audit as something else or having a different spirit or content in the way it connects to other social priorities, claims or values) are all symptomatic of our core conceptual

characterisation of audit – that audit is 'thinking differently'. Accordingly, the education and development of auditors need to cover different modes of thought that can be activated in any business or audit situation. For instance, thought can flow forwards and/or backwards in ways that are pervasive, creative, linear, circular, roundabout, reverberative or formed of combinations of these to construct different networks. Thought can flow as a mix of logic and emotion.

8 As a form of social conscience, audit must balance acceptance by society (through a sharing of its values) with the requirement of auditors to think differently to society (in order to have influence when circumstances necessitate). Audit has to stand as a different or distinctive voice, thinking/feeling/saying things that others do not or will not. It is through this commitment that audit helps to build and maintain deserved confidence in the entities being audited – and, in the process, becomes more trusted, admired and desired itself.

9 Audit's relationship with the notion of existence and what matters is rooted in the nature and importance of connection(s). Audit is a process of search and research (identification, evaluation, understanding and explanation), aligning conceptually with what physics teaches us about the nature of matter and what matters, and how purpose can both emerge from and lead to a disrupted world. As such, audit becomes a form of sense making through the connections it helps us draw; reminding us of what values count and what needs to be counted and appreciated. Through such analysis and consideration, audit, in turn, can shape and reshape societal and corporate activity, behaviour and performance.

10 While the spirit of auditing is often said to be to seek the truth, 'truth' can be viewed in more pragmatic or less absolute terms wherein truth, reality and existence are equated with a coherent set of connections that 'hang together'. Further, coherence is not bounded by our current existence and audit can draw on both imagination and creativity to shape and stimulate a new coherent existence. As such, we can think of audit as establishing better truths; of drawing valued connections that demonstrate that the confidence we place in our businesses, organisations and institutions is deserved and/or pinpointing ways by which such entities can change and transform for the better.

11 The independence of audit can be seen to be fundamentally intellectual in spirit – resting less so in the formal specification of regulatory requirements and restrictions and more in the audit's ability to undertake and inspire different thinking and its accompanying transformative effects and consequences. Accordingly, the arrangements for the appointment and remuneration of auditors should be designed to protect the ability to think differently, and should not inhibit the ability of audit to help those subject to audit to improve.

12 Audit is not 'standard' and we need only one audit standard that says just that. Individual audits can be viewed as having their own distinctive characteristics, with audit capable of working in different ways to build and maintain confidence. In terms of the audit market, we should be seeking to encourage competition on concept and product improvement; even innovating through collaboration (inviting new entrants).

13 The inclusion and positioning of the auditor's report in a company's annual report that is put together by management might be unsatisfactory. The auditor's role is to communicate their feelings about the audited subject and not just to comment upon management's feelings. Auditors who can think differently to management should consider having their own, 'different' medium of communication with stakeholders including society.

14 Wherever possible the audit report should help ensure that something happens rather than just assuring something already stated. Audit should shape the future rather than confirm the past. It is about creative divergence rather than conformity. If audit causes people to revise their expectations then, ultimately, there is an expectations gap that directly serves to justify audit - because audit enables and encourages people to think, to feel and to act differently, in ways that they had not previously contemplated.

We believe this summary provides a vivid conceptual foundation for the future transformation of audit – wherein the future of audit comes to be regarded not just as the audit of the future, but one in which audit shapes the future: the future of society and the economy, the natural and physical environment and the use and development of technology. It is a future that is creative, sustainable and resilient and engages its stakeholders. It is a future that is 'audit-centric'; one that moves audit centre-stage in terms of the development of society and business – but in a way that transforms audit away from its standard representation as a 'burden' to one where it is seen as a key enabler in the progression to a 'better' society and a 'better' economy.

We see audit as an example of 'recombinant innovation' (Syed, 2021, p. 135) or similarly 'dynamic repair' (Humphrey et al., 2021, 2024, Sennett, 2008; 2012). Syed states that "Recombinant Innovation is often dramatic because it bridges between domains or breaks down silos altogether, opening up new seams of possibility" (p. 135). We can see audit as recombinant innovation, for example initially separating correspondence and progression and then bringing them together again in new ways inspired by thinking differently and creatively. To quote Syed further,

> The growth of the future will be catalysed by those who transcend the categories we impose on the world, who have the mental flexibility to

> bridge between domains .... that is why the outsider mindset is set to become such a powerful asset .... We need to be strategically rebellious.
> (p. 141)

Syed's book is titled *Rebel Ideas: The Power of Thinking Differently*. Audit at its core is strategically rebellious. The power of audit is the power of thinking differently to achieve betterment. Audit should serve to promote and stimulate recombinant innovation and other forms of creativity.[3] It should challenge rather than confirm, developing an audit and a society (a 'New Audit Society') that is positive, progressive and optimistic; encouraging society to promote values and attitudes that are consistent with these ideals whilst respecting society's right to decide. However, the contemporary audit arguably falls way short, both reflecting and enabling a society that is increasingly restrictive and pessimistic.

Society and the audit profession have failed to contemplate what would happen if we permitted audit to develop – to become something else. For instance, auditors can be objective and, at the same time, add value. They can exercise judgement but also be rigorous in the process. They can verify and validate but they can also advise and facilitate improvement. Their capacity to do so depends on how much they are allowed or assigned to do rather than what they are prevented from doing – moving from constructing boundaries around audit that define what is not audit to breaking down boundaries and allowing audit to become something that it has never been. Instead of trying to manage, suppress, eliminate or even deny trade-offs and tension in the pursuit of a more secure or comfortable audit, the conceptual reframing of audit is one that embraces them. As a function, audit will never be comfortable because it is through asking the difficult questions, about proposing or challenging things that others have not or will not, that audit provides value, assures, verifies, enhances confidence, improves things, facilitates and/or delivers progress. Audit adds comfort by being discomforting.

Critical reflection, a contemplation that brings together the rational and the sensual in order to think differently, is a crucial cognitive process within audit. To achieve a better society each individual, each organisation and society itself should continuously contemplate what it is to be a better individual, a better organisation and a better society and how to act in order to achieve progress. The role of audit is to lead the way in this critical reflection. And to be a leader requires daring. We referenced in the opening chapter the notion of '*supere aude*' ('dare to know') and the capacity to think differently is directly related to this – the core value of audit depends on the daring or pertinence of auditors' thought processes and the analytical investigations that such thinking drives. Saying that audit is 'thinking differently' means that it is centrally engaged with notions of contradiction, of contrasts and tensions. If an asserted perspective claims one thing, audit's responsibility is to consider, or encourage consideration of, the opposite or alternative perspective. Audit in questioning or challenging, in thinking or saying something that others have or would not, in acting as a conscience or a counter-weight, encourages the development of fresh or different perspectives. Thinking differently also entails different modes of thinking as well as the taking of different perspectives on a given topic or claim. So, where the dominant thoughts are linear, audit can take a circular or roundabout thought process. Where certainty is expressed or asserted, audit may seek out ambiguity and uncertainty. Where arguments are assertive and reverberative, audit can engage with what has been suppressed or muted. Audit may do many of these things at the same time, to both determine and respond to what matters – what is material – in the circumstances of the audit. In our view 'thinking differently' becomes the defining characteristic of audit.

In summary terms, we have utilised the notion of 'thinking differently' in a range of ways. At one level, we have used 'thinking differently' as a vehicle to enable people to move away from treating the existing (business) audit as given or fixed. Secondly, we have used 'thinking differently' to capture the progressive dimensions of audit – which, through the fresh connections, insights and perspectives made or provided by the auditor, facilitates corporate and social advancement. Thirdly, we have promoted 'thinking differently' as a sensitising device for auditors to review what is done (and what is changed) on any given audit assignment. Finally, we have recognised that 'thinking differently' introduces a dynamic that extends to the very concept of audit itself. We see the book as the trigger or stimulus for much needed conceptual debate around what is audit, what it can become and, in the process, best live up to and sustain claims to be a public interested and responsive professional activity. Since the book is thinking differently and making recommendations for improvement it might itself be considered an audit of audit that is intended to inspire and make a difference.

As a way of thinking, audit is not limited to those who are designated as an 'auditor'. Audit thinking is available to all; for instance, it can be utilised by management, other committed stakeholders, those responsible for governance and those on the 'front line' charged with making and delivering goods and services. Our conceptualisation of audit is not bounded by any singular 'regime' of appointment, access, reporting, protection and sanction but, crucially, is underpinned by a commitment to betterment – of society, the economy, the environment and the use of technology. Accordingly, the design of an audit 'regime' necessitates a deep understanding of how audit supports and develops society's values and our book has sought to provide a pathway to such understanding. An audit regime should be one of stimulation and inspiration rather than compliance and regulation, respecting both the distinctiveness of individual audits and their development over time.

Audits are going to be practised in and governed by different conditions, utilising differing focal points and approaches and accommodating different forms of responsibility in the pursuit of assessing and developing deserved confidence in the audited entity. The aim of the book has been to pinpoint the potential for developing a much wider and progressive conception of audit. Our primary intent has been one of opening up rather than closing down the boundaries that surround constructions of what is audit; emphasising what audit could become rather than what it cannot be; acknowledging that too much time has been lost and that there have been too many failed initiatives trying to change the contextual circumstances associated with the current company audit. Ultimately, if audit at its conceptual core is a way of thinking, or rather a way of thinking differently, this means that audit is not standardised, nor generic. Proposals for auditors to do something different or additional should not be rejected by presuming that existing institutional arrangements are fixed and not themselves capable of being changed.

Our conceptual framing of audit has taken us from the traditional point of emphasis of what is not audit to a standpoint that audit could be anything or everything – it depends on what you, or society, want to make it. Starting from audit 'as everything' is ambitious, creative and liberating. It is just what 'thinking differently' requires – a lack of constraint and a freedom to engage. In one sense, it is a fresh, deeper level of conceptualisation that can enable 'dynamic repair'. Above all, it is a case of recognising that audit itself is dynamic. This also means we have to recognise that definition (or an absolute delineation of what is audit) is something that serves correspondence rather than progression. For progression in audit, we have to move beyond, or be more relaxed about, and break free from, formal definitions of scope. This is the audacity of thinking differently and what makes audit a fundamentally social concept. It is not so much what defines audit but what audit can enable or make possible that we should focus on, being more concerned with the idea of audit or the ideas stimulated by audit. In this regard, audit is anything but dull – it is rebellious, demanding and a source of innovation. Like electricity, which is widely recognised for the impact it has on the development of modern society, a conceptually reconfigured audit not only has the capacity to shock but also the capacity to inspire and enable.[4]

Audit is not just socially constructed but socially constructing in ways that deliver organisations and society that are not only deserving of our confidence but better. In an era increasingly associated with AI, it is important to recall that a core ambition of AI has been to develop machines that think or act like a human.[5] Accordingly, the capacity for humans to stay ahead of AI (to stay relevant and valuable) requires them to keep developing how they think. Audit, as such, is fundamentally human. It is the art of thinking differently - an expression of human creativity, skill and imagination. Its future is our future.

Notes

1 For further discussion of the pertinence of the Groundhog Day analogy for audit and its future development, see Humphrey et al. (2024).
2 For example, see www.deloitte.com/et/en/services/audit-assurance.html.
3 See, for example, the earlier discussion of creativity through combination and transformation in Chapter 7 (p. 166) and Chapter 8 (pp. 183–184).
4 "Electricity is an invisible force that has become an integral part of modern society … the history of electricity is a story of human ingenuity and innovation. It has transformed the way we live and work, and has provided us with countless benefits. However, it also poses significant challenges, and it is up to us to find ways to address these challenges in a responsible and sustainable manner. By continuing to push the boundaries of what is possible, we can ensure that electricity remains a force for good in the world for generations to come" (https://internationaljournalofresearch.com/2023/04/04/the-history-of-electricity-and-its-impact-on-modern-society/).
5 For an illustrative definition, see (https://nasa.gov/what-is-artificial-intelligence/.).

References

Auditing Practices Board, 1992, *The Future Development of Auditing: A Paper to Promote Public Debate*, (APB, London).

Baggini, J., 2017, *A Short History of Truth: Consolidated for a Post-Truth World*, (Quercus Publishing, London).

BEIS, 2022, *Restoring Trust in Audit and Corporate Governance: Government Response to the Consultation on Strengthening the UK's Audit, Corporate Reporting and Corporate Governance Systems*, (Department for Business, Energy and Industrial Strategy (BEIS), London), https://assets.publishing.service.gov.uk/government/uploads/system/uploads/attachment_data/file/1079594/restoring-trust-in-audit-and-corporate-governance-govt-response.pdf.

Brydon, D., 2019, *Assess, Assure and Inform: Improving Audit Quality and Effectiveness, Report of the Independent Review into the Quality and Effectiveness of Audit*, https://assets.publishing.service.gov.uk/media/5df8edfced915d0938597e1f/brydon-review-final-report.pdf.

Curtis, E. and S. Turley, 2007, 'The business risk audit – A longitudinal case study of an audit engagement', *Accounting, Organizations and Society*, 32:4–5, pp. 439–461, https://doi.org/10.1016/j.aos.2006.09.004.

Hatherly, D., 2009, 'Travelling audit's fault lines: A new architecture for auditing standards', *Managerial Auditing Journal*, 24:2, pp. 204–215, https://doi.org/10.1108/02686900910924581.

Hayward, J., 2003, *Thinking not Ticking: Bringing Competition to the Public Interest Audit*, (Centre for the Study of Financial Innovation (CSFI)), https://assets.publishing.service.gov.uk/media/5329dbc0ed915d0e5d0000bd/130516_independent_audit_ltd_monograph.pdf.

Humphrey, C., O'Dwyer, B. and M. Martinoff, 2024, 'Escaping Groundhog Day: The transformative possibilities of reconceptualising audit', *Accounting and Business Research*, 55:6, pp. 668–692, https://doi.org/10.1080/00014788.2024.2375713.

Humphrey, C., Sonnerfeldt, A., Komori, N. and E. Curtis, 2021, 'Audit and the pursuit of dynamic repair', *European Accounting Review*, 30:3, pp. 445-471, https://doi.org/10.1080/09638180.2021.1919539.

International Auditing and Assurance Standards Board (IAASB), 2020, *Fraud and Going Concern in an Audit of Financial Statements: Exploring the Differences Between Public Perceptions About the Role of the Auditor and the Auditor's Responsibilities in a Financial Statement Audit,* Discussion Paper, www.iaasb.org/publications/fraud-and-going-concern-audit-financial-statements.

Kasparov, G., 2018, *Deep Thinking: Where Machine Intelligence Ends and Human Creativity Begins* (John Murray Publishers, London).

Knechel, W.R., 2022, 'Who stands for audit? A commentary on the 'Brydon Report'', *International Journal of Auditing*, 26:1, pp. 27–31, https://doi.org/10.1111/ijau.12265.

Knechel, W.R., Thomas, E. and M. Driskill, 2020, 'Understanding financial auditing from a service perspective', Accounting, Organizations and Society, 81:February, https://doi.org/10.1016/j.aos.2019.101080.

Lenz, R. and B. Enslin, 2025, *The Gardener of Governance: A Call to Action for Effective Internal Auditing*, (CRC Press, Abingdon).

Lenz, R. and K. Jeppesen, 2022, 'The future of internal auditing: Gardener of governance', *The EDP Audit, Control and Security Newsletter*, 66:5, pp. 1–21, https://doi.org/10.1080/07366981.2022.2036314.

Martin, R., 2007, *The Opposable Mind: 'How Successful Leaders Win Through Integrative Thinking'*, (Harvard Business Review Press, Boston).

Mautz, R. and H.A. Sharaf, 1961, *The Philosophy of Auditing*, (American Accounting Association, Sarasota, Florida).

McGilchrist, I., 2021, *The Matter with Things: Our Brains, Our Delusions, and the Unmaking of the World*, (Perspectiva Press, London).

Miller, P. and T. O'Leary, 2007, 'Mediating instruments and making markets: Capital budgeting, science and the economy, *Accounting, Organizations and Society*, 32:7–8, pp. 701–734, https://doi.org/10.1016/j.aos.2007.02.003.

Perrin, S., 1998, 'Spot the difference', *Accountancy*, June, pp. 84–85.

Puxty, A., Sikka, P. and H. Willmott, 1997, 'Mediating interests: The accountancy bodies' responses to the McFarlane Report', *Accounting and Business Research*, 27:4, pp. 323–340, https://doi.org/10.1080/00014788.1997.9729558.

Riel, J. and R. Martin, 2017, *Creating Great Choices: A Leader's Guide to Integrative Thinking*, (Harvard Business Review Press).

Rovelli, C., 2021, *Helgoland*, (Allen Lane, London).

Sennett, R., 2008, *The Craftsman*, (Yale University Press, New Haven).

Sennett, R., 2012, *Together: The Rituals, Pleasures and Politics of Cooperation*, (Yale University Press, New Haven).

Sturge, G., 2023, *Bad Data: How Government, Politicians and the Rest of Us Get Misled by Numbers*, (Bridge Street Press, London).

Syed, M., 2021, *Rebel Ideas: The Power of Thinking Differently*, (John Murray Publishers, London).

INDEX

For Product Safety Concerns and Information please contact our EU representative GPSR@taylorandfrancis.com Taylor & Francis Verlag GmbH, Kaufingerstraße 24, 80331 München, Germany

Batch number: 10844619

Printed by Printforce, the Netherlands